Frontiers in Economic History

Economic historians have contributed to the development of economics in a variety of ways, combining theory with quantitative methods, constructing new databases, promoting interdisciplinary approaches to historical topics, and using history as a lens to examine the long-term development of the economy. Frontiers in Economic History publishes manuscripts that push the frontiers of research in economic history in order to better explain past economic experiences and to understand how, why and when economic change occurs. Books in this series will highlight the value of economic history in shedding light on the ways in which economic factors influence growth as well as social and political developments. This series aims to establish a new standard of quality in the field while offering a global discussion forum toward a unified approach in the social sciences.

More information about this series at http://www.springer.com/series/16567

Sambit Bhattacharyya

A History of Global Capitalism

Feuding Elites and Imperial Expansion

Springer

Sambit Bhattacharyya
Department of Economics
University of Sussex
Brighton, UK

ISSN 2662-9771 ISSN 2662-978X (electronic)
Frontiers in Economic History
ISBN 978-3-030-58735-2 ISBN 978-3-030-58736-9 (eBook)
https://doi.org/10.1007/978-3-030-58736-9

This Springer imprint is published by the registered company Springer Nature Switzerland AG.
The registered company address is: Gewerbestrasse 11, 6330 Cham, Switzerland

To Anna, Maria, Nicholas, Sahana, Swapan, and Natasha.

Preface

> Hegel remarks somewhere that all great world-historic facts and personages appear, so to speak, twice. He forgot to add: the first time as tragedy, the second time as farce.
>
> —Karl Marx [1852 (2012)], The Eighteenth Brumaire of Louis Bonaparte, Chapter 1.

This book is an attempt to examine the history of global capitalism through the lens of elite competition. Here, I make a case that numerous conflicts, hot and cold, are a direct consequence of elite competition and rivalry, which is inevitable under an expansionist economic system that heavily relies on access to scarce resources. Episodes of elite competition also tend to repeat itself. For instance, after a prolonged pause since the disintegration of the Soviet Union, geopolitical competition and the proverbial cold war are back as a new reality. This is very much apparent in the new American National Defense Strategy. So history indeed repeats itself. Even though this theme appears quite frequently in the popular press, a holistic political economy approach to understand issues seems to be absent. Such an approach is useful because socio-economic outcome under any system is a resultant vector of cumulative economic and political forces. Especially no studies or commentary takes the long view or adopts a historical perspective. My aim is to fill this gap with this timely publication. I hope that the book would be topical and relevant for graduate teaching in the fields of economics, geography, politics, and history. This topic is very widely studied, and a timely publication of this nature could potentially have significant appeal both within the academy and beyond.

Capitalism evolved as an expansionist system over the last 500 years. Due to its expansionist nature, it generates both intra- and international elite conflict which often turns violent. This aspect even though highlighted in passing by Karl Marx, Friedrich Engels, and Vladimir Lenin[1] is somewhat absent from all the current discourse regarding the evolution of capitalism as an economic system. This book

[1]Note that Marx highlights exploitation of labour by capital as the key factor that generates surplus value (or economic rent). In his view, suppression of wages by the capitalists (or owners of capital) is the main vehicle of exploitation. In contrast, in this book, I argue that 'economies of scale' is the main incentive behind imperial expansion under a capitalist economic system.

aims to explicitly explore the origins of intra- and international conflicts within a capitalist economic system using both a theoretical framework and extensive historical narratives spanning almost all the continents. The introductory chapter forcefully (and perhaps convincingly) makes the point that the long view of elite feuds as a by-product of the expansionist capitalist system is also the key to understanding the current geopolitical tensions and macroeconomic fragilities. The book also aims to examine the political economy of macroeconomic policies (especially interest rate policies) in the modern post-1991 era. The book is divided into five parts. Part I presents a theoretical framework. Part II deals with the history of early modern and modern Europe. It captures elite competition, rivalry, and imperialism in Europe across different European empires. Part III deals with the history of the post-war period till the present. Part IV concludes with some predictions for the future. Part V presents a comprehensive review of the literature. The aim of the book is to impartially and objectively describe the historical evolution of capitalism as a politico-economic system.

The book addresses two fundamental research questions in economics. First, what factors explain the divergence in living standards across countries? Second, what ensures internal and external stability of the capitalist economic system? The book adopts a unified approach to address these questions. Using the neoclassical growth model, it shows that economic growth (or improvements in living standards) is dependent on access to raw materials, labour, capital, technology, and perhaps most importantly 'economies of scale'. Then it modifies the neoclassical growth model by introducing power relations (both internal and external to a nation) which ensures scale economies through guaranteed access to markets and raw materials, hence the role of empire in a capitalist economic system. The stability of the system depends on growth and distribution, and it is not possible to have one without the other. However, the quest for growth and imperial expansion implies one empire is invariably encroaching on the territory of another empire. This is perhaps the most unstable and potentially dangerous characteristic of the capitalist system. Using a near comprehensive historical narrative, the book shows that this inherent tension in the capitalist system can be best managed by acknowledging great power spheres of influence within the international system. In other words, the book argues that any attempt towards unipolarity is inherently unstable, while multipolarity is much more stable. History is replete with such examples which are discussed in the book. Acknowledgement of mutual spheres of influence is perhaps the single most important reason that explains the success of the Vienna Congress in post-Napoleonic Europe and Bretton Woods following the Second World War. It also explains the failure of Versailles in interwar Europe.

The book presents a model of an early modern state which uses natural resources, labour, and capital as inputs for production. It assumes that such states consist of approximately four arms—finance, military (military includes intelligence and police), media, and welfare. The first three are part of the national security state. It argues that these state arms work together to create legitimacy and manufacture consent from the non-elites. These different arms of a modern state collaborate to create corporations to exploit economies of scale. Economies of scale create economic rent which is then protected by the national security elite using the state. Elites cooperate with each other if there is common economic and political interest. Otherwise, they compete with each other and elite split occurs. This pattern of cooperation and rivalry is observed both within and across national boundaries. For example, political crisis and elite disunity in the Western world (the USA and the EU in particular) are broadly a consequence of poor economic performance since the 2008 Global Financial Crisis.

This model is then applied to explain European imperial history with a special focus on the British and Russian empires. Examples of the British and the Russian imperial experiments are useful here as they are both large in terms of geographic expanse. Furthermore, they offer both common and contrasting perspectives. Their similarities, differences, and other nuances are examined. In addition, the book examines the history of the French and the Spanish empires. It also looks at the 300 year history of slave trade from the European imperial perspective.

In addition, the model is used to explain core-periphery relationship. In other words, the relationship between the European imperial elite and the elite in the colonies of Africa, Asia, and Latin America is examined. The book also explores the relationship between the imperial elite and the settlers or the emerging elites of the new world.

This is then followed by an analysis of the great power conflicts of the twentieth century or the World Wars. The expansionist motives and the breakdown of the international system during that period are carefully analysed. This is followed by the analysis of the post-war or the cold war period. The book devotes a chapter into analysing the geopolitical and internal political economy contexts behind the disintegration of the USSR.

Finally, the book analyses the new cold war. Here, the shifts in the rules of international trade and commerce since the disintegration of the USSR and its geopolitical implications are analysed. It pays special attention to geopolitical and military flashpoints in a rapidly changing world. The book concludes with some predictions on how a future international system would look like.

The aim of the book is to disseminate this new research in a tractable and user-friendly manner. The target audience are experts and students in the fields of economics, political science, strategic studies, geography, and history. The book aims to offer experts a broad view of history and an analysis of current geopolitical events through the lens of a novel political economy theory. Students and especially graduate students in the above-mentioned areas would benefit from the wide coverage of historical events and deep analysis. This will enrich their knowledge and perhaps provide them with a framework for future research and scholarship. Finally, I hope that the book will also appeal to the informed layperson by providing them with new information and fresh analysis with the subsequent enrichment of civil society.

Brighton, UK Sambit Bhattacharyya

Acknowledgements

The global order is in a state of flux. The established post-cold war rules of commerce are unravelling. Trade wars and threats of unilateral trade restrictions are becoming common practice when it comes to relations between great powers. Therefore, we are witnessing the gradual demise of the old politico-economic order, but the new is yet to be born. Witnessing the rapidly changing landscape of international relations deeply influenced my desire to catalogue the events and find an explanation. The uncanny similarity between the past and the present also encouraged me to search for an explanation that can stand the test of time. This quest of analysing economic and political history from a long-run perspective lies at the heart of this book. Without running the risk of oversimplification, the book emphasizes the role of economic factors in great power conflict, hot or cold. Therefore, a common error would be to view this as another attempt of offering unidimensional explanation to a multidimensional and complex phenomenon. It is anything but. As the creator of this ambitious project, I am acutely aware that the trajectory of human history is the resultant vector of a combination of factors many of which are extremely complex. Therefore, caution is exercised wherever possible to limit the risk of oversimplification while interpreting historical events. Nevertheless, it is perhaps prudent to acknowledge right at the outset that omissions are inevitable. They are in no way deliberate.

Going back to the days of my doctoral studies in Canberra, I always wanted to write a book about the history of long-term economic development. My advisor late Professor Steve Dowrick introduced me to this topic and the treasure trove of literature around it in 2003. I will always remain indebted to him for his guidance and encouragement especially during those early years which helped shape my ideas on this topic. This is a debt which I can only hope to repay.

Writing a book of this nature is not possible without the help of many individuals. I would like to extend my utmost thanks to my colleagues and collaborators. Working jointly with them on related collaborative projects helped shape my ideas for which I remain grateful. In particular, I would like to extend my gratitude to Prema-Chandra Athukorala, Paul Collier, Gaurav Datt, Tim Hatton, Hal Hill, Roland Hodler, Raghbendra Jha, Pushkar Maitra, Maurizio Intartaglia, Vasily Kozlov,

Alexander Moradi, Rick van der Ploeg, Kunal Sen, Budy Resosudarmo, David Vines, Jeffrey Williamson, Arief Yusuf, and many others. They have been wonderful colleagues, excellent collaborators, and good friends.

I would also like to thank my doctoral students Nouf Alsharif, Michael Keller, and Nemera Mamo. I have immensely benefitted from reading their research on the natural resource curse and other related topics. They have helped me stay up-to-date in terms of the latest in their respective scientific fields. I have always learnt something new through our interactions for which I remain grateful. In addition, Nouf, Michael, and Nemera have been excellent collaborators in research projects closely related to this book.

Thanks are due to five anonymous reviewers for reviewing the book proposal and offering detailed comments. Two anonymous reviewers looked at the proposal informally and offered comments at the pre-submission stage, while the other three were part of the formal review process. In addition, I would like to extend my sincere thanks to the editors for their thoughtful comments and discussions. Needless to say that all the comments, discussions, and scholarly exchanges helped me immensely to reshape and advance my ideas.

Last but not least, I would like to thank my family for their love, affection, words of encouragement, and unwavering support.

Contents

List of Figures

Chapter 1
Capitalism and Elite Feud: A Short Introduction

Abstract This chapter presents a short introduction and chapter wise summary. The book sets out to confront the question what motivates imperial expansion under the capitalist economic system? In particular, it focuses on the economic motivations of expansion. This undoubtedly is related to two fundamental research questions in economic sciences. First, what factors explain the divergence in living standards across countries? Second, what ensures internal and external stability of the capitalist economic system? Overall, the book is divided into five parts. Part I presents a theoretical framework. Part II deals with the history of Early Modern and Modern Europe. Part III deals with the history of the Post-war period till the present. Part IV concludes with an analysis of the geopolitical implications of COVID 19 and some predictions for the future. Part V presents a literature survey.

Imperial expansion is perhaps as old as civilisation itself. The drive towards territorial, commercial, and soft power expansion is intrinsic to all ancient civilisations. Agrarian societies such as the Ancient Rome started as a small city-state, which subsequently expanded into an imperial behemoth unprecedented in human history. A similar pattern is observed not just in the classical world of ancient Greece and Rome but also in other parts of the globe. Human history is replete with the rise and fall of empires. Maya, Inca, Ancient Egypt, Ancient and Moghul India, China, the Mongol Khanate, Ottoman Empire, British, French and Russian empires, Spanish Hapsburgs all initiate at a very small scale and then experience expansion and eventually die. The current reincarnation of superstates or conglomerates such as the Union of Soviet Socialist Republics (USSR), the European Union (EU), or the United States led post-war order are not exceptions to this pattern. The pattern is also unaffected by the nature of the empire—agrarian, industrial, post-industrial, or otherwise. What is puzzling though are the factors that drive this pattern. Beard (2015) in her influential book *SPQR: A History of Ancient Rome* writes,

> The Romans did not start out with a grand plan. Although eventually they did parade their empire in terms of some manifest destiny, the motivations that originally lay behind their military expansion through the Mediterranean world and beyond are still one of history's great puzzles. (p. 2, Prologue: History of Rome)

S. Bhattacharyya, *A History of Global Capitalism*, Frontiers in Economic History,
https://doi.org/10.1007/978-3-030-58736-9_1

This book sets out to confront the question what motivates imperial expansion under the capitalist economic system? In particular, it focuses on the economic motivations of expansion. It argues that expansion is essential for the internal and external stability of the system. It shows that elite feud and conflict is a natural consequence of the tensions arising out of expansion. This is not to say that economic factors are the only cause of elite feud and conflict. Great power conflict and geopolitical rivalry is a multidimensional phenomenon influenced by a myriad of complex factors. The objective here is to emphasise one of the important factors without belittling the role of other factors. Being mindful of the folly of a unidimensional design, the book deliberately uses a mixed method approach to make the key argument. It presents both a theoretical framework and an extensive historical narratives spanning almost all the continents. It makes the point that this long view of elite feuds as a by-product of the expansionist capitalist system is also the key to understanding current geopolitical tensions and macroeconomic fragilities. The book also aims to examine the political economy of macroeconomic policies (especially interest rate policies) in the modern post-1991 era. The book is divided into five parts. Part I presents a theoretical framework. Part II deals with the history of Early Modern and Modern Europe. It captures elite competition, rivalry, and imperialism in Europe across different European empires. Part III deals with the history of the Post-war period till the present. Part IV concludes with some predictions for the future. Part V presents a survey of the literature.

The aim of the book is to impartially and objectively describe the historical evolution of capitalism as a politico-economic system. The book deliberately avoids discussing the merits and demerits of a particular political system or state. Even though the nature of a political system or ideological differences engenders heterogeneous politico-economic outcomes, it hardly limits elite feud or conflict. The current tension between North Atlantic Treaty Organisation (NATO) powers (e.g. United States, the European Union, and Turkey) or within the European Union (e.g. Britain and the rest of European Union regarding Brexit) are a case in point whereby tensions simmer while economic and geopolitical interests diverge. The book also avoids drawing comparisons between political systems or empires in terms of their benevolence, cruelty, or propensity to violence. Rather it acknowledges that all the competing powers are equally driven by their national/state interest and compete fiercely to achieve their goals. Some succeed, while others fail. In what follows, I present a short chapter-by-chapter summary of the entire book.

Chapter 2 entitled *A Unified Theory of Rent, Elite Feuds, and Imperial Expansion* studies the structure of a capitalist state. Following is a brief schematic description.

The core idea of the model is to demonstrate that capitalism is an expansionist system. It heavily relies on the expansion of the resource base, expansion of the labour force, expansion of the market, technology upgrading, and most importantly 'economies of scale' for growth. Growth generates economic rent and the incumbent elite protect their rent by creating entry barriers for new entrants often by using brute force. In the event of a growth slowdown, the system enters a phase of crisis and stress. In such situations elite competition, rivalry, and feud ensue. Feuds and military conflict are often the tools at the disposal of the incumbent elites to achieve expansion of their resource base to sustain growth. This dynamic of expansion, crisis, feuds, and further expansion is the toolbox that could be used to explain the history of global capitalism.

The model presents a taxonomy of elites. It classifies them as three types—national security elite, financial and large corporation elite, and media elite. All of these elites have a vested interest in imperial expansion. As the empire expands (either directly or indirectly, more on this later), the size of the rent that these elite groups could extract also expands. Large corporations setting up production within strategic sectors provide the benefit of scale economy, monopoly power, and rent maximisation. Rent is maximised via restricting entry and increasing the size of the market through imperial expansion. This takes place irrespective of ideologies and political preferences. For example, both liberal and left-wing socialist philosophies are internationalist as they both rely on the capitalist mode of production. Therefore, globalisation of the mode of production and expansionism is at the heart of the sustainability of these systems. Hence, imperialism and elite feuds emerge after a certain stage as an inevitable consequence of the capitalist economic system.

The national security elite is relatively more nationalistic to start with as defence industries typically have a home bias. However, this changes over time. Political systems (democracy, autocracy etc.) are largely instruments of legitimacy of the elite rule. They are generally not universal and appear to be correlated with local traditions, culture, and religion. Imposition (often violently) of one type of political system (preferred by the imperial elite) over another is also common and correlated with the forces of expansionism and globalisation.

Relations between the imperial elite (the core) and the colonial elite (the periphery) is also very important. This relationship appears to be heterogeneous. Trust plays a role along with distribution of rent and patronage. For example, the European imperial elites trust the European colonial elite more than they trust the natives. This could be due to cultural ties. This could also be due to sociocultural constraints faced by the European imperial elite located at the imperial core in terms of exercising unmitigated violence or coercion towards the European colonial elite at the periphery. For instance, any atrocities or acts of coercion committed against the native population in the colonies would not affect public opinion much in the imperial core.[1] Therefore, it is unlikely to threaten legitimacy of the imperial elite's rule in the imperial core. In contrast, a conflict with the colonial elite of European descent could endanger the legitimacy of the imperial elite's rule at the imperial core due to deep cultural ties. Overall, a patron–client relationship typically evolves.

Technological progress increases rent and supports expansionism thereby making the system sustainable. It also aids legitimacy of the ruling elite by improving average living standards. However, the spasmodic nature of technological progress

[1]Frequent famines in India under British colonial rule that were often manufactured by the colonial administration to bolster war efforts or other similar atrocities or mismanagement had very little influence on the public opinion in the colonial core at that time. In contrast, British belligerence during the American War of Independence led to a backlash against the pro war Tories. Whigs assumed power in the parliament that led to the Treaty of Paris and peace in 1783.

makes expansion through this channel uncertain. Typically, diminishing return sets in triggering elite competition and feuds over existing resources.

When the elite use coercion and violence (both internally and externally)? When all else fails and the elite becomes desperate and fearful about their existence. In other words, when there is a credible threat to their authority and power they resort to violence. Therefore, empires in their declining phases are often the most dangerous because of their increased propensity to resort to violence.

Elites (especially large corporations) use their economic power to control media (the information space) and hence manipulate public opinion. This is a crucial instrument for the elite for manufacturing consent and legitimacy. In addition to controlling the information space, the imperial core also uses international assistance and non-governmental assistance to buy influence and promote hegemonic interest in the periphery.

Politicians/leaders in the imperial core are only one component of the elite. Their actions are often heavily constrained by the national security and the economic/financial (large corporations) elite.

This system (or social contract) works fine as long as there are economic growth and inequality at a tolerable level. In other words, the social contract offering some improvement in living standards for everyone in the society albeit at an unequal pace. The system gets challenged when growth slows down or stops (diminishing returns), inequality rises, and growth becomes skewed (only the very top benefits from growth). Redistributive demands at the imperial core magnify. This inevitably leads to expansionist pressures with the aim of expanding access to resources (material and human) and access to markets. This lies at the heart of elite feuds, wars, and violent conflicts.

Part II of the book deals with *Rent, Elite Feuds, and Imperial Expansion in Early Modern and Modern Europe*. Chapter 3 entitled *Atlanticism, the Slave Trade, and the Westward Expansion of Western Europe* chart the history of Atlanticism and slave trade in Western Europe. It describes what prompted the Spanish and the Portuguese to engage in Atlantic or westward expansion. It covers Portuguese and Spanish involvement in maritime spice, precious metals, cotton textile, and silk trade connecting Asia, Africa, and Latin America. It describes the process of Dutch and British takeover of this trade. It covers the history of maritime trade triangle in goods, commodities, and slaves between Europe, Africa, Asia, and Latin America. In the process, it highlights imperial competition and elite feuds in the form of Anglo-Hispanic wars, Anglo-French wars, Anglo-Dutch conflict, and the American war of independence. It pays special attention to the history of the relationship between imperial elites and settlers in the new world.

Chapter 4 entitled *The Adventures and Misadventures of Imperial Expansion in Eastern and Central Europe* covers the history of eastward expansion attempts by imperial Sweden and Polish Lithuanian Commonwealth. It also covers the history of Russo-Turkic wars and expansionism by the Russian and Ottoman empires. The Crimean War between the Russian, Ottoman, Austro-Hungarian, British and French empires receives special attention, as this is a prime example of expansionism by the European empires in the dying days of the Ottomans. The chapter emphasises that one of the key motives of this conflict was to share the spoils of the disintegrating Ottoman Empire. In addition, this chapter examines the Napoleonic invasion of Russia and the broader Napoleonic wars. The defeat of Napoleon initiated the concert of Europe, an important institution that preserved peace in the continent for almost a century. This chapter also discusses the role of the Westphalian system in preserving peace when there are competing imperial interests.

Chapter 5 entitled *Western Europe and Colonialism in India and East Asia* chart the history of expansionism by several East India Companies in India, Indonesia, and other parts of Asia. The chapter focuses on the relationship between the colonial elite and the local elite in colonial India and Indonesia. The theories of client patron relationship are analysed. Pivotal events such as the Battle of Plassey and the Mutiny is covered.

Chapter 6 entitled *Expansionism in the American and Australian Colonies* covers expansionism in the American and Australian continents. The Thirteen American colonies of Britain stayed loyal to the Monarch throughout the seventeenth and most part of the eighteenth century. The Anglo European settlers of the colony benefitted extensively from becoming a part of the British global trading network. Lucrative trade in commodities such as tobacco, cotton, sugar, indigo, tea, coffee, timber, and others substantially increased the economic power of the settlers. With growing economic power, political demands increased. Britain's global war with France also challenged the security of the British colonies in America. However, the imperial parliament in London led by William Pit was reluctant to pay for the security of the American colonies. He wanted tax revenue from the colonies to pay for its security. This led to widespread discontent among settlers that finally transpired into an open conflict in the form of the American War of Independence. Following the conclusion of the American War of Independence and British withdrawal in 1783, the building blocks of an independent American nation was formed. A strong central government under the leadership of George Washington was formed. Over time, it expanded both west and southwards gaining territory from France, Spain, and Mexico. The chapter discusses this expansion.

A similar pattern appeared in Australia. Penal colonies in the states of New South Wales and Tasmania and settler colonies in the states of Victoria and South Australia transformed it into a large continent-sized country. Chapter 6 also describes the expansion process in Australia.

Chapter 7 entitled *Expansionism and the Cataclysm of Two World Wars and the Russian Revolution* deals with the two world wars, the Russian Revolution and the interwar period. The collapse of the international system (the concert of Europe) that managed competing European imperial interests ushered in an era of uncertainty and extremely violent imperial conflicts. This had catastrophic consequences for both elites and non-elites in Europe. Chapter 7 is broadly divided into three sub-chapters. The first sub-chapter deals with the period leading up to WW1. This is followed by a detailed description of the Bolshevik Revolution and the formation of the Soviet Union. Finally, the chapter ends with the audit of the history of the Second World War (which is effectively a continuation of the First World War). Key military and political events leading up to the Second World War is analysed. The toxic ethnonationalist ideology of German exceptionalism as promoted by the National Socialists is examined. Key economic events such as the Great Depression and the role of the financial elites are discussed in this context.

Part III of the book deal with *The Post War Period*. Chapter 8 entitled *Cold War Rivalry in a Bipolar World* covers the history of the Cold War. It starts with the fall of Berlin and subsequent division of Berlin as the genesis of the cold war. It examines the Bretton Woods system, reconstruction of post-war Europe (predominantly Britain, Germany, and France), and the usage of the dollar as the currency for international commerce and maintaining reserves. This chapter examines the economic benefits accruing to the American financial elites under this new system. It also examines to what extent Soviet Union's refusal to participate in the Bretton Woods financial and economic system transpired into the cold war. The Cuban Missile Crisis, Soviet invasion of Czechoslovakia and Afghanistan, the Vietnam War, the Korean War, Sino-Soviet Split, the Oil Standard, and Sino-American Rapprochement are also analysed.

Chapter 9 entitled *Dissolution of the USSR and Russian Decline in the 1990s* covers the episodes leading up to the dissolution of the Soviet Union. In particular, it analyses the impact of political, economic, and social policies such as Perestroika and Glasnost. This is followed by analysis of the events surrounding the unconstitutional dissolution of the USSR and the rise of Boris Yeltsin as the new leader. The chapter analyses foreign policy of the Yeltsin government in the 1990s along with domestic economic policies of privatisation and liberalisation led by Yegor Gaidar and Anatoly Chubais. Special focus is given to the economic events leading up to the Russian Bond crisis and default in 1998.

Chapter 10 entitled *End of History and Exceptionalism: International System after 1991* focuses on the events after 1991. The withdrawal of the Soviet Union from Eastern Europe created enormous expansion opportunities for the American and Western hegemonic interests. This period oversaw economic and territorial expansion of the European Union. The financial, trade, and military architecture of this expansion is discussed in detail. The role of dollar as the currency that underpins this system is explored. Therefore, the role of monetary policy in conjunction with trade and security policies is discussed. The chapter demonstrates how these policies ran their course over the next three decades as diminishing returns kicked in. Excessive reliance on credit creation as opposed to manufacturing growth brought about volatility and financial crisis of 2000 and 2008.

Offshoring jobs to China and the Asia Pacific and their subsequent impact on the American labour market and income are discussed in this chapter. The cold war origins of this policy (United States—China Détente of 1972) is investigated along with internal political economy factors. The chapter covers the long-term consequences of replacing income with credit to support consumption. In other words, it entertains the thesis how excessive reliance on the monetary policy credit channel leads to asset price bubbles.

On the security side, special attention is given to conflicts in the Middle East (Iraq, Libya, Syria, and Afghanistan) and Yugoslavia leading to foreign and security policy overreach. Attention is given to tensions in the South China Sea and the

Korean Peninsula. Ever-expanding military and security budget, growing national debt, and the stability of the national currency is analysed.

Chapter 11 entitled *The Rise of China, India, and Russia: The Building Blocks of a New International System* analyses the spectacular rise of China as a global economic powerhouse. This narrative is entertained in conjunction with the rise of India and the BRICS[2] as a group. The chapter discusses ramifications of new international institutions such as the New Development Bank (BRICS Bank), Asian Infrastructure Investment and Development Bank (AIIDB), The Shanghai Cooperation Organisation (SCO), and the Eurasian Economic Union (EAEU). Infrastructure initiative such as the China led One Belt One Road (OBOR) initiative and the Russia–India–Iran North-South corridor is discussed. This analysis is undertaken at the backdrop of the Asian Development Bank's estimate that Asia would need $1.7 trillion infrastructure investments annually to sustain its growth momentum.

Part IV of the book entitled *Going Forward: What to Expect* offers certain predictions. Chapter 12 under the title *Rivalry, Expansionism, and the Future of the International System* revisits the main thesis of the book—capitalism is an expansionist system fraught with risks of violent confrontation. History should guide us to manage these conflicts effectively and draw lessons from them. Barring major armed or nuclear conflicts (flashpoints of such incidents are many), the world will perhaps converge towards multipolarity whereby the economic and political powers of the BRICS nations are likely to increase at the expense of Western Europe and the United States. This process is accelerated by the ongoing public health crisis and the global economic crisis. The international trade and financial systems are likely to change. Whether this transition will take place in a peaceful and orderly manner is an open question. Given the dangers of a nuclear conflict, it is likely that a Thucydides' Trap[3] would be avoided this time.

Part V and Chap. 13 presents a survey of the literature.

Bibliography

Allison, G. (2017). *Destined for war: Can America and China escape Thucydides's Trap*. Boston: Houghton Mifflin Harcourt.

Beard, M. (2015). *SPQR: A history of ancient Rome*. London: W.W. Norton.

[2]BRICS is an association of Brazil, Russia, India, China and South Africa.

[3]Thucydides in the ancient Greek text *The History of the Peloponnesian War* wrote, 'What made war inevitable was the growth of Athenian power and the fear which this caused in Sparta'. He meant a rising power (Athens) will inevitably come into conflict with a dominant power (Sparta) because they have conflicting interests. Following Thucydides' work, Allison (2017) coined the phrase 'Thucydides' Trap' describing conflicting interests of the United States and China.

Part I
Theoretical Framework

Chapter 2
A Unified Theory of Rent, Elite Feud, and Imperial Expansion

Abstract This chapter presents the theoretical framework. The framework addresses two fundamental questions in economic sciences. What factors explain the divergence in living standards across countries and what ensures internal and external stability of the capitalist economic system? The framework adopts a non-technical and unified approach. Using the neoclassical growth model, it shows that economic growth is dependent on access to raw materials, labour, capital, technology, and perhaps most importantly 'economies of scale'. Then it modifies the neoclassical growth model by introducing power relations (both internal and external to a nation), which ensures scale economies through guaranteed access to markets and raw materials. Thus, imperial expansion is a natural consequence of the capitalist economic system. The stability of the system depends on growth and distribution and it is not possible to have one without the other. However, the quest for growth and imperial expansion implies one empire invariably enters into conflict with another empire. Such inherent tension in the capitalist system can be best managed by acknowledging great power spheres of influence.

2.1 The Unified Framework

In this chapter, I describe the theoretical foundations of this book: how economic factors motivate expansionism, elite rivalry, and conflict which in turn shapes history. We consider a model that demonstrates resources, technology, and power as the three pillars of the capitalist system that evolved over the last 500 years. In particular, the production process is characterised by the following relationship:

$$Y = F(R, L, K) \tag{2.1}$$

where the output Y is produced using a combination of the inputs natural resources R, labour L, and capital K. For tractability, we consider all firms in the economy to be identical. Therefore, the macro output of the economy is the product of the micro output of the representative firm and the number of firms in the entire economy. Note that we do not distinguish between land and natural resources here to keep the

S. Bhattacharyya, *A History of Global Capitalism*, Frontiers in Economic History,
https://doi.org/10.1007/978-3-030-58736-9_2

structure parsimonious and tractable. Land could be considered as a natural resource, which hosts factories, farmlands, offices, mines, and oil rigs (in case of subsoil wealth), and forests. The inputs of production (natural resources, labour, and capital) receive compensation through wages or rental payments equal to their contribution to production at the margin.[1] The compensation schemes could be different between the market and planned variants of capitalism. We will elaborate later in the chapter that the production process is similar across the two systems with the main difference emerging out of redistribution.

Technology and power[2] relations across inputs determine the most suitable combination of inputs. To illustrate the role of technology, let us consider the following Cobb-Douglas production function $Y = R^{\alpha}L^{\beta}K^{1-\alpha-\beta}$. If all inputs are increased by a fraction θ then the output also increases by a fraction θ. Hence, the production function exhibits constant returns to scale technology. For the sake of minimising complexity, we consider the combination of inputs used here as knowledge or production technology. Alternatively, one could define the production function as $Y = AR^{\alpha}L^{\beta}K^{1-\alpha-\beta}$, where A represents technology. In that event, $A = 1$ would represent constant returns to scale technology while $A > 1$ would represent increasing returns to scale technology.

Power relations between the different owners of inputs (or factors of production) are enforced through rules such as factory discipline, law and order etc. In the power hierarchy, the state typically enjoys 'monopoly of violence'. It can also exert 'threat of violence'. Thus, it acts as the main enforcer of power relations. The production process converts inputs into outputs for mass consumption. Even though technology plays a critical role in the production process, power relations also matter at the margin. For instance, given a certain level of technology, inputs can gain at each other's expense if the existing set of rules or institutions are biased in their favour thereby assigning more power. The owner of capital can extract payment greater than their marginal product using the power hierarchy while depressing wages of workers using violent repression.[3] As technology is upgraded, the combination of inputs required for production changes thus altering power relations over time. Moreover, with technology upgrade the need for skilled labour increases relative to unskilled or low skilled labour thereby introducing hierarchy within labour.

Under this system of production, within country inequality and poverty stems from the relative payments received by the inputs of production, skills, and power relations. Power relations act both at the micro and macro levels and can be either progressive or regressive. For instance, if a particular technology is biased in favour of skills and capital then a progressive power relations system practiced either by the

[1]A system run by slave labour (such as the plantation economy) relies entirely on coercion and thus workers are not compensated.

[2]Power can be both economic and political. In fact, one can lead to the other. See Bhattacharyya (2011a) for more discussion.

[3]Production systems based on slave labour (i.e. plantation economies) and colonial institutions demonstrate such characteristics.

state or an enterprise can correct for the resultant inequality through redistribution or reskilling of workers. In contrast, a regressive power relations system if practiced can perpetuate inequality and cause extreme poverty. Plantation economies in the Americas and other former colonies in Africa and Asia are good examples of such systems. Similarly, across country inequality and poverty could stem from skill and technology gap, and a political system perpetuating regressive power relations.

As described above, a fraction of the output produced in a capitalist economy using the production function (2.1) is used for factor payments. A fraction of the output is also used for investments, consumption, government expenditure, maintenance of the existing stock of machines (or capital), and endow children of the owners of capital with capital.[4] Government expenditure includes spending on military, police, law enforcement, public sector employees, and welfare. At least in theory, under perfectly competitive market structure there will be free entry and exit of firms. Therefore, there will be no surplus value (or rent) generated by the firms. In practice, all market economies exhibit oligarchic or monopolistically competitive market structure. For interested readers, I would refer to the literature on Schumpeterian growth. This literature demonstrates the prevalence of non-competitive market structures in market economies. Under conditions of oligarchy or monopolistic competition with at best partial free entry, all firms and by extension the entire economy generates positive rent. In socialist economies, the entire rent is appropriated by the state. A part of it is redistributed to the population and a part of it is saved in the form of precious metals or other liquid or illiquid financial assets. The per capita redistributed rent for the elite is greater than the same for the non-elite population. For a complete account of growth and distribution in socialist economies, see Kalecki (1990, 1992, 1993). We discuss more on this in Chaps. 8 and 9. In contrast, in market economies, the state uses tax as the main instrument to appropriate a proportion of the surplus or rent from the private actors (mainly owners of capital). Labour can also generate a surplus in the form of savings but this is small relative to the surplus generated by firms. Therefore, market-oriented states typically do not tax small savings.

The economy illustrated above attains steady state when per capita capital stock and per capita output stops growing over time. Note that we are assuming exogenous population growth at a constant rate. The steady-state level of per capita capital stock and output is dependent on the factors of production including natural resources and capital. Long-run growth in per capita income is possible with steady technological progress, which continually shifts the production frontier given production inputs (or factors of production). An increase in the access to natural resources or capital also increases the steady-state level of income and the economy shifts from a lower level steady state to a higher level steady state. This expansionary shift is described

[4]This is identical to the resource constraint equation in an optimal growth model (commonly known as the Ramsey Model) with a moderate twist. The optimal growth model assumes all new born babies are assigned with capital, whereas here we assume that only the children of capitalists are endowed with capital.

as the 'transitional dynamics'. Note that the steady-state result appears due to the theoretical assumptions of constant returns to scale (CRS) and diminishing returns to the factors of production. It is also possible for economies to make efficiency gains by using the inputs better if they are not producing on the production possibility frontier.

Let us now examine the factors that can trigger expansion in the abovementioned model. Under the strict contours of the model, an *expansion in the resource base R* leads the economy to a higher steady state. Therefore, access to new natural resources is expansionary. The effect of the *expansion of the labour force* on the economy is manyfold. A larger labour force would imply a greater share of the output is used to equip more new workers with capital. This would leave less output for the purpose of investments, which would be contractionary. However, a larger labour force can also reduce cost of production and increase rent for the firms if the institutional structures allow them to discriminate across different groups of the labour force. This can effectively create a constant pool of surplus labour for the owners of capital. Overall, it is expected that the latter effect would dominate over the former and therefore would be expansionary.

The model illustrated above is a supply-side model, as it does not deal explicitly with the demand side. It implicitly assumes that in the long run, supply creates its own demand. *Expansion of the size of market* would present a positive demand shock to the economy and therefore undoubtedly would be expansionary. It would provide new incentives for firms and the economy to expand output supply. Access to a bigger market would open up additional opportunities for firms to exploit scale economies and maximise rent.

Finally, exogenous technological progress in the form of A as noted above would also be expansionary. The dynamic here is identical to a textbook Solow model. Even if we introduce the flexibility of endogenous technological progress as in Schumpeterian growth models, the effect of a positive technology shock is always expansionary.

The model as described above does not take into account the distributional consequences of economic expansion. It implicitly assumes that there are no distributional consequences as all the factors of production receive payments equal to their marginal product. In reality, factor markets in a capitalist system are segmented not just by skill levels but also by social status. Therefore, economic expansion as illustrated above inevitably delivers skewed distributional outcome, which unleashes antagonistic political forces. The balance of power between these antagonistic political forces constitutes the political equilibrium or steady state, which is not explicitly discussed in the model so far. For example, a somewhat simplistic description of the political economy equilibrium would be that the production process is capital and skill intensive and therefore the distributional outcome inevitably favours the owners of capital and skills relative to the owners of other factors of production, especially unskilled or semi-skilled labour. In reality, the political economy dynamics is far more complex which I aim to describe next.

The above model is capable of delivering a stable steady state without the need for continual expansion. Therefore, a valid question would be why the system needs to be expansionary. The answer stems from the stability of the political equilibrium that emerges from the distributional consequences of the economic steady-state equilibrium. The political equilibrium shapes the rules of the economic equilibrium. Therefore, political instability leads to economic instability. The political equilibrium remains stable as long as the majority population perceives the distributional outcome fair. Overall, the majority care about their absolute income as opposed to their relative income. Therefore, the majority are willing to tolerate inequality as long as their absolute income is going up over time. In other words, the unskilled and semi-skilled labour force would perceive the distributional outcome fair as long as their absolute income is increasing over time but albeit at a slower pace relative to the owners of capital and skills. The only way to deliver such an outcome is through continual expansion or economic growth. If this is not the case then the legitimacy of political equilibrium is called into question. Questionable legitimacy destabilises the political equilibrium and in turn the economic equilibrium or the steady state.

Furthermore, expansion generates economic rent and the incumbent elite protects their rent by creating entry barriers for new entrants often by using brute force. We will describe the role of brute force later in the book. In the event of a growth slowdown, the sharp distributional contradictions inherent to the system are unleashed and consequently, the system enters a phase of crisis and stress. A politico-economic system in crisis and stress gives rise to elite competition, rivalry, and feuds. In turn, the incumbent elites also use feuds and military conflict as tools to achieve expansion of their resource base in order to sustain growth and maintain stability. In what follows, I argue that this dynamic of expansion, crisis, feuds, and further expansion is the toolbox that could be used to explain the history of global capitalism. I elaborate on the mechanism described above a bit further in the following paragraphs.

In order to describe the political economy dynamics, let us stratify the society into elites and non-elites. Elites are a minority. However, they exert substantial influence on the political equilibrium and shape the rules that govern economic and political life. Elites are typically the owners of natural resources and capital. The non-elites could be divided into broadly two groups—skill endowed and unskilled. The skilled endowed non-elites are typically upwardly mobile. Since returns to skills are substantial, therefore they are presented with the opportunity to save, invest, and own capital. Examples of such groups of non-elites are the merchants in the early modern era with their entrepreneurial and military skills and the urban university-educated middle class in the contemporary world with their engineering or information technology skills.

Let us also impose a taxonomy of elites. Elites can be classified as three types—national security elite, financial and corporate elite, and media elite. All of these elites have vested interest in expansion which I will call imperial expansion. As I will demonstrate later in the book that expansion beyond a point becomes well outside the territorial and cultural boundaries of the core and hence imperial in nature. As the empire expands, the size of the rent that these elite groups could extract also expands. The empire could expand directly by setting up colonies and absorbing more and more territory through military conflicts. It could also expand through proxies and via controlling the economic and political means of others. The former is observed leading up to the Second World War whereas the latter is a method of choice for imperial expansion in post-colonial societies after the Second World War.

Large corporations set up production within strategically important sectors. They provide the benefit of scale economies, monopoly power, and rent maximisation to the sections of elite who own natural resources and capital. Rent is extracted via restricting entry and increasing the size of the market through imperial expansion. Note that both of these shocks would result in a positive shift in the economic steady state. This takes place irrespective of ideologies and political preferences of the elite. For example, both liberal and socialist philosophies are internationalist in nature as they both rely on the capitalist mode of production. Again, it is important to emphasize that the motivation behind expansion here is twofold. First, the profit and power motives of the incumbent elite. Expansion increases the size of the rent and hence increases the economic and political power of the incumbent elite. We assume that political power is derived from economic power. Greater political power allows the incumbent elite to tilt the rules in their favour that in turn ensures favourable distributional outcome and greater rent in the subsequent periods. Second, the stability of the entire system. Expansion creates enough surplus for redistribution. Redistribution in turn helps the incumbent elite to dampen sharp contradictions within the society emerging from the skewed distributional outcome of the capitalist system.

Therefore, globalisation of the mode of production and imperial expansion is central to the capitalist system and its survival. Globalisation of the mode of production implies creating a global network of raw materials, labour, production, and markets to sell goods and services. Militarism is an integral part of this system, as one would need muscle power to secure the networks. Competing empires would like to expand and secure their respective global networks. Given that resources and markets are finite, confrontation, or what I call 'elite feuds' emerge as an inevitable consequence of such imperial rivalry. It is of course in the mutual interest of these competing empires to manage such conflict. Management can take place through a global security architecture or global institutions. Alternatively, it can also take place through some form of unwritten rules, bilateral or multilateral treaties, and sheer luck. However, all of these mechanisms are subject to commitment problems. In other words, there is no effective enforcement mechanism at the global level. If one empire perceives itself to be too strong or too weak they might deem the perceived cost of a direct violent confrontation to be acceptable and thereby violate the existing agreements. We will return to this discussion again later.

The national security elite within the society looks after security and defence of the production and raw materials networks. Therefore, they look after the industries related to national defence. It is relatively more nationalistic to start with as the defence industries typically have a home bias. This however changes over time and with the size of the empire. Larger empires also internationalise their defence production networks in order to reduce costs and exploit economies of scale. Therefore, they tend to become more internationalist over time.

The financial elite derives their wealth and power from controlling the supply of money. Money is the mode of transaction in capitalist societies. As I have described earlier, large corporations and skilled non-elites generate surplus from exploiting economies of scale or partaking in skill-intensive production. Generating these surpluses and day-to-day economic exchanges involve potentially infinite number of transactions. To reduce transaction costs requires a mode of transaction and hence the role of money. The surpluses also need to be saved for the purpose of investments or future consumption. Therefore, they need a store of value. Money and other forms of liquid and illiquid assets act as a store of value (or instruments of saving). The conversion of savings into investments, the management of assets, and pooling of risk associated with saving and investing require intermediation. Financial institutions provide this service of intermediation and the financial elite controls these institutions.

The power of the financial elite evolves over time. As the size of the empire grows, so is the power of the financial elite. Outward orientation is natural to the financial elite as it collectively increases their power and wealth. In particular, when the size of the imperial state is relatively small, the financial elite derives their wealth from issuing currency on behalf of the state and buying state securities and debt. The imperial state pays interest to the financial elite in return for holding their debt. The currency issuance (or the IOUs) by the financial elite[5] is typically backed by precious metals such as gold and silver. The stock of the precious metal dictates how much currency the financial elites can issue and therefore acts as a constraint from the supply side. In addition, the total volume of economic activity acts as a constraint from the demand side. For example, if there is an economic expansion (or output growth) then it is expected that the number of transactions in the economy would grow thereby increasing demand for money. The supply of money (or currency in circulation) would need to be increased accordingly. If there is imbalance in the form of excess supply of money then it would trigger inflation. In contrast, if there is excess demand for money (or not enough currency in circulation) then that would trigger a collapse in bond prices and an increase in interest rate. Bond prices would fall as wealthy citizens would try to sell bonds and other financial assets in order to satisfy their demand for liquidity. Borrowers and bond issuers such as the imperial state would have to pay more to borrow thereby increasing bond yield. Subsequently, economic contraction would ensue.

As the empire expands, so is its access to raw materials and markets. Large corporations typically lead this process on behalf of the empire. Under a globalised system of trade and commerce, at least within the imperial boundary, expanding commerce demands expansion in the financial system as well. This implies expansion in currency issuance by the financial elite. The colonies are encouraged (or forced) to use the imperial currency as their mode of transaction. At the very best, the colonies set up currency boards by pegging their local currency to the currency of the imperial core thereby giving up their monetary policy independence.

[5]Note that I am using the phrases 'financial elite' and 'financial intermediary' interchangeably here.

Colonial governments are also forced to hold sovereign debt of the imperial core. This creates additional demand for the imperial currency in terms of both transactions and assets outside of the imperial core.

Furthermore, an expanding empire brings in new security challenges in terms of protecting trade routes. Maintaining military presence in strategically important locations gain increasing importance. A network of overseas military bases become essential for the management of the empire. Needless to say that this imposes a significant burden on the imperial state budget. Therefore, imperial states have to engage in deficit financing to satisfy the financing needs. In other words, the budgetary challenges are addressed intertemporally by imperial states through borrowing from the future. Imperial states issue bonds which are then bought, sold, and managed by the financial elite. This also creates a symbiotic relationship between the financial and national security elites. The national security elites do not mind military conflicts as long as it is below their threshold level of cost in terms of personnel and equipment loss. Personnel loss acts as a constraint in any armed conflict for the national security elite.

All of the above taken together contributes to the wealth and power of the financial elite. Note that the sole instrument to power for the financial elite is currency issuance. The constraints on currency issuance are primarily twofold. First constraint is the transactions demand for currency. Imperial expansion is an obvious response to increase transaction demand. Second constraint is the reserve requirement. Having precious metals of equal value (or a fraction of the value) in reserve against currency issuance is the key to the stability of any fractional reserve financial system. This allows the financial elite to hedge against the risk of herd behaviour and bank runs. Obviously, the financial elite also strives to minimise this constraint but there is a trade-off. Strengthening regulatory environment, property rights, contracting institutions could encourage peripheral players to invest in imperial core currency denominated assets. This could increase transaction demand. Furthermore, the currency could be used in the international trade of strategic commodities such as energy. Money supply could be increased accordingly without expanding the reserve requirements (i.e. the need to hold precious metals). However, there is always a limit to this expansion as it depends on third parties choosing to use the imperial currency. Military threats could be used to compel third parties into trading using the imperial currency but there is a cost in terms of personnel and other losses. In the end, controlling human behaviour and currency preferences is not costless.

The three elite groups within the political system wield enormous political and economic power. This is irrespective of the political system that is in place. Political systems (democracy, theocracy, autocracy etc.) are largely instruments of legitimacy of the elite rule. They help address the political succession problems inherent in any political system. Democracies choose their elite from a wider pool using plebiscites, theocracies use religious and moral authority, whereas autocracies rely on heredity or the selectorate.[6] Note that political systems are generally not universal and appear to be correlated with local traditions, culture, and religion. Imposition (often violently) of one type of political system (preferred by the imperial elite) over another is also common and correlated with the forces of expansionism and globalisation. Sometimes moral arguments are used to justify violent expansionism but they are never credible when judged through the lens of imperial interest.

Relationship between the imperial elite (elite in the core) and the colonial elite (elite in the periphery) is also very important. The core imperial elite tolerates some degree of autonomy of the peripheral elite depending on the level of trust between them. The core–periphery relationship appears to be heterogeneous. Trust plays a very important role along with the distribution of rent and patronage. The role of the peripheral elite is primarily to collect rent on behalf of the core. It facilitates extraction of raw materials, manages physical and human resources, and maintains military presence in the event of any security threat. It also maintains local infrastructure facilitating primarily resource extraction and other economic activities.

An example of the heterogeneous nature of core–periphery trust, we could look at colonies populated by European settlers as opposed to non-settler colonies. European imperial elite trusts the European colonial elite more than they trust the natives. This could be due to cultural ties. This could also be due to sociocultural constraints faced by the European imperial elite located at the imperial core in terms of exercising unmitigated violence or coercion towards the European colonial elite at the periphery. For instance, any atrocities or acts of coercion committed against the native population in the colonies would not affect public opinion much in the imperial core.[7] Therefore, it is unlikely to threaten legitimacy of the imperial elite's rule in the imperial core. In contrast, a conflict with the colonial elite of European descent could endanger the legitimacy of the imperial elite's rule at the imperial core due to deep cultural ties. Overall, a patron–client relationship typically evolves.

Technological progress facilitates growth thereby increasing rent. This, in turn, supports expansionism and thereby makes the system durable. It also aids legitimacy of the elite rule if it improves average living standards. However, the spasmodic nature of technological progress makes expansion through this channel uncertain. Typically, diminishing returns to the factors of production given a certain level of technology sets in. This triggers elite competition and feuds over the existing resources.

When is the elite likely to use coercion and violence (both internally and externally)? When all else fails and the elite becomes desperate and fearful about their existence. In other words, when there is a credible threat to their authority and power they resort to violence. Therefore, empires in their declining phases are often the most dangerous because of their increased propensity to resort to violence.

Elites (especially large corporations) use their economic power to control media (the information space) and hence manipulate public opinion. This is a critical

---

[6]Selectorates are a small group of very influential individuals.

[7]For two contrasting examples from British involvement in India and America, see footnote 1.

instrument for the elite in order to manufacture consent and seek legitimacy. Note that the incumbent elite cannot rule the masses without legitimacy. Therefore, in any political system, the incumbent elite would require a critical minimum support from the masses in order to be legitimate. The media elite colludes with the incumbent in order to manufacture consent and seek legitimacy on behalf of the incumbent. In return, the media elite receives a share of the rent. Note that, the media elite faces competition in the information space. Therefore, the appearance of neutrality is important for the colluding media elite in order to remain a credible source of information. Hence, they devote significant resources to appear impartial while defending the legitimacy and imperial interests of the incumbent elite at both home (imperial core) and abroad (periphery). In addition to the information control, the imperial core also uses international assistance and non-governmental assistance to buy influence and promote hegemonic interest in the periphery. We have not discussed the media arm of the elite in detail thus far. This is more modern than all the other elites. We will talk more about it in due course.

Politicians/leaders in the imperial core do not act independently. They are only one component of the elite and is often chosen by the underlying powerful group and then legitimised by a popular vote or other forms of institutions. Their actions nonetheless are often heavily constrained by the national security and the economic/financial (large corporations) elites.

This system of social contract works fine as long as there is economic expansion and tolerable inequality. In other words, some improvement in living standards for everyone in the society albeit at an unequal pace. The system gets challenged when growth slows down or stops (diminishing returns), inequality increases, and growth becomes skewed (i.e. only the very top benefits from growth). This inevitably leads to expansionist pressures with the aim of expanding access to resources (material and human) and markets. This lies at the heart of elite feuds, wars, and violent conflicts.

In what follows, I present a rapid-fire illustration of the theory in action to explain the economic histories of the global North and South. I will of course enter into much more detailed discussion in Parts II and III of the book.

2.2 Theory in Action: The Capitalist System, Imperialism, and the North-South Divide

The global North and especially Britain was one of the early movers towards an energy and technology-intensive production process commonly known as the industrial revolution. Many other countries had the initial conditions to undergo such transition in the production process but Britain was the first among equals. In Bhattacharyya (2016), I discuss the process and geographic preconditions that led to the industrial revolution therefore will not repeat it here. However, the key point to note is the desire to expand output. Expansion can take place via new technology, access to abundant raw materials (including energy), and access to new markets. All of this taken together offers economies of scale, which further reduces the unit cost of production and facilitates expansion. The desire to expand not only stems from greed and scale economies but also from maintaining legitimacy of the ruling elite. Without growth in output, the redistributive demands by the disadvantaged input (labour) could increase making it increasingly expensive for the owners of the winning inputs (capital and skills) to preserve the prevailing power relations. We can call the owners of the winning inputs the elite who typically gets to set the rules both at the micro and macro levels.

In the global North, the Spanish and the Portuguese were the first to embark on this expansion drive once they organized themselves as imperial nation-states. Under an early modern pre-industrial production relation, nation-states offered the desired optimal scale economies and therefore we notice the mass extinction of feudal states in Western Europe. In Bhattacharyya (2011a, 2016), I discuss what transpired such transition and to what extent geography contributed to it. The Iberians had ocean navigable ships but did not have the gift of steam power. Britain managed to make that significant technological leap first. Moreover, even prior to the technological leap England shattered the expansion prospects of the Spanish in the North Atlantic by defeating their Armada.

The industrial revolution put Britain in a dominant position as an industrial power. The initial access to abundant coal in England and Wales facilitated the transition towards a coal-fired energy-intensive and steam-dependent production process. Military success contributed towards access to new markets and new resources, which offered scale. In case of Britain, the initial expansion occurred in North America and the Indian sub-continent. The energy-intensive production process and technology gradually diffused to other parts of continental Europe. What followed is intense competition for market access and natural resources between different European imperial states. A complicated system of alliances, betrayals, and treaties between European empires signify this epoch with the French, and the Dutch and the British dominating the global map of trade and commerce at different points in time. This intense competition gave rise to three major conflicts—the Napoleonic wars, World War I and World War II. Following World War II the European colonial world order collapsed.

The global South during this time was colonised. It collectively did not manage to make the transition towards an energy-intensive steam-based production system and as a result lagged behind. Some societies in the South did have the initial conditions to make such a transition but failed to do so in time (Bhattacharyya 2011b). Moreover, the South systematically succumbed to the military and technological prowess of the North losing key battles and conflicts and thereby giving way in terms of access to markets, raw materials, and strategic control over logistics. As a result, the elite in global South and its population ceded control of the production process and power relations within their society. Power relation was dominated by the colonizers who could set the rules regarding access to raw materials, technology, capital, and distribution. This triggered deindustrialization and deskilling of the local population, which perpetuated inequality and extreme poverty.

After the Second World War, many of these former colonies became independent and embarked on nation-building. Nation-building during this epoch was driven by self-reliance in order to protect the hard-earned sovereignty and independence. This strategy led to some improvements in the living standards of the masses but largely failed to deliver on the promise of growth and mass eradication of poverty. The strategy was over reliant on the internal market, which hardly offered economies of scale. As a result, it failed to deliver the growth and distribution needed to transform these societies.

Following the conclusion of the Cold War in 1991 new opportunities emerged for the global South from a reinvigorated model of globalization. Globalization and international trade offered the scale economies and access to technology required to generate growth and reduce poverty. Sovereign, independent and accountable governments in the South also helped in improving power relations, which helped reducing poverty. Southeast Asia, China, and India are useful examples of such success stories. Therefore, one could argue that the lessons from history going forward is that the most effective poverty reduction strategy is to engage in international trade and commerce in a competitive global economy where the rules of engagement are fair and respect the sovereignty of every nation-state.

The theoretical framework introduced above is directly related to a large literature on long-run economic growth and development. I have discussed them elsewhere (see Bhattacharyya 2011a) and in various journal publications. Therefore, I will not include them here. However, Chap. 13 offers a fairly comprehensive review of this literature for interested readers.

The framework is partially related to the politics, sociology, and international relations literature. Wallerstein (1983) describes capitalism as a historical social system with an imperial core and colonial periphery. Political scientists Hardt and Negri (2000) describe the transition from a nation-state imperialism to a postmodern empire. Brewer (1991) and Meiksins Wood (2003) offer theoretical explanations of imperialism. In particular, how the political power of capital evolves with capitalism. Another related literature is the work that followed Carr (1937) and Morgenthau (1948) commonly referred to as the realist traditions of international relations theory. Note that, the primary subject matter of this book is the economic history of capitalism. Therefore, any relationship to the social and political theories are at best partial and somewhat remote. Furthermore, to the best of my knowledge, none of these studies in sociology and politics discuss the role of economies of scale in economic expansion and empire, a key subject matter here. The contributions in sociology and politics also do not offer a holistic and long view of economic and political history as is offered here.

A more relevant framework however is North et al.'s (2009) 'natural state' thesis. The key idea is the following. Elites within a state are able to form coalitions. They do so in order to restrict entry and protect their rent from potential challengers. However, the forces of free market, trade, economic growth, and liberal democracy challenge these restrictions. The forces unleashed by the process of economic growth and liberal democracy challenge incumbent elite power in illiberal polities and therefore the elites suppress economic growth and democratization in order to hold on to power. In contrast, states that are able to transition towards free market and liberal democracy are competitive, durable, and prosperous.

North et al.'s (2009) 'natural state' thesis explain the development process of countries in the North Atlantic. In particular, it explains Anglo-American engagement in Atlantic trade and subsequent economic and political changes. However, it ignores the role of the Atlantic slave trade, colonialism, and institutionalised racial discrimination in shaping the economic fortunes of the Atlantic economies (Williams 1944; Findlay 1990; Inikori 2002).[8] More importantly, the 'natural state' thesis fails to explain the decline in economic and political powers of post-imperial societies possessing the twin institutions of free market and liberal democracy. The relative decline of British economic and political power post-Second World War is a case in point. Furthermore, the relative decline of the continental European economies of the Atlantic Alliance since 2008 Global Financial Crisis also cannot be explained by the 'natural state' thesis. This trend is only likely to accelerate in a post-COVID-19 pandemic world.

North et al.'s (2009) 'natural state' thesis does not explain institutional capture in Western liberal democracies. The thesis assumes that the twin institutions of free market and liberal democracy is sufficient to guarantee perpetual economic expansion and fair distributive outcome. Yet lobbying and institutional capture erode institutional capacity in free market liberal democracies delivering weak growth and skewed distributive outcome. Rising income and wealth inequality in the United States since 2008 is a case in point (Saez and Zucman 2019). Indeed, a fraction of it could be explained by technological progress. Nevertheless, institutional capture and tax evasion by the elite remains a potent factor.

The 'natural state' thesis also fails to explain the rise of China, a country that did not embrace Anglo-American liberal political institutions. China's expansion strategy is not dissimilar to the European Imperial powers of the eighteenth and nineteenth centuries. The European monarchies created monopolies using the institutional mechanism of the Royal Charter granting the bourgeoisie monopoly rights over trade in certain commodities. Several East India Companies emerged out of this process. The intention was to exploit scale economies and eliminate competition. Similarly, modern China's expansion strategy relies on trade, foreign direct investment, and state monopoly in strategic sectors. Trade increases the size of the market thereby offering scale economy. Foreign direct investment works symbiotically with the state monopolies offering scale. Privately owned small and medium-size businesses evolve as part of the supply chain of the monopolies.

In contrast, my theoretical framework as described above is able to adequately explain the relative decline of British and continental European economic and political power. The loss of empire limits accesses to markets, raw materials, and human resources. At the very least, it makes the inputs of production relatively more expensive thereby reducing economic rent. Loss of markets also limits the ability to

---

[8]For an alternative view on the effect of Atlantic slave trade on British industrial revolution, see Harley (2013).

exploit economies of scale and therefore reduces rent. What ensues is a decline in economic and political power.

My framework is also able to explain institutional capture within the Atlantic Alliance and the rise of China and the BRICS. I revisit these issues in Chaps. 3, 5, 8, 11, and 12 of the book.

Bibliography

Bhattacharyya, S. (2011a). *Growth miracles and growth debacles: Exploring root causes*. Cheltenham: Edward Elgar.

Bhattacharyya, S. (2011b). Five centuries of economic growth in India: The institutions perspective. In R. Jha (Ed.), *Handbook of South Asian Economics* (pp. 32–43). London: Routledge.

Bhattacharyya, S. (2016). The historical origins of poverty in developing countries. In D. Brady & L. Burton (Eds.), *Oxford handbook of the social science of poverty, Chapter 12* (pp. 270–292). New York: Oxford University Press.

Brewer, A. (1991). *Marxist theories of imperialism: A critical survey*. London: Routledge.

Carr, E. H. (1937). *International relations since the peace treaties*. London: Macmillan.

Findlay, R. (1990). *The triangular trade and the Atlantic economy of the eighteenth century: A simple general-equilibrium model* (Essays in International Finance, No. 177, Princeton: Department of Economics, Princeton University)

Hardt, M., & Negri, A. (2000). *Empire*. Cambridge, MA: Harvard University Press.

Harley, C. K. (2013). *Slavery, the British Atlantic economy and the industrial revolution*. Discussion papers in economics and social history number 113, University of Oxford.

Inikori, J. (2002). *Africans and the industrial revolution in England: A study in international trade and economic development*. Cambridge: Cambridge University Press.

Kalecki, M. (1990). Political aspects of full employment. In M. Kalecki (Ed.), *Collected works of Michael Kalecki* (Vol. I). Oxford: Clarendon Press.

Kalecki, M. (1992). Central price determination. In M. Kalecki (Ed.), *Collected works of Michael Kalecki* (Vol. III). Oxford: Clarendon Press.

Kalecki, M. (1993). Introduction to the theory of growth in a socialist economy. In M. Kalecki (Ed.), *Collected works of Michael Kalecki* (Vol. III). Oxford: Clarendon Press.

Meiksins Wood, E. (2003). *Empire of capital*. London: Verso Books.

Morgenthau, H. (1948). *Politics among nations: The struggle for power and peace*. New York: Alfred A. Knopf.

North, D., Wallis, J., & Weingast, B. (2009). *Violence and social order*. New York: Cambridge University Press.

Saez, E., & Zucman, G. (2019). *The Triumph of injustice: How the rich dodge taxes and how to make them pay*. New York: W.W. Norton.

Wallerstein, I. (1983). *Historical capitalism with capitalist civilization*. London: Verso.

Williams, E. (1944). *Capitalism and Slavery*. Chapel Hill: University of North Carolina Press.

Part II
Rent, Elite Feuds and Imperial Expansion in Early Modern and Modern Europe

Chapter 3
Atlanticism, the Slave Trade, and the Westward Expansion of Western Europe

Abstract This chapter charts the history of Atlanticism and slave trade in Western Europe. It describes what prompted the Spanish and the Portuguese to engage in Atlantic or westward expansion. It covers Portuguese and Spanish engagements in the maritime spice, precious metals, cotton textile, and silk trade connecting the continents of Asia, Africa, and Latin America. It describes the process of takeover of this trade by the Dutch and then the British. It covers the history of maritime trade in goods, commodities, and slaves between Europe, Africa, Asia, and Latin America. It highlights imperial competition and elite feuds in the form of Anglo-Hispanic wars, Anglo-French wars, Anglo-Dutch conflict, and the American War of Independence as a by-product of this trade. It pays special attention to the history of the relationship between imperial elites and settlers in the new world.

Various empires graced the Eurasian continent during her long history of human habitation. Jared Diamond, in his book entitled Guns, Germs, and Steel describes how a small and extremely fertile landmass of Eastern Mediterranean, the 'Fertile Crescent' yielded wild varieties of crops such as rice, wheat, and others more than 40,000 years ago. The local human inhabitants who turned from hunter gathering nomads to sedentary cultivators subsequently domesticated these wild crops. A turn from hunter gathering nomadic lifestyle to sedentary agriculture did wonders to their nutrition and protein intake. With food supply relatively secure, the local population also domesticated wild animals that acted as an important source of protein. Therefore, sustenance became less of a challenge freeing up time. Fertile agricultural land also became a valuable asset with different groups competing for it on the battlefield.

The above narrative fits my theoretical framework well. What we observe here is a change in the production process (from nomadic hunter-gatherers to sedentary agriculture) yielding rent in the form of surplus grains. The desire to expand rent (or surplus grain) even further leads to trade between groups. Competing tribes realise that there are gains from trade but the gains from plunder and violent conflict are even more if it is worthwhile taking that risk. Competing tribes also realise that they can exploit scale economies with the expansion of territory (land input) and livestock (capital).

S. Bhattacharyya, *A History of Global Capitalism*, Frontiers in Economic History,
https://doi.org/10.1007/978-3-030-58736-9_3

The obvious geographic advantage of the Eastern Mediterranean as described above gives rise to powerful land-based imperial civilisations such as ancient Greece, Rome, Egypt, Babylon, Persia, Mesopotamia, and others with the Eastern Mediterranean as their imperial core. All of these empires turn out to be land-based because of the nature of the production function. Their reliance on agriculture as the main economic activity rendered land as an extremely valuable asset worthwhile competing for. All of these ancient civilisations were also reliant on important river systems as their farming practice depended on the availability of freshwater. Therefore, not surprisingly, the Tiber is associated with Rome, the Nile is associated with Egypt, and the Tigris and the Euphrates are associated with Mesopotamia etc. All the while Western Europe remained relatively backward periphery with low population density and mainly nomadic population.

The Eastern Mediterranean's established stable trade links and a system of inter-imperial relations with other mighty land and river-based empires of the East such as Yangtze valley civilisation of China, Indus valley, and Gangetic civilisations of India. This system of trade, inter-imperial relations lasted for thousands of years. However, they were also marred by violent conflicts originating from expansion attempts by Alexander the Great of Macedonia (around 330 BC), Cyrus the Great of Persia (around 500 BC), Nader Shah of Persia (around 1750 AD), and others. With the rise of Ancient Rome, Eastern Mediterranean witnessed the largest empire in her imperial history with Rome and later Constantinople (modern-day Istanbul) as the imperial core.

The Western European periphery was first colonised by Ancient Rome with the extent of the empire stretching as far as the islands of Britain. The periphery received latest technology, ideas, a tax system, and other institutions as a colony. This led to improvements in agricultural productivity and population growth. The positive trends were frequently interrupted by pestilence. Most notable among them were the 'Black Death' in fourteenth century (Voigtlander and Voth 2008). War was also a common feature with a growing population as various small and medium-sized feudal states competed for land. Western Europe as a periphery of the Eastern Mediterranean imperial core, remained extremely violent (Beard 2015).

The initial stages of expansion in Western Europe could be described as the era of Malthusian cycle. The main economic activity was food production which made use of land, labour, and technology as inputs. Production was also affected by exogenous shocks such as climate and pestilence. Cultivable land was fixed and was owned by the feudal lord or a small group. Peasants cultivated the land on behalf of the feudal lord and received grain wage in return. The feudal lord also had to pledge allegiance to the imperial core seated in Rome by collecting taxes on its behalf.

As the Western Roman Empire[1] disintegrated around 400 AD, the power of the local feudal lords increased and various new polities emerged. These successor polities in Western Europe were feudal in nature. They started competing with

[1]Note that the Eastern Roman Empire survived another couple of centuries with Constantinople as the capital.

each other, often violently, in order to expand. New technologies such as the water mill emerged and proliferated over the period 400–900 AD. The technological advancements boosted food production and war fighting capabilities, but overall the economy remained trapped in the Malthusian cycle. The Malthusian cycle continued in Western Europe during the dark ages leading up to the fourteenth century. Robbins (1928) provides evidence that supports the Malthusian narrative that I have described above. In her paper on the impact of Black Death in France and England, she records that France was hit by famine on at least 15 occasions during the fourteenth century alone. Good harvest and population growth were followed by crop failures, climate shocks, pestilence, and famines.

The transition from technological backwardness to advancement took place gradually over the period 1000–1400 AD and beyond. Most of the early advancements in technologies in Western Europe were due to knowledge and technology transfer from the East. In particular, technology and knowledge transfer from the Chinese to the Arabs and to the Romans via the ancient trade route (Mokyr 1990). The merchants travelling on the ancient trade route from China to the Middle East and Eastern Mediterranean were the main emissaries of knowledge. However, knowledge transfer also took place through military conquest. Cataloguing the direction of knowledge transfer, Jared Diamond (1997) in his book Guns, Germs, and Steel writes:

> Until the proliferation of water mills after about A.D. 900, Europe west or north of the Alps contributed nothing of significance to Old World technology or civilisation; it was instead a recipient of developments from the eastern Mediterranean, Fertile Crescent, and China. Even from the A.D. 1000 to 1450 the flow of science and technology was predominantly into Europe from the Islamic societies stretching from India to North Africa, rather than vice versa. (pp. 409–410)

With the demise of the Western Roman Empire, the state capacity and the economic power of the resultant competing polities improved over time. New technology and better farming techniques gradually increased food production and nutrition levels. Food surplus also increased fertility and reduced mortality raising the total population. Repeated territorial conflicts, wars, and Crusades ensued which in turn increased the state's ability to mobilise militarily and collect taxes. In spite of advancements in capabilities, Eastward expansion attempts by the Western European polities ended up in a deadlock. Crusades and other raids to the East did not result into large-scale territorial expansion. As a result, the Western European polities focused on the west instead.

The key motivation behind looking towards the West was to discover an alternative route to the Far East bypassing the Arab (or Moorish) intermediaries and other Eastern imperial powers. Under the mercantilist paradigm prevalent at that time, the wealth of a kingdom was measured by its stock of precious metals such as gold and silver. The polities in Western Europe desperately needed to expand wealth in order to finance local conflicts and Crusades. The legend of limitless wealth in the Far East motivated many to explore alternative seafaring routes. With the advancement of cartography and the understanding that earth is spherical, explorers understood that it is theoretically possible to reach the Far East if one travels west from Western

Europe. Describing such process Michael Beaud (2000) in his book entitled 'A History of Capitalism: 1500–2000' writes, 'Monarchs greedy for greatness and wealth, states battling for supremacy, merchants and bankers encouraged to enrich themselves: these are forces which inspired trade, conquests, and wars (p. 14)'.

Monarchs in Western European polity invested heavily into the discovery and conquest of new land. For example, financed by Queen Isabella I of Castile, King Ferdinand II of Aragon and a consortia of Genoese and Florentine bankers in Seville Christopher Columbus set sail from Palos de la Frontera, Spain into the Atlantic in search of the Far East hoping to establish a new trade route and benefit from the lucrative spice and silk trade. It did not materialise the way he expected and he ended up discovering the new world instead. The prevailing mercantilist philosophy of the time and the quest for bounty induced many more explorers to follow the footsteps of Christopher Columbus and bring back wealth to their motherland. The Spanish explorer Hernan Cortez and his band of conquistadors set sail for the new world where they encountered Montezuma's Aztecs. Cortez and his men overpowered the Aztecs and conquered their capital Tenochtitlan. Atahualpa's Inca encountered a similar fate when Francisco Pizzaro's army of two hundred conquistadors defeated them in Cajamarca in 1532. The Capture of Atahualpa by Pizzaro's men yielded the largest ransom recorded in human history.

The ceaseless pillage of wealth and precious stones from the new world continued. The Portuguese and the Spanish were the pioneers in discovering the new world and setting up maritime contact. They possessed the best ocean navigable vessels at that time. The business of plunder was lucrative but the early explorers and conquistadors also brought continental infectious diseases such as smallpox with them which were alien to the native population of the new world. It had a devastating impact on the native population as they perished in the face of Eurasian diseases such as pneumonic plague, influenza, and smallpox. The Spanish and the Portuguese colonialists arrived in numbers and over time took control of the gold and silver mines of the Mayas and the Incas. Pillage and plunder became the norm. It was not just gold and silver; the colonialists also brought back new crops such as potatoes, tomatoes, cocoa beans to Europe. This trade was lucrative which encouraged more and more individuals to set sail.

Extraction of precious metals from the mines using a native labour force became challenging in the face of a declining native population. Historians have documented declining native population in South America following European contact and they identify violence and disease as key contributing factors (Stannard 1993; Diamond 1997). In order to tackle labour supply shortages, the early colonialists started replacing the native labour force by importing slaves from Africa. The colonialists also set up plantations of lucrative cash crops such as sugarcane, cotton, coca, cocoa beans, rubber, and others. The plantation owners initially relied on native labour but imported slaves from Africa gradually replaced the natives.

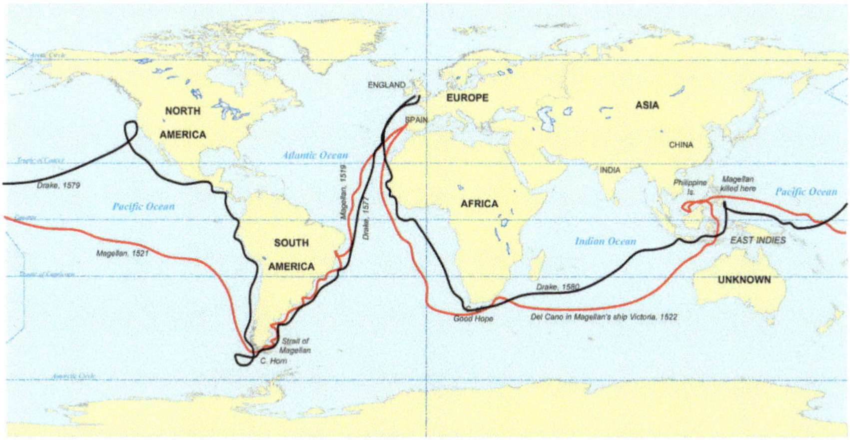

Fig. 3.1 Ferdinand Magellan and Francis Drake: first voyages around the globe. Notes: Author's construction using the ArcGIS software. Data on the voyage paths is from Encyclopaedia Britannica. Black line indicates Drake's Voyage (1577–1580) while the red line indicates Magellan and Del Cano's Voyage (1519–1522)

The Portuguese and the Spanish had the most advanced ocean-going vessels at that time.[2] Vasco da Gama, the Portuguese explorer was the first to reach India from Europe via the sea route covering the Atlantic and Indian oceans. He reached the Sothern Indian port city of Calicut in 1498. Ferdinand Magellan, another Portuguese explorer reached the spice islands of Southeast Asia in 1511 travelling east via the Indian Ocean. Later he also reached the Philippines by travelling west via the Atlantic and the Pacific oceans where he was killed in a battle. Figure 3.1 illustrates Magellan's and later Francis Drake's first voyages circumnavigating the globe. Armed with superior ocean-going vessels, the Spanish and the Portuguese not only dominated the Atlantic trade route with the new world, but also took over the maritime trade routes in Asia.

The Arab traders dominated the sea trade routes in Asia prior to the arrival of the Portuguese (Prakash 2004). However, the vessels used by them were small and unsuitable in the high seas. These vessels mainly traced the coast from Arabia to India and to the spice island in Southeast Asia. The Portuguese and the Spanish gunboats were bigger and far more superior to the vessels of the Arab traders. The Portuguese and the Spanish took over the lucrative trade in spices, cotton, and silk along the coastal route from the Arabs.

A complex international trading system emerged. The trade network is illustrated in Fig. 3.2. The maritime traders from Portugal and Spain armed with their superior gunboats sourced precious metals (gold and silver) from the new world. These

[2]The Chinese exploratory voyages preceded the Spanish and the Portuguese by approximately 100 years. Their superior vessels took them as far as East Africa. However, they retreated due to internal political reasons which I will cover in Chap. 5.

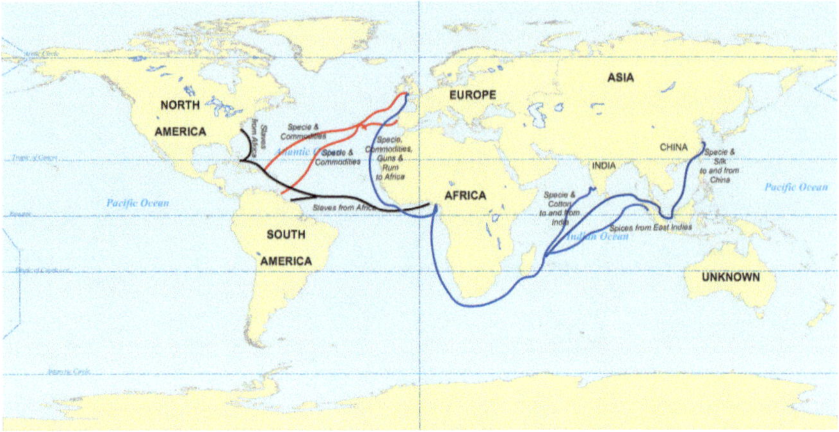

Fig. 3.2 The pre-modern and modern global trading system: commodities, specie and slaves. Notes: Author's construction using the ArcGIS software

precious metals were then used as a specie to source cotton textile from India, silk from China, and spices from the Far East. These commodities were then sold in Europe to predominantly wealthy buyers. The size of the European market was large enough to support this lucrative trade. The traders enjoyed economies of scale. Moreover, the maritime traders also engaged in local trade. For example, they sourced cotton textiles from India and sold them at the Far Eastern markets. Silk from China and spices from Malaya and Indonesia were also sold at the Indian market. The medium of exchange was a mix of barter and specie. The maritime traders also engaged in arms trade. In West Central Africa (mainly modern-day Angola), they sourced slaves and transported them to the new world on slave ships. They remunerated the African inland slave raiders and warlords using specie, guns, and gunpowder sourced from Europe and China, silk from China, cotton textile from India, and spices from Indonesia. In addition, the traders also supplied alcohol to the African market in return for slaves. The plantations set up in the new world cultivated sugarcane that was then turned into fermented sugar. The fermented sugar was transported back to Europe for the production of rum which was then exchanged for slaves in Africa.

In the sixteenth century, the Spanish Hapsburgs dominated this trade. The Hapsburg Empire not only included Spain, but also the Netherlands. In late sixteenth century, the Hapsburg merchants increasingly started facing challenges from English and Dutch mercenary ships. English naval power has increased substantially by late sixteenth century. Francis Drake, the Elizabethan explorer, slave trader, and pirate has already completed his circumnavigation of the globe in 1580 (see Fig. 3.1). The English and Dutch ships at that time conducted armed robbery and pillage in the high seas targeting Spanish vessels and interfering with Spanish Hapsburg interests in the Americas. For example, Francis Drake regularly engaged in pillage and piracy of Spanish ships carrying specie from South America. After entering the Pacific Ocean,

Drake also claimed California which brought him into direct conflict with the Spanish. By late sixteenth century, several Dutch provinces also declared independence from the Hapsburgs and created a republic. Dutch republic vessels were also competing with the Spanish in the lucrative spice trade in the Far East. In 1588, the skirmishes came to a head and the Spanish took decisive action by sending their 130 ships strong Armada against Elizabethan England.

The Catholic Hapsburg aggression against Protestant England had a religious dimension to it. However, the clash of commercial interests of two expanding empires cannot be downplayed here. Defeat of the armada exposed Spanish weaknesses in the high seas. Soon after the English and the Dutch started dominating the North Atlantic. In 1607, the English established their first American colony in Jamestown Virginia. The English also prevailed against the Dutch in the North Atlantic as they exposed Dutch vulnerabilities in the narrow passages of the English Channel. The English Channel was vital for Dutch access to the Atlantic. The alternative northern route via the North Sea existed in theory, but it was far more treacherous. English dominance in the channel meant that the Dutch had to play by English rules.

During the seventeenth century, Britain gradually took control of most of the trading routes. The Spanish were relegated to the trade between their European core and the colonies in South Central America. The Dutch held on to its colonies in the Far East and the lucrative trade in spices. As the volume of trade grew, the Dutch merchants set up the Dutch East India Company. The Company was a corporation to manage trade and exploit economies of scale. This is consistent with our model in Chap. 2. The Dutch far Eastern colony was called the Dutch East Indies (modern day Indonesia) with its capital in Batavia (modern day Jakarta). The Dutch East India Company had extensive commercial interests ranging from spices, silk, cotton, rubber, and other plantations. The plantations were run using native workforce and a strict race-based hierarchy was imposed. The hierarchy and other discriminatory practices were enforced using violent methods.

The Dutch West India Company established its colony of New Netherlands in North America in 1624, which included New York City, Long Island, Connecticut, and New Jersey. The capital of the colony was New Amsterdam (modern day New York) in which both Dutch and English settlers lived side by side. The settlement colony caused violent displacement of the native Indian population, especially from the Manhattan Island. As Dutch power waned, the English took control of the settlement colony in 1664 and renamed its capital as New York in honour of the Duke of York who was instrumental in defeating the Dutch.

Initially, the English colonial monopolies such as the Virginia Company and the Providence Island Company had the same motive as their Spanish and Portuguese counterparts. To make money out of the commodity trade. However, this proved difficult in a continent that was labour scarce and resource poor. There were no gold or silver mines to exploit thus eliminating the prospect of a specie trade. Indeed these monopolies did not make money and went bankrupt. However, fortunes reversed with the arrival of the settlers. Over time as more and more settlers arrived from

Europe, a lucrative trade network involving settlers, slaves, raw cotton, sugarcane, rum, guns, cotton textile, silk, and spices emerged under the British.

In 1615, Thomas Row's arrival to Mughal emperor Jahangir's court in India marked the beginning of British involvement in the subcontinent. Sir Thomas Roe was the emissary of King James I and he gained for the British the right to establish a factory in Surat, a port city where the British East India Company's ships first anchored following arrival. The Surat factory became part of an expanding British trade network.

In North America, the trade network included establishment of settlement colonies. The settlers predominantly from the North-western European stock set up cotton plantations and family farms cultivating wheat. The produce of the settler colonies were exported to Britain and other parts of Europe by corporations such as the Plymouth Company and the Virginia Company. These companies enjoyed monopoly power and amassed enormous rent from this trade. The cotton plantations in Virginia and elsewhere were run using slave labour. Slaves were sourced from the Gold Coast region of West Africa. The Royal African Company enjoyed monopoly right over this trade, which was backed by a royal charter. Slaves were also transported to the Caribbean island colonies of Britain to work in sugar plantations. Sugar produced in the Caribbean supported British breweries producing rum. The slave traders then used rum and other alcoholic beverages as a currency to purchase slaves in West Africa.

The Royal African Company also sourced gold from mines up the Gambia River. This gold converted into specie was then used to source Calico cotton from India and silk from China for the European and African markets. Over time, the market expanded even further with more gold and wool sourced by the British from Australia.

The mercantilist philosophy of importing precious metals and specie from overseas triggered inflation in the home country as too much money chased too few goods. To counter inflation, the state imposed restrictions on imports but encouraged exports so that the state does not run out of wealth. This policy led to the expansion of maritime trade and commerce even further. The 'no import' ideology also boosted domestic manufacturing providing it with a large domestic as well as overseas market. Outward orientation and trade in manufacturing led to specialisation, division of labour, and gains from trade. The distributional outcome of the gains from trade changed the structure of the political economy and the distribution of political power. Rent increased manyfold and so is the political power of the bourgeoisie in control of trade and commerce. A transition from a monarchic state to a bourgeois one was in progress. For example, 1642 Civil War, 1688 Glorious Revolution, and 1570 Dutch war of independence were all political transitions where the bourgeoisie gained at the expense of the monarch. Describing the events in Britain and the Netherlands Acemoglu et al. (2005b) writes:

> The victory of Parliament in the Civil War and after the Glorious Revolution introduced major checks on royal power and strengthened the rights of merchants. After the Civil War, the fraction of MPs who were merchants increased dramatically. (p. 564)

> Dutch merchants always had considerable autonomy and access to profitable trade opportunities. Nevertheless, prior to the Dutch Revolt, the Netherlands (in fact, the entire Duchy of Burgundy) was part of the Habsburg Empire, and the political power of Dutch merchants was limited.... The critical improvement in Dutch political institutions was therefore the establishment of the independent Dutch Republic, with political dominance and economic security for merchants, including both the established wealthy regents and the new merchants immigrating from Antwerp and Germany. (p. 566)

3.1 Britain, France, America, and Three Centuries of Slave Trade

> But now what? Why, now comes my master, takes me right away from my work, and my friends, and all I like, and grinds me down into the very dirt! And why? Because, he says, I forgot who I was; he says, to teach me that I am only a nigger! After all, and last of all, he comes between me and my wife, and says I shall give her up, and live with another woman. And all this your laws give him power to do, in spite of God or man. Mr. Wilson, look at it! There isn't one of all these things, that have broken the hearts of my mother and my sister, and my wife and myself, but your laws allow, and give every man power to do, in Kentucky, and none can say to him nay! Do you call these the laws of my country? Sir, I haven't any country, anymore than I have any father. But I'm going to have one. I don't want anything of your country, except to be let alone,—to go peaceably out of it; and when I get to Canada, where the laws will own me and protect me, that shall be my country, and its laws I will obey. But if any man tries to stop me, let him take care, for I am desperate. I'll fight for my liberty to the last breath I breathe. You say your fathers did it; if it was right for them, it is right for me! Harriet Beecher Stowe, Uncle Tom's Cabin; or, Life Among the Lowly, pp. 167–168

In the mid-seventeenth century, the Royal African Company (RAC) was set up by the Stuart Monarch James II and merchants from the City of London in order to trade in commodities (mainly gold) in West Africa. Its precursor, the Company of Royal Adventurers Trading to Africa received a Royal Charter in 1660 granting it monopoly over English trade in West Africa. The intention was to promote trade in gold and silver along the Gambia River. However, the company started engaging in slave trade and soon after it received another Royal Charter granting it monopoly right over slave trade. Thus, began the British involvement in the Atlantic slave trade.

Seventeenth century witnessed a gradual decline in Spanish maritime power. As a result, Spanish control over the Caribbean islands weakened. By 1655, the British seized control of Jamaica from the Spanish. In addition, the British also held the island of Barbados, St. Kitts, and Antigua. The permanent presence of a Royal Navy fleet guaranteed security. The economies of these islands were heavily dependent on plantation of commercial crops such as tobacco and sugarcane. These plantations were run exclusively by slave labour. Slaves were imported by the Royal African Company (RAC) from West Central Africa and sold to the plantation owners in British, Spanish, and French Caribbean islands. As the global demand for sugar grew, the Caribbean island economy flourished and so is the demand for slaves. Slaves faced harsh living conditions in the plantations. As a result, their mortality rates in the islands were high and birth rates low. Furthermore, the voyage across the Atlantic was precarious for the slaves and many perished. The unsustainable nature of the slave population in the plantations meant that the plantation owners constantly replaced their existing stock and thereby created a steady demand. Sugar plantation was extremely labour intensive and without the steady supply of slave labour it may not have been cost effective. In addition to the sugarcane plantations in the Caribbean, slaves were also exported to the cotton plantations in the colonies of Virginia in North America. In the North American colonies, plantation economies based on slave labour evolved along the Mississippi River.

Similar to Britain, the French involvement in the Atlantic Slave Trade was mainly related to supporting the plantation economies in the French Caribbean otherwise known as the French West Indies. This trade remained viable due to the high demand for sugar and the cost of production using slave labour relatively low.

3.2 Slave Trade and Its Effect on Africa and Beyond

Atlantic slave trade enriched the European merchants and strengthened the imperial interests of Britain, France, Spain, and Portugal. However, it had a devastating impact on the victims, the Africans. The trade dehumanised the African population and robbed them of their dignity. It perpetuated racial discrimination and propagated racism and violence, the effects of which are felt throughout the world even today. In addition, it also had a profound impact on Africa's current development trajectory and institutions. I discuss them in turn.

The theories of the impact of slave trade on Africa's current development can be classified into two broad categories: the depopulation view, and the socio-political view.

The strong proponents of the depopulation view are the historians Joseph Inikori and Patrick Manning. Gemery and Hogendorn (1979) also add an alternative dimension to the view basing their argument on trade theory. Inikori (1992) argues that the slave trade out of Africa during the period 1450–1870 resulted into massive depopulation of the continent. The population all throughout this period remained too low to trigger division of labour, growth in internal trade, specialisation and diversification, transformation of the technology, and organisation of production in the manufacturing sector. As a result, manufacturing in pre-colonial Africa could not develop beyond the handicraft stage. In the agricultural sector, the effects were more immediate. The low ratio of population to cultivable land encouraged dispersed settlements all throughout the continent, particularly in sub-Saharan Africa. The population moved towards extensive rather than intensive form of agriculture, which made subsistence and local self-sufficiency predominant. This had a dampening effect on technology adoption and production organisation in the long run. African agriculture largely remained primitive and under commercialised during this period.

Fage (1978) and Lovejoy (1982) strongly disagree with Inikori's view. They argue that Inikori's claim of an absolute decline in the African population due to slave trade is unfounded. Fage (1978) also adds that the trade had a minimal impact demographically. However, Manning (1981, 1982) and Thornton (1980) show that the demographic effects are significant no matter what the absolute totals are.

Manning (1981, 1982) adds another dimension to the depopulation view. He shows that the African continent faced with an increasing demand for slaves from the new world reacted by increasing the supply of slaves. This increase in availability of slaves also raised the African demand for slaves. Africans preferred female slaves whereas young age male slaves were exported across the Atlantic to work in the plantations. This engendered huge imbalance in African sex ratios which had a long-term impact on the continent's demographic structure. According to his estimates, the continent's population was held in check during the eighteenth and nineteenth century by the slave trade restricting economic progress.

Gemery and Hogendorn (1979) add that the mass removal of working age population from the continent caused an implosion of the African production possibility frontier as the lost labour input affected virtually all production choices. This resulted into unambiguous reduction in welfare of the continent. The secular decline in welfare continued over more than two centuries plunging the continent into economic backwardness.

The major contributors to the socio-political view are Inikori (1977, 1992), Manning (1981, 1982), and Miller (1988).

Inikori (1992) argues that a vast majority of slaves who were exported were free individuals captured by force. The capture took a number of forms notably kidnapping, raids organised by the state, warfare, pawning, via the judicial procedures, tributes etc. Firearms were imported from the Europeans in exchange for slaves particularly during the period 1750–1807, which were used for capturing more slaves (Inikori 1977). Rodney (1966) and Meillassoux (1976) show that increase in the Atlantic slave trade led to more capturing and expansion of the African slave trade often marred by violence. Lovejoy (1994) shows that warfare, raiding, and kidnapping were the means of enslavement for more than three quarters of the slaves captured during 1805–1850 from Central Sudan. The judicial process became a tool for enslaving people within the community (Klein 2001). Klein (2001) observes that judicial penalties in the form of compensation, exile, or beatings were converted to enslavement. Inikori (2000) argues that the increase in the trade for captives institutionalised banditry and corruption for more than 300 years in the continent, which retarded socio-economic development.

Curtin (1975) partially disapproves of Inikori's view. He argues that it is improper to view conflicts that arose from political causes in Africa in the same light as those that originated from purely economic motives such as the slave trade. Inikori (1992), however, questions the usefulness of this dichotomy as these relationships were far more complex. According to his view, 'attempts to establish any form of simplistic relationship are therefore misleading' Inikori (1992, p. 26).

Manning's work focuses on Dahomey which is roughly the area around the Bight of Benin during the period 1640–1860 (Manning 1981, 1982). He observes that the immense increase in slave prices with a price elasticity of supply of 1.5 created the incentive for capturing more slaves. Institutions were set up during 1640–1670 in this area, which was conducive to capturing slaves. The institutions included warfare, raiding, kidnapping, judicial procedures, and tributes. Manning (1982) writes, 'These structures further reinforced a willingness to tolerate or justify the enslavement of one's enemies or even one's own' (p. 9). In case of Dahomey, the state became an active participant in the collection and delivery of slaves, which is an evidence favouring Inikori's argument.

Miller (1988) gives an account of the deadly nature of the process of capture in Angola. He writes that warfare and violence stimulated the capture of slaves in West Central Africa often capturing slaves in exhausted, shaken, or physically wounded conditions. Populations were raided consistently by stronger neighbours and harassed and driven out from their homes and land. Gemery and Hogendorn (1979) add that the culture of raiding and warfare created a distinct minority class in the African society who became far more powerful than the rest of the population both in economic as well as political terms. The slave traders of Africa started enjoying European goods, currency, and guns in return for slaves. They made significant gains from trade at least in the short run even though everyone was unambiguously worse off in the long run due to the implosion of the production possibility frontier (Gemery and Hogendorn 1979). The extreme inequality of wealth distribution tilted the existing institutions in favour of the slave traders, which created the foundation for further inequality in the future. This is consistent with the theory of institutions, inequality, and growth proposed by Engerman and Sokoloff (1994) and Acemoglu et al. (2005a) with respect to the new world. These institutions persisted all throughout the pre-colonial period further intensifying the problem. After colonisation, the colonial powers did not interfere with the existing extractive institutions of the natives. It was reinforced by them instead (Robinson 2002). Persistence of weak institutions had a negative impact on the long-run economic development of the continent.

Nunn (2008) also provides a similar account. He shows that slave trade prevented state development, encouraged ethnic fractionalisation, and weakened legal institutions. Through these channels, slave trade continues to affect current economic development in Africa. However, Bhattacharyya (2009) shows that Nunn's evidence is not robust to the inclusion of malaria and other geography variables.

African institutions also underwent profound changes due to the Atlantic Slave Trade and other factors (Easterly and Levine 1997; Herbst 2000; Acemoglu et al. 2001, 2002). The institutions' school argue that the weak institutions in Africa largely explain her state of underdevelopment. Easterly and Levine (1997) use several indicators of public policy, which can also be categorised as institutional measures even though they were not explicit about this in their study. They argue that the lack of growth in sub-Saharan Africa is associated with poor public policy such as low schooling, political instability, underdeveloped financial systems, high government deficits, and insufficient infrastructure. They link the choice of poor public policies on the part of the African governments to Africa's high ethnic fragmentation. In other words, they argue that high ethnic fragmentation increases polarisation and the degree of social conflict in terms of policy choice in African societies. This increases the cost of conflict resolution. The government often fails to internalise these costs and selects socially suboptimal policies. This is perhaps the first systematic attempt to explore African institutional weaknesses and the reason behind it in our profession. Even though Easterly and Levine (1997) were the first to apply this idea in Africa, it is older than this. Alesina and Tabellini (1989) and Alesina and Drazen (1991) theoretically modelled this idea almost a decade before their article was published.

Herbst (2000) also seeks an explanation for institutional weakness in Africa. Robinson (2002) provides an excellent review of Herbst's book. Herbst's work predominantly focuses on the following questions. Why states are so ineffective in Africa? Why African states are often plagued by chaos and lawlessness? He comes up with an interesting answer.[3] He argues that in Africa, labour was scarce and not land which is reflected by the low population density figures across the continent. Therefore, the pre-colonial states in the continent did not fight over land but they fought over people. This explains why property rights over people were so well defined in the form of slavery whereas property rights over land were not as many of the lands were held communally. This implies that it was not necessary for the pre-colonial states to defend a well-defined territory as there was no fierce competition over land. In other words, there was less need to invest in defence and maintain bureaucracies. Therefore, tax collections in these states were poor and often absent. This allowed African states to survive without having to engage in institution building (tax collection, invest in defence, maintain bureaucracies, and provide rule of law) which made them very fragile. The trend of almost no external threat coupled with low population density persisted during the colonial period. Therefore, the colonisers had little incentive to develop institutions either. After independence, the situation did not change. The United Nations decision to enforce the colonial boundaries as national boundaries and the Cold War politics reinforced this trend. Hence, what we observe now is the weak institutions of contemporary Africa. Herbst's argument is an extension of the work done by Max Weber on the development of European states.

Even though Herbst's thesis has received kudos for its intuitive appeal, it is still not free from criticism. Robinson (2002) criticises Herbst for not emphasising the impact of colonialism on institutions and state formation in Africa. He also adds that the relationship between population density and institution building gets a bit unclear particularly in case of Africa when one takes into account the 'reversal of fortune' effect and the impact of colonialism (Acemoglu et al. 2001, 2002). The following paragraph deals with this theory in more detail.

Acemoglu et al. (2002) observe that the relatively prosperous and densely populated areas of the world outside Europe prior to 1500 are relatively poorer now whereas the less prosperous and sparsely populated regions outside Europe before 1500 are relatively prosperous at present. This empirical fact is termed by Acemoglu et al. (2002) as the 'reversal of fortune'. They argue that this is because of

[3]Herbst's thesis is not standalone. Bates (1983) and Stevenson (1968) also provide some tentative evidence within Africa which is in agreement with the population density argument of the thesis.

the nature of colonial policy pursued by the European colonisers. In colonies with high population density prior to 1500, the European colonisers faced relatively more resistance from the natives which ruled out the possibility of settlement and hence they erected extractive institutions without bothering about the overall protection of private property. On the other hand, in colonies with low population density prior to 1500, the European colonisers faced less resistance from the natives and decided to settle and erect institutions with better protection of private property. This argument may not be true in case of Africa. The African continent has always been a place with low population density. In spite of the low population density, the colonisers decided not to settle in Africa and build 'institutions of plunder' instead.[4] The answer to this apparent paradox perhaps lies in the argument of Acemoglu et al. (2001). Acemoglu et al. (2001) argue that one of the key factors that influenced the decision of not settling in Africa by the European colonisers was the continent's disease environment which is well reflected by the settler mortality figures from the colonial records. They use settler mortality data mostly constructed out of the historian Philip Curtin's work on the disease environment of the European colonies to establish a statistically significant inverse relationship between the disease environment and institutional quality. As Robinson (2002) puts it, these factors are not taken into account in Herbst's story.

3.3 Anglo-French Conflict Over Atlantic Trade

The French were a late entrant in the Atlantic trade in commodities and slaves. However, due to high demand for slaves in the plantation economies of the West Indies and commodities such as sugar, French interest, and power expanded rapidly. The colony of New France was set up which at its peak included territories stretching from the Hudson Bay in the north to the Gulf of Mexico in the south. The colony encompassed territories of modern-day Canada, the island of Newfoundland, the state of Louisiana, and parts of Mexico. In spite of the enormity of the territory, the French had far fewer settlers compared to the British or Dutch settler colonies of North America. The French also engaged in the lucrative fur trade with the native Indian communities in New France.

This rapid expansion invariably brought them into conflict with the other dominant colonial power in North America, Britain. In 1754, this conflict culminated into the Seven Years War between Britain and France on the American continent. Britain prevailed in this conflict with France ceding territories to Britain in both North America and the Caribbean. Yet, this conflict was hardly decisive. It continued as part of the global rivalry between the colonial interests of Britain and France not just in the Atlantic but also in the Indian Ocean and India. This conflict also morphed into

[4]The exceptions are the settler colonies of South Africa, Zimbabwe, Namibia, and Kenya.

a global imperial conflict during the latter part of the eighteenth century. Spain sided with France and Russia stayed neutral during this conflict.

In summary, Britain was victorious in many of the key battles allowing her to dominate France in the imperial trade and commerce involving lucrative commodities and slaves. However, this did not deter the rivals into further conflicts over the next 100 years and beyond. The expansionary urge fuelled by the mode of production and economic system as described in Chap. 2 meant that conflict continued unabated over the next 100 years with some interregnums in between.

3.4 The American War of Independence Through the Prism of Settler Colony and Imperial Core Relationship

The British settler colonies of North America were collectively known as Thirteen Colonies and composed of the territories of Massachusetts Bay, New Hampshire, Connecticut, Rhode Island, Delaware, New York, New Jersey, Pennsylvania, Virginia, Maryland, and Georgia. These colonies were English speaking as Protestant English migrants from Britain predominantly settled there. The economic power of the settlers grew over time as they made their fortune from the lucrative trade in cotton, tobacco, indigo, corn, wheat, rice, sugar, and other commodities. The settlers also benefitted from the Atlantic Slave Trade by employing enslaved Africans in the plantations Deep South along the Mississippi River. As the settler economy flourished, these colonies also became a major destination of the British East India Company traded commodities such as tea, coffee, indigo, rubber, and spices.

The growing economic power of the settlers quickly translated into political demands. Local representative legislatures were set up by the imperial core in London to placate tensions. However, contradiction over jurisdiction of the different legislatures sharpened. The local legislature run by the English bourgeoisie of settler origin started questioning the legitimacy of the Parliament in London in enacting laws that govern the colonies. Additional tariffs on imported commodities such as tea were deeply unpopular. In 1765, the Parliament in London passed the Stamp Act in order to pay for the British troops present in the colonies following the Anglo-French Seven Years War. This acted as a spark in an environment of popular discontent. Skirmishes followed with the settlers in New England destroying a shipment of tea in Boston Harbour in 1773. The skirmishes culminated into a war in 1775–1776, which lasted till 1783. This war is commonly known as the American War of Independence. France and Spain, the other rival imperial powers entered the war in 1778 and 1779, respectively, and sided with the settlers. The war ended in 1781–1782 with the surrender of the British under army general Charles Cornwallis. The following year, the pro-war Tories lost their parliamentary majority to the Whigs who officially ended the American campaign. However, the wider war against France continued.

Again, the American history of independence is illustrative that under the expansionist capitalist economic model, the periphery can amass enough power to challenge the imperial core. The power of the periphery is derived from their participation in the Atlantic trade and the resultant accumulation of rent. Once the periphery acquires a critical minimum rent and military might, they break from the core and start protecting their rent independently.

Bibliography

Acemoglu, D., Johnson, S., & Robinson, J. (2001). The colonial origins of comparative development: An empirical investigation. *The American Economic Review, 91*(5), 1369–1401.

Acemoglu, D., Johnson, S., & Robinson, J. (2002). Reversal of fortune: Geography and institutions in the making of the modern world income distribution. *Quarterly Journal of Economics, 117*, 1231–1294.

Acemoglu, D., Johnson, S., & Robinson, J. (2005a). Institutions as the fundamental cause of long-run growth. *Handbook Economic Growth, 1*, 385–472.

Acemoglu, D., Johnson, S., & Robinson, J. (2005b). The rise of Europe: Atlantic trade, institutional change and economic growth. *The American Economic Review, 95*, 546–579.

Alesina, A., & Drazen, A. (1991). Why are stabilizations delayed? *The American Economic Review, LXXXI*, 1170–1188.

Alesina, A., & Tabellini, G. (1989). External debt, capital flight and political risk. *Journal of International Economics, 27*, 199–220.

Bates, R. (1983). The centralisation of African societies (Chapter 2). In *Essays on the political economy of rural Africa*. Berkley: University of California Press.

Beard, M. (2015). *SPQR: A history of ancient Rome*. London: W.W. Norton.

Beaud, M. (2000). *A history of capitalism: 1500–2000*. New York: Monthly Review Press.

Bhattacharyya, S. (2009). Root causes of African underdevelopment. *Journal of African Economies, 18*(5), 745–780.

Curtin, P. (1975). *Economic change in precolonial Africa: Senegambia in the era of the slave trade*. Madison: University of Wisconsin Press.

Diamond, J. (1997). *Guns, germs and steel: The fate of human societies*. New York: W.W. Norton.

Easterly, W., & Levine, R. (1997). Africa's growth tragedy: Policies and ethnic divisions. *Quarterly Journal of Economics, 112*(4), 1203–1250.

Engerman, S., & Sokoloff, K. (1994). *Factor endowments: Institutions, and differential paths of growth among new world economies: A view from economic historians of the United States*. NBER working paper no. w066.

Fage, J. (1978). *A history of Africa*. London: Hutchinson.

Gemery, H., & Hogendorn, J. (1979). The economic costs of West African participation in the Atlantic Slave trade: A preliminary sampling for the eighteenth century. In H. Gemery & J. Hogendorn (Eds.), *The uncommon market: Essays in the economic history of the Atlantic Slave trade*. New York: Academic Press.

Herbst, J. (2000). *States and power in Africa: Comparative lessons in authority and control*. Princeton: Princeton University Press.

Inikori, J. (1977). The import of firearms into West Africa, 1750–1807: A quantitative analysis. *The Journal of African History, 18*, 339–368.

Inikori, J. (1992). *The chaining of a continent: Export demand for captives and the history of Africa South of the Sahara, 1450–1870*. Institute of social and economic research, University of the West Indies, Mona, Jamaica

Inikori, J. (2000). Africa and the trans-Atlantic Slave trade. In T. Falola (Ed.), *Africa Vol 1: African history before 1885* (pp. 389–412). Durham, NC: Carolina Academic Press.

Klein, M. (2001). The slave trade and decentralized societies. *The Journal of African History, 42*, 49–65.

Lovejoy, P. (1982). The volume of the Atlantic Slave trade: A synthesis. *The Journal of African History, 23*, 473–501.

Lovejoy, P. (1994). Background to Rebellion: The Origins of Muslim Slaves in Bahia. *Slavery Abolition, 15*(2), 151–180.

Manning, P. (1981). The enslavement of Africans: A demographic model. *Canadian Journal of African Studies, 15*(3), 499–526.

Manning, P. (1982). *Slavery, colonialism and economic growth in Dahomey, 1640–1960*. Cambridge: Cambridge University Press.

Meillassoux, C. (1976). The role of slavery in the economic and social history of Sahelo-Sudanic Africa. In J. Inikori (Ed.), *Forced migration: The impact of the export slave trade on African societies* (pp. 74–99). Hutchinson: London.

Miller, J. (1988). *Way of death: Merchant capitalism and the Angolan Slave trade, 1730–1830*. Madison: University of Wisconsin Press.

Mokyr, J. (1990). *The lever of riches: Technological creativity and economic change*. New York: Oxford University Press.

Nunn, N. (2008). The long-term effects of Africa's Slave trades. *Quarterly Journal of Economics, 123*(1), 139–176.

Prakash, O. (2004). *Bullion for goods: European and Indian merchants in the Indian Ocean trade, 1500–1800*. New Delhi: Manohar.

Robbins, H. (1928). A comparison of the effects of the black death on the economic organization of France and England. *Journal of Political Economy, 36*(4), 447–479.

Robinson, J. (2002). States and power in Africa by Jeffrey I. Herbst: A review essay. *Journal of Economic Literature, 60*, 510–519.

Rodney, W. (1966). African Slavery and other forms of social oppression on the Upper Guinea Coast in the context of the Atlantic Slave trade. *The Journal of African History, 7*, 431–443.

Stannard, D. (1993). *American Holocaust: The conquest of the new world*. Oxford: Oxford University Press.

Stevenson, R. (1968). *Population and political systems in tropical Africa*. New York: Columbia University Press.

Thornton, J. (1980). The Slave Trade in the eighteenth-century Angola: Effects on demographic structures. *Canadian Journal of African Studies, 14*(3), 417–427.

Voigtlander, N., & Voth, H.-J. (2008). *The three Horsemen of growth: Plague, war and urbanization in early Modern Europe*. Department of Economics, Universitat Pompeu Fabra.

Chapter 4
The Adventures and Misadventures of Expansion in Eastern and Central Europe

Abstract This chapter covers the history of eastward expansion attempts by imperial Sweden and Polish–Lithuanian Commonwealth. It also covers the history of Russo-Turkic wars and expansionism by the Russian and Ottoman empires. The Crimean War between the Russian, Ottoman, Austro-Hungarian, British, and French empires receives special attention as this is a prime example of expansionism by the European empires in the dying days of the Ottomans. The chapter emphasises that one of the key motives of this conflict is to share the spoils of the disintegrating Ottoman Empire. In addition, this chapter examines the Napoleonic invasion of Russia and the broader Napoleonic wars. The defeat of Bonaparte initiated the concert of Europe, an important institution that preserved peace in the continent for almost a century. Finally, this chapter discusses the role of the Westphalian system in preserving peace under competing imperial interests.

Portuguese and Spanish merchants were early entrants in maritime Atlantic trade. Their engagement goes back to the late fifteenth century. Dutch, English, and French merchants ably followed them. Therefore, it was extremely difficult for merchants from Central, Northern, and Eastern Europe to penetrate an already saturated Atlantic trade space. Furthermore, the military power of the central and Eastern European merchants was relatively inferior to pose any serious challenge to the Western European Atlantic traders. The Western European merchants possessed far superior ocean going vessels compared to their counterparts from the Baltics. The Baltic merchants had no realistic chance of overpowering Western European (especially Dutch and English) control over choke points in the North Sea and the English Channel. Northern route towards the Atlantic bypassing the islands of Britain was far more dangerous to navigate. Therefore, any realistic expansion opportunity for these aspiring imperial powers exploiting early capitalist production technology were eastwards. In this chapter, I will outline the expansion attempts of Sweden, Polish–Lithuanian Commonwealth, Austro–Hungarian Empire, Ottoman, French, and Russian empires.

S. Bhattacharyya, *A History of Global Capitalism*, Frontiers in Economic History,
https://doi.org/10.1007/978-3-030-58736-9_4

4.1 Eastward Expansion Attempts of Sweden

Eastward expansion attempts of Sweden perhaps go as far back as the preindustrial periods of the thirteenth century. The Battle for control over the Neva river system and Finland in the thirteenth century perhaps is the first such attempt by the combined armies of Sweden and Norway. The objectives of these conflicts were perhaps to unite the Scandinavian lands before moving further east. The eastward movement was also driven by the desire to take control of the lucrative river-based trade route connecting the north, the Black Sea basin, and the Eastern Mediterranean by displacing the powerful states of Novgorod and Karelia.

In the early thirteenth century and 100 years prior, the powerful state of Novgorod had a monopoly over the trade route stretching from the mouth of the Neva River on the Baltic Sea to the Black and Caspian sea regions in the south. Lucrative trade in timber, grain, animal hide between northern and southern Europe were conducted via the internal river systems of Neva, Volga, and Dnieper. The combined forces of Sweden, Norway, and Finland made several attempts to take control of this trade route. However, they largely failed to dislodge the Novgorod Republic. They were resoundingly defeated on the battlefield by the Novgorod price Alexander Yaroslavich (also known as Alexander Nevsky).

Five centuries later in early eighteenth century, Sweden made another attempt to expand eastwards. Charles XII of Sweden was an able military commander. At the start of the eighteenth century, he was facing the combined military power of Denmark, Poland, and Russia. The initial challenge was to take control of the Baltic Sea. The Baltic Sea was a key maritime trade route connecting Eastern and Western Europe. Lucrative commodities traded using this route were grains, wool, animal hide, and timber. Therefore, taking control of this trade route was essential for the protection of monopoly power of the merchants and exploit scale economies. At the initial stages, Sweden enjoyed some military success. Charles XII was able to easily overcome resistance from Poland and Denmark. After suffering significant defeats at the hands of their Swedish tormentors, Poland and Denmark had to accept political regimes pliant to Sweden. Buoyed by his initial success, Charles XII ventured further east with a plan to defeat Russia. However, this did not run according to plan for Charles XII. The Russians under the command of Peter the Great inflicted heavy defeat on the Swedes on the battlefield of Poltava in 1709. In addition to the able military leadership of Peter the Great, the harsh Russian winter also played its part. The Russians under Peter practiced scorched earth policy while retreating. They dispersed cattle and hid grains from the advancing armies of Charles XII in order to deny them access to provisions while on the offensive. They also outflanked them by successfully thwarting the arrival of reinforcements. Being short on provisions, Charles XII was relying heavily on the arrival of reinforcements and alliances with local warlords and Cossacks. However, the Russians resoundingly defeated these loyal forces even before they could unite with Charles' army. As a result, Charles' 40,000 strong army was reduced to approximately 24,000 even before he could face

Peter's men at Poltava. Dorrell (2009) presents a comprehensive account of Charles' Russian campaign.

The defeat in Poltava extinguished imperial prospects of Sweden in Central and Eastern Europe. Even though significantly weakened by the defeat in Poltava, Charles' imperial ambitions did not subside until 1711. He continued to encourage his Ottoman ally into a fight with Russia. The conclusion of a peace treaty between the Ottoman Turks and the Russians effectively ended Charles' and Sweden's imperial ambitions. Russia under Peter, powered by her newly developed shipbuilding industry emerged as the undisputed leader in the Baltics. Russia dominated the trade in timber, wool, grains, and animal hide between eastern and western Europe. Peter consolidated his dominant position in the North even further by establishing the new city of St. Petersburg.

4.2 Polish–Lithuanian Commonwealth and Eastward Expansion Attempts

The Polish–Lithuanian Commonwealth was established in the mid-sixteenth century but its glory days arrived in the seventeenth century. The Commonwealth experienced territorial expansion and became one of the largest territories in Europe. The Commonwealth's economic and political power expanded through the lucrative trade in commodities such as timber, wool, and grains with Western Europe via the Baltic Sea route. It also engaged in trade with the Ottoman Turks in the south and Black Sea regions. At its peak, the Commonwealth expanded eastwards and even held Moscow for the period from 1610 to 1612.

The Commonwealth's dominance over Moscow was short lived as the Russians regrouped under the Nizhny Novgorod merchant Kuzma Minin and the Prince Dmitry Pozharsky. Minin and Pozharsky's army successfully defeated the Polish invaders and expelled them from the Moscow Kremlin and Russia in late 1612. Furthermore, with the acquisition of new resource-rich colonies in America by Britain, France, Spain, and the Netherlands, the demand for commodities such as timber and grains from the east declined dramatically. Consequently, the economic, political, and military power of the Polish–Lithuanian Commonwealth also declined. The last hurrah for the Commonwealth was perhaps the decisive Battle of Vienna in 1683. The Commonwealth allied with the Holy Roman Empire decisively defeated the Ottomans and permanently confined them to the south of the Danube River. Devoid of expansion opportunities to the East or the South and a steady decline in revenue from trade, internal battles flared up within the Commonwealth. A strong and assertive Russia under Peter the Great made the Commonwealth a protectorate of the Russian Empire. Towards the end of the eighteenth century, the Commonwealth's three powerful neighbours Prussia, Russia, and the Hapsburgs carved up its entire territory. By 1795, the Commonwealth ceased to exist on the European map.

4.3 Expansion in Central Europe: The Austro–Hungarian Empire

The Holy Roman Empire of the German Nation was a loosely defined confederation of Imperial estates in Central Europe spanning from the North Sea to the Adriatic. It was one of the successor states of the Hapsburg Empire following the Peace of Westphalia in 1648. The Peace of Westphalia was a series of treaties between conflicting European kingdoms to end the Thirty Years of religious conflicts between Catholics and Protestants. The treaty was based on non-interference in the internal affairs of the constituent states and respect for sovereignty. This is often identified as the genesis of the modern international system which I will discuss more later on.

Due to its decentralised character, the Holy Roman Empire never managed to establish strong central government control. Even though merchants from the northern cities of Antwerp and Amsterdam engaged in Atlantic trade in commodities such as tea, coffee, chocolate, alcoholic beverages, calico, and grains, the revenue earned from indirect trade taxes and tolls were negligible. The firm control over the Atlantic trade route by Britain, France, Spain, and the Netherlands meant that there was very little room for the Holy Roman Empire to expand westwards. The empire was effectively squeezed between the powerful neighbours in the west, east, and south in the form of French, Russian, and Ottoman Empires, respectively. The empire maintained its fragile existence till 1805 when it finally collapsed following defeat at the hands of Napoleonic France at the Battle of Austerlitz. The Kingdoms of Prussia and Austria succeeded it.

Following the defeat of Napoleon Bonaparte's Grande Army in Russia in 1812, the Austrian Empire reappeared. The Prussians also switched sides sensing French weakness. By mid-nineteenth century, the Austrian Empire evolved into a constitutional monarchy called the Austro–Hungarian Empire. The Austro–Hungarians were a loose confederacy with weak centralised control. Following its creation in 1867, it rapidly industrialised. Towards the end of the nineteenth century, it became major exporters of machine tools, locomotives, automobiles, electrical power generators, and processed wheat. Its major trading partners were Germany, Britain, the United States, and Russia. In spite of its immense technological advances, the expansion opportunities encountered by it were largely limited. Following the defeat of Napoleon, the European Imperial States were bound by the Westphalia system of international relations. Thus, expansion through military conquest was not in the offing. Military campaigns became increasingly expensive in terms of human lives and material equipment. Therefore, the new reality encouraged states to find compromise. At its peak, the Austro–Hungarian Empire spanned from the northern city of Krakow to the Adriatic in the south. With the advent of the First World War, the Austro–Hungarian Empire disappeared from the European map.

4.4 Ottoman Empire

The genesis of the Ottoman Empire traces back to the late thirteenth century when it was founded by a Turkic tribal dynasty from northern Anatolia. The Ottomans were a key node on the Eurasian land-based trade route connecting the East and the West. Lucrative trade in commodities such as silk, cotton, dry fruits, spices, saffron, and others passed through the Ottoman towns and civilisational centres. The economic, political, and military power of the Ottomans grew over time. The Ottoman rulers also had a religious mission. They viewed themselves as the legitimate heir of the Prophet and took it among themselves to spread the religion of Islam. The Ottomans formed a Caliphate. In mid-fourteenth century, the Ottomans ventured into Europe and conquered the Balkans. Rapid territorial expansion transformed the Ottomans into a continental sized empire. In the fifteenth century, as the Byzantine Empire disintegrated, the Ottomans took control of Constantinople (modern day Istanbul). At its peak in the sixteenth and seventeenth century, the Ottoman Empire controlled large swathes of territory in Southern Europe, the Black Sea basin, Central Asia, the Horn of Africa, North Africa including Egypt, and the Eastern Mediterranean.

The rise of the Ottoman Empire was fundamentally based on its monopoly over the East-West land-based trade. However, with the discovery of the maritime trade routes between the East and the West via the Cape of Good Hope, the monopoly of the Ottomans were finally broken. Portuguese and Spanish traders established direct maritime contacts with the Far East via the Indian Ocean. The Ottomans made several attempts to challenge Portuguese merchants on the Indian ocean. However, Portuguese vessels were far more superior on the high seas rendering Ottoman resistance largely fruitless. The Ottomans continued to benefit from the rent generated by the coastal trade along the Arabian and Indian peninsula for a while. However, their stranglehold on the East-West trade was broken. In the sixteenth and seventeenth century, the Tsardom of Russia became powerful and increasingly assertive. The Russians started challenging the Ottomans in Eastern Europe and the Black Sea basin. In the eighteenth century, Catherine the Great took control of Crimea and most of the Black Sea basin from the Ottomans. Devoid of expansion opportunities, the Ottoman economy suffered from inflation and lack of modernisation. In contrast, the European neighbours of the Ottoman Empire benefitted immensely from the Atlantic and far Eastern maritime trade. Several military defeats and loss of territory followed for the Ottomans. The empire still remained relevant till the Crimean campaign of the nineteenth century and the First World War. After the First World War, the Ottoman Empire collapsed and the modern Turkish state emerged.

4.5 French Revolution and Expansion in Imperial France

Symbolically the revolution in France began with the storming of the Bastille in 1789. Powered by the ideals of enlightenment (citizenship, abolition of feudalism and monarchy, and declaration of the rights of man) the revolution swept away the orthodoxy in France. Within the next 3 years, France became a republic and executed its monarch, Louis XVI. The revolutionary rage abolished slavery from all French colonies in 1794 only to be reintroduced a decade later. The revolutionary period and the associated instability lasted for a decade when it finally ended under the dictatorship of Napoleon Bonaparte.

The French Kingdom, even though a late entrant to Atlantic trade compared to Spain, Portugal, Britain, and the Netherlands, immensely benefitted from trade with the New World and her colonies in the Caribbean. The Kingdom's involvement in the lucrative commodity trade along with the Atlantic Slave trade over the seventeenth century ensured a steady supply of revenue into the state coffers. However, the perpetual global war with Britain took a heavy toll on state finances (Doyle 1990). The Seven Years War in North America which transformed into the American War of Independence turned expensive for the French imperial state. The state borrowed heavily to finance these colonial wars and stood at the precipice of bankruptcy leading into the nineteenth century. At home, almost two-thirds of the French population were peasants working on the farms. The farms were owned mainly by the nobility and the clergy and practiced inefficient farming techniques. Majority of the peasant population lived at or below the subsistence level. Bad harvest meant food shortages which fuelled population discontent. The popular discontent turned into rage against a heavily indebted and weakened state. A combination of these factors transpired into the revolution.

During the revolutionary period, war and external conflicts ravaged the French state. The revolutionary liberal and republican ideals were not confined to France as they spread across Europe. Pan Europeanism emerged in France and other parts of Europe as the new French elite consolidated their power by expanding into the Low Countries, Germany and Italy. The instability ended in 1799 when Napoleon Bonaparte assumed power in a coup, established a dictatorship and declared himself the emperor.

France maintained her North American and Caribbean colonies under Bonaparte. However, sourcing commodities from the new world became increasingly difficult under the British naval blockade. The British instituted the blockade following their crushing victory over the French and Spanish navy at the Battle of Trafalgar. Bonaparte concentrated on Eastward expansion instead and instituted a Continental blockade against the British. France found continental allies in Spain and Prussia. Napoleon reformed the bureaucracy, instituted a new legal system called the Code Napoleon, introduced a tax system, and presided over a powerful army.

Russian economy suffered due to the Continental blockade instituted by France, as it was reliant on the export of raw materials to Britain. As a result, Russia frequently violated the French blockade. Napoleon used the protection of Polish sovereignty from the Russian as a pretext to march eastwards. The first major encounter in the east was in 1805, when the French Grande Army met the allied forces of Austria and Russia at Austerlitz. The Austrians and the Russians were defeated. Following the defeat, the Russians retreated. There were other battles between the Grande Army and the allied forces of Russia and Prussia. However, they all remained inconclusive, as Napoleon did not achieve the decisive victory against Russia that he was hoping for. In June 1812, Napoleon invaded Russia but the Russians refused to engage. Only in September, the two armies finally met near Moscow at Borodino. Borodino was one of the bloodiest battles during the French invasion of Russia. The French army narrowly prevailed but the losses for both sides were significant. The Russians abandoned Moscow, which was engulfed in fire. Napoleon was hoping to replenish his supplies in Moscow but the Russians practiced scorched earth policy leaving nothing behind when they withdrew from Moscow. Facing a supply shortage, Napoleon decided to retreat. As winter set in, the pressure on dwindling supplies magnified. The Russians mounted more surprise attacks on the retreating army from the rear. Battling hunger, diseases, a resurgent Russian army, and the harsh Russian winter the Grande Army disintegrated. Napoleon lost more than half of his fighting forces in the Russian campaign.

The painful defeat of the Grande Army took its toll on Napoleon. He was finally deposed in 1815 and France lost her Pan European Empire.

4.6 The Russian Empire

The origins of the Russian imperial state could be traced back to the Rurik Dynasty in the late ninth century. The Rurik Dynasty hailed from Novgorod. At its peak, the territory of this loose federation stretched from the White Sea in the north to the Black Sea in the south. Prince Oleg of Novgorod expanded south along the Dnieper river valley uniting eastern Slavic tribes against Khazarian invaders from the east and setting up Kiev as the strategic capital to protect the Dnieper trade route. This is outlined in the chronicles of 'Nestor the Chronicler', who was a monk in eleventh century Kiev (Chisholm 1911). The chronicles are likely a mix of legends and facts. Nevertheless, this is the earliest historical record of 'Kievan Rus' that we currently have. 'Kievan Rus' came into prominence when Prince Vladimir the Great introduced Christianity in late tenth century.

The other Russian medieval states were centred around Vladimir Suzdal (twelfth to fourteenth century), the Novgorod Republic (twelfth to fifteenth century), and Muscovy (thirteenth century). All of these nascent states were vulnerable to Mongol invasion from the east. They were repeatedly defeated on the battlefield by the Mongol invaders who installed their proxies as vassals.

The first significant breakthrough for the Russian principalities came on the Battlefield of Kulikovo in September 1380 where a united army of the Russians successfully defeated the army of the Golden Hordes led by Mamai. Over time, Muscovy or the Grand Dutchy of Moscow became the dominant principality and united all the Russian tribes through loose federation or annexation. As Mongol power waned, the Russian principalities expanded their territory in the east.

With centralisation of power, trade and commerce flourished in these medieval states. For example, lucrative grain trade along the Volga and wool trade with England via the Baltics flourished with centralisation of power. Apart from faith and religion, protection of trade routes was the main military motive at that time. For example, Kuzma Minin and Dmitry Pozharsky's successful defence against Polish invasion was partially motivated by the necessity of protecting the Volga and Dnieper trade routes. Alexander Nevsky's defence of Novgorod against Swedish and Norwegian invaders was partially motivated by the necessity of protecting the northern river-based Baltic trade routes.

Note that the key resource at this stage of economic development is land. As the territorial expanse of the imperial state grew, so is its economic, political, and military power. Modernisation of the state and its military machine began at the earnest with Peter the Great's assumption to the throne. He introduced internal, external, and military reforms. He significantly modernised the navy sensing its importance in the protection of the lucrative Baltic Sea-based maritime trade route. The Baltic trade route allowed imperial Russia to import exotic commodities such as tea, coffee, spices, calico, and sugar from the East India Company and export grains, wool, and timber to Western Europe. Merchants realised that transporting physically heavy commodities such as timber via the river and sea route is much more cost-effective relative to the land route.

Sensing technological change, Peter imported vital shipbuilding technology from the Netherlands. Modernised army and navy significantly increased Russian military potential in the Baltics. Russia soon came into conflict with Sweden. In early eighteenth century, Charles XII of Sweden invades Russia but gets defeated. Consequently, Russia became perhaps the dominant military and naval power in the Baltics and Eastern Europe. Sensing the military strategic importance of the Baltic coastline, Peter moved the capital of Imperial Russia from Moscow to St. Petersburg in 1713. St. Petersburg is the imperial city that Peter established in early eighteenth century.

Under Peter's rule, the Russians expanded east and south and successfully defeated the Ottomans. Under Catherine the Great in mid-eighteenth century, Russia expanded even further. Russian military conquest displaced the Ottomans from the northern Black Sea and Caucasus regions. In 1783, Catherine absorbed the territory of Crimea into the Russian Empire following the crushing defeat of the Crimean Khanates and the Ottomans. Catherine not only embarked on territorial expansion, she also set up major settlement programmes in Crimea and the Black Sea region in order to boost the labour force. Her administration encouraged Greek, Armenian, Russian settlers to settle these lands. The Russian settlers were mainly freed serfs.

As the Russians became powerful, the balance of power in Europe shifted in favour of Britain, France, and Russia—three major imperials powers at the time. With revolution in France in the nineteenth century and subsequent rise of Napoleon

Bonaparte, the balance of power shifted again. In 1812, France under Napoleon invaded Russia, which was subsequently thwarted following the battle of Borodino.

After the fall of Napoleon, as conflicts became increasingly expensive in terms of resources and human lives, the Imperial Powers of Europe (Britain, France, Prussia, Russia, and Austria) came to the realisation that it is much more cost-effective to settle disputes using non-military means and multilateral treaties. Hence, the Concert of Europe was born at the Congress of Vienna in 1815. The Concert was modelled on the Peace of Westphalia and was a precursor to the modern United Nations-based system of international order in order to manage large-scale conflict between Imperial Powers. The Treaty of Vienna was aimed at weakening revolutionary movements such as the French Revolution, and curbing nationalism. More importantly, it recognised the balance of power. In other words, it recognised imperial spheres of influence and offered a rule-based system to limit infringement into each other's sphere of influence. As the capitalist system of global trade and commerce evolved and conflicts became expensive, the imperial powers saw the merit of managing conflict using rules rather than armed confrontation.

The system worked well until mid-nineteenth century when the expansionary instincts of the underlying capitalist system reared its ugly head again in the form of the Crimean War. By mid-nineteenth century, the Ottoman Empire was weak and in serious need of modernisation (Figes 2010). It gradually started disintegrating and the other major European powers (Russia, France, and Britain) were positioning themselves to pick up the pieces. For imperial Russia under Nicholas I, the priority was to extend power and influence into the Ottoman territories of Balkans along the Danube and further south. It was also to protect Russian interest in the Baltics and Poland. Nicholas wanted to achieve these goals without triggering a large-scale conflict with Britain and France (Figes 2010). To this end, he engaged in personal diplomacy by visiting London in order to meet Queen Victoria and Prince Albert directly. Towards the end of Nicholas' trip to London, Queens Victoria wrote a penetrating assessment of the Tsar in a letter to her uncle.

> There is much about him I cannot help liking, and I think his character is one which should be understood, and looked upon for once as it is. He is stern and severe—with fixed principles of duty which nothing on earth will make him change; very clever I do not think him, and his mind is an uncivilized one; his education has been neglected; politics and military concerns are the only things he takes great interest in; the arts and all softer occupations he is insensible to, but he is sincere, I am certain, sincere even in his most despotic acts, from a sense that that is the only way to govern. (cited in Figes 2010, p. 67)

Britain's primary intention was to contain Russia. Increasing Russian power in Europe and beyond were perceived by many in the parliament as ominous to Britain's increasingly global imperial interest. Palmerston perceived Russian control over the geostrategically important Ottoman territories in the Middle East to be a threat to Britain's maritime trading interests with the Far Eastern and South Asian colonies. In addition, Palmerston's political ambition also played a part. Figes (2010) writes that Palmerston was perhaps the first modern politician to successfully use the media and further his interest. A war with Russia captured the imagination of the British public and established Palmerston as a wartime leader.

Nicholas I badly misread the British political system. He exerted most of his diplomatic efforts on the Royal Family while the real power resided with Lord Palmerston and the corridors of parliament. He was caught unaware when Britain decided to join the anti-Russian alliance with France, Ottoman Turkey, and Sardinia.

France's motivation was similar to Britain but with limited resources. Following the defeat of 1812, French power in Europe was limited. French elite also wanted to exact revenge against the Russians and viewed the Crimean conflict as a payback opportunity (Figes 2010). Therefore, France had two primary interests. First, France wanted to protect its imperial interests in the Middle East and North Africa by limiting Russian power and carve up the dying Ottoman Empire. Second, France wanted to drag Britain into a conflict with Russia to further its interest in Europe.

The Crimean war ensued in 1853 and it was one of the bloodiest conflicts in Europe. The proximate cause is identified as religious but the underlying politico-economic factors are undeniable which I have discussed above. Following the Crimean War, the Concert of Europe mechanism collapsed. Russia lost the conflict and the Allies were nominally victorious. The losses in terms of human lives were enormous on both sides. Russia recovered all the Crimean War territorial losses and rested more territories from the Ottoman Empire during the Russo-Turkish War of 1877–1878. By 1878, Russia was firmly back in control of the Black Sea region, the Caucuses, and parts of the Balkans. In 1878, via the Treaty of Berlin, the spirit of 'Concert of Europe' was revived. International relations returned to a rule-based path with the great powers again recognising their mutual spheres of influence. It proved extremely successful as peace prevailed in Europe and beyond until 1914. The 1880–1914 period, often dubbed as the first wave of globalisation, experienced unprecedented expansion in trade, commerce, and living standards across the imperial core (Williamson 2011).

4.7 Summary

Technological progress and modernisation in early modern Europe significantly reduced the unit cost of production. Advancement in maritime transport meant that the unit cost of transporting goods across borders declined dramatically. Cross border trade and commerce flourished which contributed to the ever-growing rent of merchants and state entities. New goods and new commodities unleased the forces of supply which were searching for demand in new markets. Rapid growth in supply of manufactured and processed goods meant higher demand for raw materials. Exploiting scale economies dictated the necessity to establish a global supply chain. Empires protected their respective supply chains using military force. The desire to exploit scale economies even further meant expansionism. As a result, imperial confrontation was commonplace in this nascent system of global capitalism. Competition was brutal so the system lacked sophistication. So violent conflict was the only way to resolve disputes. However, over time conflict proved to be burdensome as it put severe demands on scarce resources and human lives. This necessitated the need for a rule-based system to preserve peace. As a result, we observe the evolution of a rule-based system in nineteenth century Europe in the form of Vienna Congress modelled on the Westphalian Peace.

The chapter illustrates this process using examples of imperial expansionism in Central and Eastern Europe. It demonstrates that economic and commercial interests often dictate imperial confrontation even though at times they are shrouded in the ideals of democracy and citizenship (in Napoleonic France) or religion (Crimean War).

Bibliography

Chisholm, H. (ed.) (1911). Nestor (author). *Encyclopaedia Britannica* (vol. 19, 11th ed., p. 406, 407). Cambridge: Cambridge University Press.

Dorrell, N. (2009). *The dawn of the tsarist empire: Poltava & the Russian campaigns of 1708–1709* (pp. 52–62). Nottingham: Partizan Press.

Doyle, W. (1990). *The Oxford history of the French revolution* (2nd ed.). Oxford: Oxford University Press.

Figes, O. (2010). *Crimea: The last crusade*. London: Allen Lane.

Williamson, J. G. (2011). *Trade and poverty: When the third world fell behind*. Cambridge, MA: MIT Press.

Chapter 5
Western European Expansionism in India, China, and Indonesia

Abstract This chapter charts the history of expansionist adventures of European Colonial Powers in India, Indonesia, and China. The chapter focuses on the relationship between the colonial elite and the natives. It analyses the theories of client patron relationships and the role of special events such as the battle of Plassey and the Mutiny.

European imperial powers reached India, China, and the Far East via the maritime trade route as early as the fifteenth century. Chapter 3 describes this expansionary drive and the associated global trade network in commodities, specie, and slaves. Initially, the intention was to set up trading missions. For example, the Portuguese set up trading missions in Bombay (modern Mumbai), Goa, and Calicut in the fifteenth century. Two centuries later the British followed suit and set up their trading post in the port city of Surat (located in the province of Gujarat). In seventeenth-century around the same time as the British, the Dutch set up their trading post in Pulicat (located in the province of Tamil Nadu). The French trading mission was in Pondicherry and in Chandan Nagar. The trading missions sought exclusive trading rights over certain commodities from the local rulers. Their aim was to take over the maritime trade route and establish their monopoly right over their respective trade networks. Competition was fierce between various European imperial powers and they were often resolved using brute force. Over time, the various European Imperial trading companies realised that assuming political control from the local polity is the best way to enhance monopoly power and protect rent. In this chapter, I describe the process of European expansion into the important global trade nodes in India, China, and Indonesia.

S. Bhattacharyya, *A History of Global Capitalism*, Frontiers in Economic History,
https://doi.org/10.1007/978-3-030-58736-9_5

5.1 India[1]

5.1.1 Pre-modern India

India industrialised early and was a major producer of artisan cotton textile and silk long before the European arrival (Mukherjee 1939). India was an important node in the land-based trade network that connected China, Middle East, and the Eastern Mediterranean. India was an exporter of industrial goods and an importer of primary and intermediate goods when Sir Thomas Roe visited the court of Mughal emperor Jahangir in 1615.[2] As described in Chap. 3, this period also witnessed an unprecedented increase in world trade due to the discovery of the Americas and the sea route to Asia via the Cape of Good Hope. India benefited enormously from the integration of the Indian Ocean into the larger network of world trade. The early half of the sixteenth century witnessed the rise of a trading network where the European traders exchanged South American bullions (mainly silver) for manufactured goods and spices from India to be sold in Europe and Africa (Prakash 2004). This was made possible by the European conquest of South America and thereby getting access to the lucrative silver and gold mines of the continent. Vasco da Gama's arrival in Calicut in 1498 is perhaps the start of this new era of trade in the Indian Ocean. Soon after Vasco da Gama's arrival, the Portuguese Crown did not hesitate to monopolise this trade route and exclude other key European competitors. The exchanges during this time were largely restricted to spices from the Malabar region in return for precious metals. However, this trade pattern changed significantly a century later when the Dutch and later the English successfully challenged the Portuguese monopoly.

The European imperial monopolies were ruthless in thwarting each other when the opportunity arose. For example, the Dutch East India Company sensing Portuguese weakness in the Atlantic and in Europe smashed them in India. They took control of Ceylon (modern Sri Lanka) and the Malabar Coast from them in the seventeenth century. Exchanges during this period involved not only spices but also a wide variety of manufactured goods and textiles. The Dutch East India Company traded in spices, sugar, tea, indigo, jute, saltpetre (potassium nitrate), cotton textile, opium, and silk. A bulk of their trade involved manufactured goods and military supplies. Potassium nitrate is a key ingredient in the production of gunpowder. By 1750, China and India together accounted for 57% of the world's manufacturing output and therefore a substantial share of the world manufacturing exports (Bairoch 1982). The Dutch East India Company also participated in the intra Indian Ocean trade.

---

[1] Some materials in this section are reproduced from my earlier work Bhattacharyya (2011b) with permission from the publisher.

[2] Sir Thomas Roe was the emissary of King James I and he gained for the British the right to establish a factory at Surat, a port city, where the British East India Company's ships first arrived in India.

In spite of the significant capital inflows to India in the form of precious metals, the growth dividends were relatively moderate during this time. This, according to Bhattacharyya (2011a), is largely due to the institutional weaknesses. Institutions in India during this time fit the following model developed by North et al. (2009) well. States protected the monopoly power and rents of politically influential elite by restricting entry into the courts. These elites (feudal landlords and local rulers) shared a part of their rent with the state in return.[3] The main instrument used by the state to restrict entry was violence, expropriation of private property, and higher taxes. Entry restrictions were further reinforced by the caste system, which hindered social mobility. Therefore, what we observe is a rent-seeking state with very weak institutions unable to constrain the actions of the elite. Indeed the effective tax rate during the Mughal period was as high as 40% of the total farm produce which increased to 50% or more during the later periods as the central authority of the Mughal Empire waned (Raychaudhuri 1983; Bayly 1983). The farmers had very little rights over their land and any dissent would have attracted disproportionate violence from the local elites and their army. The artisans and merchants were also no exception to this treatment. The additional rents captured by the states by taxing trade with the Europeans were largely spent into conspicuous consumption. Undoubtedly, this created some short-term demand for Indian manufactured goods and textile. The long-run costs of not investing in shipbuilding, maritime trade infrastructure, army, research, and development, however, far outweighed the short-term benefits. In other words, the gains from trade failed to deliver long-run growth because a significant proportion of the surplus frittered away in conspicuous consumption. Very little of the state-appropriated-rent was invested back into the modernisation of military and bureaucracy. As we learnt from the European experience, a modernised military and bureaucracy were essential for securing maritime trade routes and protecting rent of the local monopolies.

History took this course because institutions were weak with very little political power in the hands of the artisans and merchants to constrain the actions of the Emperor and his court. The artisans largely remained atomistic producers relying entirely on the European traders for their overseas maritime trade and access to markets. The unit cost of transporting goods via the maritime trade route was far less compared to the land-based trade route. Hence, maritime trade expanded rapidly compared to the land-based trade. Religious prejudice precluded direct participation in maritime trade and therefore this lucrative trade route was left entirely into the hand of the European monopolies. They operated in the Indian territorial waters virtually unchallenged. Overall, the Indian artisans failed to exploit economies of scale and expand. Furthermore, the structure of the Mughal Empire was already very hierarchical with power concentrated in the hands of the minority elites. It also generated enormous amount of wealth that largely went into wasteful consumption. In support of this fact Landes (1998) writes,

[3]This can be in terms of precious metals, army, or crops.

> India also had a large and skilled industrial workforce, whose products circulated throughout the region. As a result, the Indians yielded a substantial surplus that supported rulers and courts of legendary opulence. (p. 156)

Sensing Mughal decline and the weakness of the Marathas, Bengalis, and the House of Mysore, the British stepped in and started gaining more political control during the late eighteenth century. In June 1757, a pivotal battle in Plassey between the British East India Company led by Robert Clive and the Nawab of Bengal Siraj-ud-Daulah who was nominally allied with the French sealed the fate of India. In spite of the overwhelming numerical superiority of the Nawab's army, he was defeated. Bribed by Robert Clive, the commander-in-chief of the Nawab's army Mir Jafar and his men stayed away from the battle. A minority of the Nawab's men did resist but the fate of the battle was sealed even before it began. The victory against the Nawab of Bengal significantly increased the power and influence of the British East India Company in India. Over the next century, British political influence in India grew exponentially.

The initial motivation of the British East India Company was not to set up a colony. However, as the political landscape in South Asia shifted, the British sensed an opportunity. The volume of rent, scale economies, and expansion opportunities political control can deliver are unmatched by what miniscule trading posts in Surat, Madras, or Calcutta can deliver. Moreover, political control delivers guaranteed long-term access to supply chain, raw materials, and markets.

Seeking political control was also a direct result of the prevailing political economy in both countries. Dutt (1992) argues that strong parliamentary lobbying by the British cotton manufacturers against the import of Indian textile forced the East India Company to resort to policies that led to a systematic destruction of the Indian textile industry. He writes, "Even in 1813, witness after witness in the Select Committee of the House of Lords testified that free Indian textile imports (of both finer and coarser varieties) would damage British industry" (pp. 148–149). The British East India Company resorted to policies of imposing internal tariffs and transit duties on Indian goods, dislocation and direct exploitation of the artisans, and forceful reduction of market demand to destroy the industry.[4] Greater political control helped the Company further these coercive policies. Indian textile also lost their overseas market due to the imposition of high import tariffs in Britain.

The Company had an influence on the land tenure system and property rights during that time. In many areas, the existing landlords received proprietary rights in land. The Company extracted rents from them without caring much about investment. The landlords passed on this burden of rent to the farmers and the poor farmers struggled to make investments in capital and technology. This system of rent seeking significantly reduced agriculture productivity and trapped farmers into a vicious

---

[4]According to Dutt (1992), many artisans were subjected to flogging, imprisonment, and worse. Cutting off the thumbs of winders of raw silk has been documented. The domestic demand for textile also reduced significantly due to the decline of the Indian royal courts, as they were the major buyers of the quality products.

cycle of poverty. It also made farmers vulnerable to adverse weather shocks. Weather shocks triggered crop failures, which invariably led to famines under the repressive rent-seeking institutions. The Great Bengal Famine of 1770 was one such momentous event where crop failure resulted into famine and famine triggered epidemics. Over ten million people perished from starvation and disease.

An example of the rent-seeking institution outlined above is the Permanent Settlement concluded by the Cornwallis administration in 1793. It was a grand contract between the Company government and the Bengal landlords. Under the contract, the landlords were admitted into the colonial state system as the absolute proprietors of landed property and the government was barred from enhancing its revenue demands from the landlords. This arrangement institutionalised the alliance between the landlords and the colonial rulers. It also legitimised rent seeking. In a recent study, Banerjee and Iyer (2005) show that these institutional arrangements had and continue to have a significant impact on economic outcome within India. Areas where proprietary rights were given to the landlords have significantly lower agricultural investments and productivity than areas where rights were given to the cultivators.

Therefore, colonisation by the British East India Company denied Indian artisan manufacturing the opportunity to expand and exploit economies of scale. Military defeats in Plassey and elsewhere rendered the Indian bourgeoisie powerless to exert any credible pressure on the European Imperial monopolies. The Europeans and later Britain were virtually unchallenged in the Indian territorial waters. Increasingly they became unchallenged on land as Mughal power waned and the remaining principalities became militarily weak. Lobbying by British cotton textile producers meant that the Company offered preferential treatment to British producers as opposed to their Indian counterparts. The native rent-seeking institutions persisted and it strengthened the feudal proprietors both economically and politically. Two centuries of deindustrialisation ensued and India soon became a net exporter of raw materials and primary products and a net importer of industrial goods.

The harsh land taxes and coercive social reforms practiced by the Company came to a head in 1857 when a large-scale revolt broke out in India against East India Company rule. It originated in the north and rapidly spread to other parts of the country. It took the Company more than a year to contain the rebellion. The Company rule ended in 1858 when the British parliament passed the 'Government of India Act 1858'. The Act brought India under direct control of the British Sovereign.

5.1.2 Deindustrialisation During the Eighteenth and Nineteenth Centuries

Economic historians debate whether India suffered deindustrialisation during the eighteenth and the nineteenth centuries (Tomlinson 1993). Roy (2002) argues that

Britain's productivity gains in textile manufacturing and the decline in sea freight rates due to world transport revolution made it increasingly difficult for Indian producers to be competitive in the world market. As a result, Britain first captured India's export market and then the domestic market. Hence, India experienced deindustrialisation. In a similar vein, nationalist authors argue that deindustrialisation was a direct consequence of British colonial rule (Dutt 1906, 1992; Nehru 1947). For example, Dutt (1992) argues that strong parliamentary lobbying by the British cotton manufacturers against the import of Indian textile forced the East India Company to resort to policies, which led to a systematic destruction of the Indian textile industry. Empirical evidence on deindustrialisation, however, is extremely sparse. Majority of the contributions on this topic rely on a few available employment and output share numbers (Clark 1950; Thorner 1962; Bagchi 1976a, b; Prakash 2005). Clingingsmith and Williamson (2008) however is an exception. They rely on relative price data to show that indeed India suffered from deindustrialisation during the eighteenth and the nineteenth century.

The key question, however, is whether deindustrialisation was harmful for India's economic performance. A simple way to visualise deindustrialisation is that a skilled manufacturing worker or artisan moving back to the farm. As a result, the entire economy becomes reliant on the farming sector and nonfarm contribution to national income declines. Modern observers regularly point out that economies over reliant on the primary sector are susceptible to global commodity price shocks and volatility. Bleaney and Greenway (2001) and Hadass and Williamson (2003) are amongst the early contributions to stress the long-run growth implications of such instability. Most theories stress the investment channel in looking for connections between commodity price shocks and growth (Dercon 2004; Fafchamps 2004). The story goes as follows. Poor households find it difficult to smooth their expenditures in the face of shocks and volatility because they are rationed in credit and insurance markets, so they lower investments and takes fewer risks. Poor firms find it difficult to smooth net returns on their assets, so they lower investment and take fewer risks. Perhaps most importantly, poor governments whose revenue sources are mainly volatile customs duties find it difficult to smooth public investment on infrastructure and education in the face of shocks. Lower public investment ensues, and growth rates fall. In short, theory informs us that commodity price shocks and volatility should reduce investment and growth in the presence of risk aversion. In addition, negative shocks are typically followed by severe cuts in investments in health and education in poor countries, which adversely affects long-term human capital accumulation and growth (Jacoby and Skoufias 1997; Jensen 2000). Therefore, economies over reliant on the commodity sector are likely to suffer from these shocks and experience lower growth over the long run. Modern evidence seems to be consistent with the theory. Using data from 92 countries between 1962 and 1985, Ramey and Ramey (1995) find that higher volatility leads to lower mean growth. This result is confirmed for a more recent cross-section of countries (Fatás and Mihov 2006; Poelhekke and van der Ploeg 2007; Koren and Tenreyro 2007; Loayza et al. 2007). Focusing on the period 1870–1939 Blattman et al. (2007) show that commodity price shocks and volatility impacts negatively on growth. Bhattacharyya and

Williamson (2011) document that the impact of volatility on growth is not uniform across countries with the rich European offshoots such as Australia are typically less affected than the poor periphery. Recent research also indicates that volatility and poor economic performance may be reflective of a much deeper institutional weakness which perhaps causes both (Acemoglu et al. 2003). Therefore, in light of the evidence presented above it is perhaps reasonable to conclude that deindustrialisation was harmful to India's economic performance.

The question that follows is why deindustrialisation took place in India? Answer to this question would lead us to the root causes of India's slow growth during the eighteenth and the nineteenth century. Clingingsmith and Williamson (2008) argue that Indian manufacturing succumbed to both globalisation price shocks as well as domestic supply-side shocks. They write,

> In sum, our view is that the long run sources of India's deindustrialisation were both the globalisation price shocks due to European productivity advance in manufacturing (and the induced demand for industrial intermediaries such as cotton and indigo) plus the negative productivity shocks to Indian agriculture induced by the earlier Mughal decline and deteriorating climate conditions. (p. 218)

They support their argument using evidence from the relative price data. However, they ignore the role of imperial expansion by the European monopolies which I have outlined above. Imperial expansion by the European monopolies through military conquest, political control, and ruthless exploitation of scale economies were the preconditions for adverse terms of trade effect experienced by the artisanal manufacturing in India.

5.2 China

The Chinese state and ruling elite were at the forefront of Old World technology and knowledge until the mid-fifteenth century. Cast iron, compass, gunpowder, paper, printing press, and many other modern technologies were first invented in China. The Chinese also were the first to introduce sophisticated irrigation canals, which increased rice production by many folds (Diamond 1997). Furthermore, the Chinese treasure fleet led by Admiral Zheng He reached as far as East Africa more than a century before Portuguese and Spanish voyages. Figure 5.1 illustrates the voyages undertaken by the Chinese Treasure Fleet under Zheng He's command. Despite this long list of technological breakthroughs and daring maritime achievements, why do the Chinese retreated from competing with the Western European monopolies in maritime trade? Why their initial advantage frittered away? Why is it Britain and not China progressed towards an industrial society? The answer perhaps lies in the internal elite feud prevalent in China at that time. This section revisits the history of that process.

Food production developed in China as early as 7500 BC (Diamond 1997, p. 100). By the start of the millennium, Chinese agriculture was able to support a

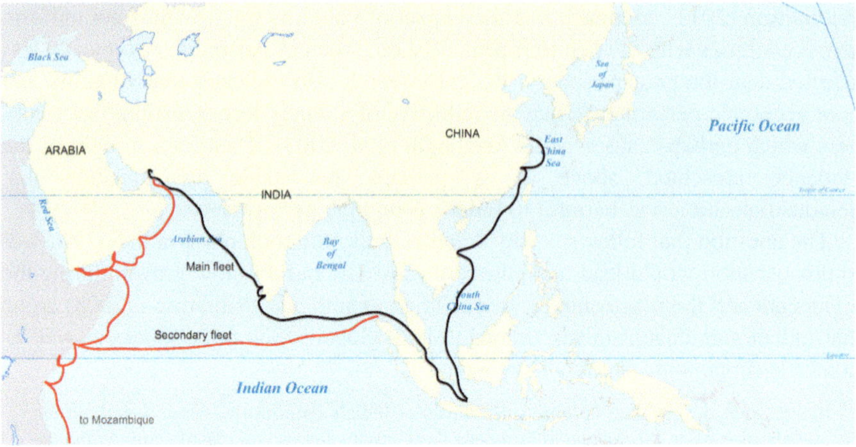

Fig. 5.1 Chinese treasure fleet: fourth voyage. Notes: Author's construction using the ArcGIS software. Data on the voyage path is from Encyclopaedia Britannica. Black line indicates the main fleet while the red line indicates the secondary fleet

large population. The hierarchical structure of the Chinese society was comparable to advanced modern political economy institutions. The treasure fleets of the early fifteenth century, the discovery of gunpowder and compass suggests that the Chinese were in a favourable position to compete with the European monopolies that were to emerge almost a century later.

The Ming Dynasty in China was the patron of the treasure fleet. The first treasure fleet set sail from Nanjing, China in 1405. Historians debate the actual purpose of the treasure fleet voyages (Finlay 2008). However, the commercial, diplomatic and security aspects of them cannot be downplayed. Prior to the first treasure fleet voyage, the Chinese coastline and especially South China Sea was treacherous and lawless (Finlay 2008). Piracy and slave trafficking was common along the islands of Malacca and modern-day Indonesia. Therefore, the proximate objective could have been to secure China's maritime security interests in its immediate neighbourhood. Indeed the large fleet and the huge army on board thrashed several pirate fleets in Palembang and Sumatra along its way to Calicut in South Asia. A broader objective was to establish state monopoly over the lucrative maritime trade with South Asia.

Prior to the treasure fleet setting sail, privateers dominated maritime trade with South Asia and especially the important port of Calicut. Sensing potential military and political threats from the privateers and the opportunity of rent, the Yongle Emperor of the Ming Dynasty invested heavily in the construction of the treasure fleet. Securing and monopolising the trade route not only opened up the prospect of Chinese maritime power projection, it also offered scale economies significantly reducing the unit cost of transporting goods to and from China. Predictably, the large fleet and its 20,000 strong army eliminated competition from the Singhalese Kotte Kingdom along with taking control of the waterways via Malacca. Note that all of these locations are important nodes or choke points in the maritime trade route and therefore had strategic significance.

Overall, the treasure fleet conducted seven voyages over the period 1405–1433 and went as far as East Africa and the Arabian port of Hormuz. It conducted diplomacy and spread the message of Chinese maritime might. It transported goods and lucrative commodities such as silk, cotton, and spices between its origins and destinations. It also carried emissaries and trade missions from their host kingdoms back to China.

However, the question remains what changed so that Imperial China abandoned the treasure fleet after their seventh successful voyage. The fate of the treasure fleet after it returned in 1433 offers a clue. After the return of the fleet in 1433, the power balance within the Chinese state changed significantly. Their opponents, the civil officials, within the Chinese court, overthrew the previously powerful eunuchs. This was partly triggered by Li Zicheng's rebellion and the collapse of the Ming Dynasty into the hands of the Manchu-led Qing. The eunuchs and the Yongle Emperor were strong supporters of the treasure fleet and centralised control over maritime trade. The commander of the treasure fleet admiral Zheng He was himself a eunuch who enjoyed strong backing of the Yongle Emperor. During the Ming reign, China witnessed rapid growth in maritime trade, the size of the navy, and construction projects related to maritime and other infrastructure (see, Ebrey 1999; Ebrey et al. 2006). These were all feasible due to the monopolisation of trade and the associated scale economies. The large rent generated by maritime international trade allowed the Ming Dynasty to finance megaprojects such as irrigation canals, Grand Canal restoration, and upkeep of the Great Wall. The civil officials were opposed to government monopoly over international trade. They were more in favour of privateers. When they returned to power under the Qing, they ceased the treasure fleets and gradually dismantled institutions of centralised state control over trade. The Qing and the civil officials viewed the formal rules set by the Ming as unsustainable with the advent of international trade with the Europeans. The unravelling of centralised control did not have any noticeable immediate impact as Asian and European privateer led trade continued. In support of this view, Ebrey et al. (2006) writes,

> In the sixteenth century, this formal system [of containing trade] proved unable to contain the emergence of an international East Asian maritime trading community composed of Japanese, Portuguese, Spanish, Dutch, and Chinese merchants and adventurers. Because the profits to be had from maritime trade were high, both open and clandestine trade took place all along the coast. (p. 277)

However, the long-term impact was significant. The loss of state monopoly meant significantly less revenue for the state and a decline in state investment in vital infrastructure supporting maritime trade. Under Ming rule, the state monopoly was a major buyer of new ships offering scale economies for the shipbuilding industry. In addition, shipbuilding also benefitted from state investments into infrastructure such as the Nanjing garrison. The demise of the state monopoly meant that shipbuilding declined as micro privateers could not compensate for the loss of a major buyer such as the state monopoly. Moreover, the decline in shipbuilding and other associated infrastructure meant the gradual dismantling of the maritime security architecture that Zheng He and his treasure fleet painstakingly assembled. The security architecture guaranteed safe passage for Chinese and other ships. In its absence, piracy and other threats returned. By sixteenth century, the initial advantage was lost. The Portuguese and the Dutch monopolies had better ships and guns. Therefore, they dictated the security architecture on the high seas. They also had a much wider trade network, which enabled them to exploit scale economies to the fullest extent. As a result, the European monopolies derived all the benefits from trade and thrived. In contrast, the Chinese producers increasingly reliant on the European monopolies for trade logistics and access to markets experienced a gradual decline.

Devoid of maritime power projection capabilities, in the nineteenth century China became increasingly vulnerable to European imperial expansionism. Buoyed by their success in India, the European Imperial monopolies imposed one demand after another on Imperial China to extract concessions in their lucrative commodity trade. One such lucrative trade was opium from India. The British East India Company illegally smuggled opium into China going back to the mid-eighteenth century. The Company would bring Opium from India to its trading post in Canton and then bribe Chinese smugglers to smuggle them inland. This practice continued for the next half a century. The Chinese Imperial administration tried to prevent it by passing many edicts and laws making the trade illegal but it did not have any real effect. The absence of Chinese naval power meant that the British could operate freely on the Chinese territorial waters and continue this morally reprehensible trade unopposed. It finally came to a head in 1839 and the First Opium War began. The Chinese Imperial administration capitulated to the British East India Company and was forced to give up Hong Kong. In addition, the British extracted reparations for war damage. The Chinese had to agree to British demands of unfettered access to five Chinese ports including Shanghai and Canton.

The uneasy peace did not last long as civil war broke out in China in 1853. The civil war morphed into the Second Opium War as some of the warring factions attacked British interest in Canton and executed a French missionary. The British declared war and the French joined in. The second war also ended unfavourably for the Chinese and they ceded control of virtually all of the coastal territory. They were also forced to make opium trade legal, pay war damages to Britain and France, and supply indentured labourers (also referred to as coolies) to the East India Company. This was after the enactment of the 1807 Abolition of the Slave Trade Act in the British Parliament forbidding slave trading in the British Empire. Therefore, slaves could no longer be used in plantations. The Chinese indentured labourers proved convenient as they could now work the British plantations in Malaya.

Similar to India, China was also outplayed and outgunned by the European monopolies. China started early. It did establish a trade monopoly in the fifteenth century under Ming rule only to abandon it three decades later. Internal political struggle played a big part in the Chinese decision. The absence of monopoly restricted scale economies and naval power projection capabilities. Over the long run, this proved costly as European Imperial monopolies ruthlessly exploited

Chinese military and naval weakness. The nineteenth-century Opium Wars are a testament to such humiliation. Devoid of sovereignty and expansion opportunity, the Imperial Chinese economy experienced stagnation and decay throughout this period.

5.3 Indonesia

The Indonesians of the fifteenth century had some initial advantage in their territorial waters, especially around the choke points of the Straits of Malacca. For example, the Kingdom of Samudra had a fleet which could dictate terms to any passing ships and collect taxes. However, Samudra's fleet was destroyed in the early fifteenth century by the ominous treasure fleet of Zheng He. From that point onwards, the Indonesian islands did not have any meaningful fleet to challenge the big players such as China, Portugal, Spain, and the Netherlands.

The Dutch East India Company (VOC) reached the Indonesian shores in early seventeenth century. It was a military commercial monopoly set up by the Dutch Republic in 1602 as an amalgamation of various Dutch maritime commercial companies of the time. It received a monopoly to trade with Mughal India in imported silk and cotton textile. It also received a monopoly to trade in spices with Southeast Asia. In 1619, the VOC violently took control of the city of Jakarta on the island of Java. They renamed it as Batavia. The VOC soon expanded into other Indonesian islands and held the territory till 1800 when the Dutch government directly took control.

During its reign, the VOC and later on the Dutch colonial government ruthlessly exploited Indonesian resources and made huge profits. Dutch industrialisation was heavily dependent on Indonesian resources. Initially reliant on the spice trade, the Indonesian island economy branched off to other raw materials as the Dutch introduced tea, coffee, rubber, cacao, tobacco, sugar, cinchona (quinine), and palm oil plantations. The plantation economy thrived on the back of steady demand from Europe and elsewhere. Exclusively slave and indentured labourers from Indonesia, India, and China ran these plantations. The Dutch imported a large number of indentured labourers from India and China (otherwise known as coolies) to work and manage the Indonesian plantations. Typically, native labourers worked on the plantations while the Chinese and Indian intermediaries collected their produce to be sold to the Dutch merchants. The colonial system in general and the plantation economy in particular were extremely hierarchical and exploitative in nature. The native peasants and the indentured labourers had no rights and extremely difficult working conditions. The mortality rates among them were high.

The 400 years of Dutch engagement in the Indonesian islands effectively turned her into an agricultural colony. Heavily reliant on raw materials exports, the Indonesian economy was vulnerable to volatility in commodity prices (Williamson 2011). This had long-term adverse consequences for Indonesian industrialisation and economic growth (Williamson 2011).

Indonesia endured this exploitative system for 400 years until the conclusion of the Second World War when the entire European Imperial system came crashing down. The Dutch gave up their Indonesian colonies as new power brokers emerged in the Asia Pacific. Following the Second World War and the surrender of the Japanese, the United States of America (USA) firmly established herself as the uncontested military commercial leader in the Asia Pacific. Globally, two major imperial power blocks emerged in the form of the USA and the Union of Soviet Socialist Republics (USSR). I discuss more on this in Chap. 8.

Bibliography

Acemoglu, D., Johnson, S., & Robinson, J. (2003). Disease and development in historical perspective. *Journal of the European Economic Association, 1*, 397–405.

Bagchi, A. (1976a). Deindustrialisation in India in the nineteenth century: Some theoretical implications. *Journal of Development Studies, 12*, 135–164.

Bagchi, A. (1976b). Deindustrialisation in Gangetic Bihar 1809–1901. In B. De et al. (Eds.), *Essays in Honour of Prof. S.C. Sarkar*. New Delhi: People's Publishing House.

Bairoch, P. (1982). International industrialization levels from 1750 to 1980. *Journal of European Economic History, 11*, 269–333.

Banerjee, A., & Iyer, L. (2005). History, institutions, and economic performance: The legacy of colonial land tenure systems in India. *The American Economic Review, 95*, 1190–1213.

Bayly, C. (1983). *Rulers, townsmen, and bazaars: North Indian society in the age of British expansion, 1770–1870*. Cambridge: Cambridge University Press.

Bhattacharyya, S. (2011a). *Growth miracles and growth debacles: Exploring root causes*. Cheltenham: Edward Elgar.

Bhattacharyya, S. (2011b). Five centuries of economic growth in India: The institutions perspective. In R. Jha (Ed.), *Handbook of South Asian Economics* (pp. 32–43). London: Routledge.

Bhattacharyya, S., & Williamson, J. (2011). Commodity price shocks and the Australian economy since federation. *Australian Economic History Review, 51*(2), 150–177.

Blattman, C., Hwang, J., & Williamson, J. (2007, January). The impact of the terms of trade on economic development in the Periphery, 1870–1939: Volatility and secular change. *Journal of Development Economics, 82*, 156–179.

Bleaney, M., & Greenway, D. (2001). The impact of terms of trade and real exchange rate volatility on investment and growth in sub-Saharan Africa. *Journal of Development Economics, 65*, 491–500.

Clark, C. (1950). *Conditions of economic progress*. London: Macmillan.

Clingingsmith, D., & Williamson, J. (2008). Deindustrialization in 18th and 19th century India: Mughal decline, climate shocks and British industrial ascent. *Explorations in Economic History, 45*, 209–234.

Dercon, S. (2004). *Insurance against poverty*. Oxford: Oxford University Press.

Diamond, J. (1997). *Guns, germs and steel: The fate of human societies*. New York: W.W. Norton.

Dutt, R. (1906). *The economic history of India*, vol. I, Under Early British Rule, 1757–1837. London.

Dutt, A. (1992). The origins of uneven development: The Indian subcontinent. *The American Economic Review, 82*, 146–150.

Ebrey, P. (1999). *The Cambridge illustrated history of China*. Cambridge: Cambridge University Press.

Ebrey, P., Walthall, A., & Palais, J. (2006). *East Asia: A cultural, social, and political history*. Boston: Houghton Mifflin.

Fafchamps, M. (2004). *Rural poverty, risk and development*. Cheltenham: Edward Elgar.
Fatás, A., & Mivhov, I. (2006). *Policy volatility, institutions and economic growth*. INSEAD, Singapore and Fontainebleau, France, unpublished.
Finlay, R. (2008). The Voyages of Zheng He: Ideology, state power, and maritime trade in Ming China. *The Journal of the Historical Society, 8*(3), 327–347.
Hadass, Y., & Williamson, J. (2003, April). Terms-of-trade shocks and economic performance, 1870–1940: Prebisch and Singer Revisited. *Economic Development and Cultural Change, 51*, 629–656.
Jacoby, H. G., & Skoufias, E. (1997, July). Risk, financial markets, and human capital in a developing country. *The Review of Economic Studies, 64*, 311–335.
Jensen, R. (2000, May). Agricultural volatility and investments in children. *The American Economic Review, 90*, 399–404.
Koren, M., & Tenreyro, S. (2007). Volatility and development. *Quarterly Journal of Economics, 122*(1), 243–287.
Landes, D. (1998). *The wealth and poverty of nations: Why some are so rich and some so poor*. London: Abacus.
Loayza, N. V., Rancière, R., Servén, L., & Ventura, J. (2007). Macroeconomic volatility and welfare in developing countries: An introduction. *World Bank Economic Review, 21*(3), 343–357.
Mukherjee, R. (1939). *The economic history of India: 1600–1800*. London: Longmans, Green and Company.
Nehru, J. (1947). *The discovery of India*. London: Meridian Books.
North, D., Wallis, J., & Weingast, B. (2009). *Violence and social order*. New York: Cambridge University Press.
Poelhekke, S., & van der Ploeg, F. (2007). *Volatility, financial development and the natural resource curse*. CEPR discussion paper 6513, October.
Prakash, O. (2004). *Bullion for goods: European and Indian merchants in the Indian Ocean trade, 1500–1800*. New Delhi: Manohar.
Prakash, O. (2005). *The Great divergence: Evidence from eighteenth century India*. Paper presented at the GEHN Conference on Imperialism, Istanbul, September 11–12.
Ramey, G., & Ramey, V. (1995). Cross-country evidence on the link between volatility and growth. *The American Economic Review, 85*(5), 1138–1151.
Raychaudhuri, T. (1983). The mid-eighteenth-century background. In D. Kumar & M. Desai (Eds.), *The Cambridge economic history of India* (Vol. II). Cambridge: Cambridge University Press.
Roy, T. (2002). Economic history of Modern India: Redefining the link. *The Journal of Economic Perspectives, 16*, 109–130.
Thorner, D. (1962). Deindustrialisation in India 1881–1931. In D. Thorner & A. Thorner (Eds.), *Land and labour in India*. Bombay: Asia Publishing House.
Tomlinson, B. (1993). *The economy of Modern India 1860–1970*. Cambridge: Cambridge University Press.
Williamson, J. G. (2011). *Trade and poverty: When the third world fell behind*. Cambridge, MA: MIT Press.

Chapter 6
Expansionism in the American and Australian Colonies

Abstract This chapter covers expansionism in the American and Australian continents. Following independence from Britain, the Thirteen American colonies expanded both west and southwards gaining territory from France, Spain, and Mexico. A similar pattern appeared in Australia where penal colonies in the states of New South Wales and Tasmania and settler colonies in the states of Victoria and South Australia transformed into a large continental state.

6.1 Expansion in America

> A new consciousness seems to have come upon us—the consciousness of strength—and with it a new appetite, the yearning to show our strength . . . Ambition, interest, land hunger, pride, the mere joy of fighting, whatever it may be, we are animated by a new sensation. We are face to face with a strange destiny. The taste of Empire is in the mouth of the people even as the taste of blood in the jungle. Editorial, *Washington Post*, 1898

> God has not been preparing the English-speaking and Teutonic peoples for a thousand years for nothing but vain and idle self-admiration. No, He has made us adept in government that we may administer government among savage and senile peoples—He has marked the American people as His chosen nation to finally lead in the redemption of the world. Senator Albert J. Beveridge, 1900

As described in Chap. 3, the Thirteen American colonies of Britain stayed loyal to the Monarch throughout the seventeenth and most part of the eighteenth century. The Anglo European settlers of the colony benefitted extensively from becoming a part of the British global trading network. Lucrative trade in commodities such as tobacco, cotton, sugar, indigo, tea, coffee, timber, and others substantially increased the economic power of the settlers. With growing economic power, political demands increased. Britain's global war with France also challenged the security of the British colonies in America. However, the imperial parliament in London led by William Pit was reluctant to pay for the security of the American colonies. He wanted tax revenue from the colonies to pay for their security. This led to widespread discontent among settlers that finally transpired into open conflict in the form of the American War of Independence. Following the conclusion of the American War of

S. Bhattacharyya, *A History of Global Capitalism*, Frontiers in Economic History,
https://doi.org/10.1007/978-3-030-58736-9_6

Independence and British withdrawal in 1783, the building blocks of an independent American nation was formed. A strong central government under the leadership of George Washington was formed. Over time, it expanded both west and southwards gaining territory from France, Spain, and Mexico. This chapter describes the process of expansion.

The American War of Independence formally ended in 1783 with the conclusion of the Treaty of Paris. Under the Treaty, Britain recognised the Thirteen Colonies as independent territories. Independence opened up new trading opportunities with imperial France and Spain. As trade and commerce expanded, new settlers arrived and the pressure on land and other resources grew. The first major territorial expansion of this nascent empire came in the form of Purchase of Louisiana from the French in 1803. The French territory of Louisiana included the modern states of Montana, South and North Dakota, Iowa, Nebraska, Wyoming, Colorado, Kansas, Oklahoma, Arkansas, Missouri, and Minnesota. This effectively more than doubled the size of the United States. The purchase added the fertile plains of the Midwest to the plantation economies of the South offering scale economy and increased rent.

The territory of Spanish Florida, which consisted of territories from neighbouring Georgia, Alabama, Mississippi, North and South Carolina, also came under the United States control in 1821 after the conclusion of the Adam Onis Treaty with Imperial Spain. Spain held this territory in addition to Cuba and other Caribbean islands since the sixteenth century with some interruptions. However, with the Napoleonic invasion and annexation of Spain in the early nineteenth century, it became increasingly difficult for imperial Spain to continue to maintain her imperial possessions in the new world. Debt skyrocketed and rebellions broke out in the Spanish South America. Severely weakened by military conflict and debt, Imperial Spain was prepared to give up Spanish Florida to the United States in return for debt forgiveness. Under the Adam Onis Treaty, the Americans were ready to renounce their claim on Spanish Mexico only to reclaim it two decades later.

Spanish Florida did not have significant economic value. It had labour scarcity rendering it unsuitable for the imposition of a forced agricultural labour system that was common in Spanish South America. This system is commonly known as *encomienda*. However, Spanish Florida did have military strategic value as it gave the United States an entry into the Gulf of Mexico to challenge its European imperial rivals (mainly Britain) in the Caribbean. Controlling and upgrading the existing Spanish naval fortresses in Pensacola, St. Augustine and St. Marks ensured security of the United States vessels along the Atlantic trade route from a potential British threat.

The Adam Onis Treaty also gave the United States entry into the Pacific as Imperial Spain relinquished all her claims on the Oregon Country (British Columbia District) in favour of the United States. The British, Canadian, French, Spanish, and Russian merchants frequented these Pacific shores in search of fur, which aided the lucrative fur trade. The Columbia River mouth was also rich in fish and timber resources. Even though not exclusive, shared access to these resources offered the United States more scale economies.

Following the conclusion of the Adam Onis Treaty with imperial Spain, the United States administration under President James Monroe was increasingly opposed to European imperial interference in the new world. As the power and influence of a rising empire grew, it became increasingly assertive. It put the other European empires into notice in its desire to carve out its own sphere of influence in the western hemisphere. The immediate challenge came from the Russian Empire, which claimed exclusive access to the Pacific Northwestern coastline (modern day Alaska). The United States and Britain were opposed to this claim. The concept of America's own sphere of influence in the western hemisphere was only formalised three decades later in 1850 in the form of the Monroe Doctrine. This doctrine was pivotal in America's war effort against Imperial Spain in late nineteenth century. More on this later. The Monroe Doctrine survived for centuries and continues to have a significant influence on American foreign policy.

In 1845, the United States annexed Texas to further bolster its presence in the Gulf of Mexico. A war with Mexico ensued. The American forces were victorious. They captured Mexico City, the Rio Grande, and pushed further west into California. After 2 years of conflict, the war ended with the Treaty of Guadalupe Hidalgo. Mexico ceded vast swathes of territory to the United States. The war and the treaty thrashed Mexican imperial ambitions. The United States became the undisputed continental leader and a leading empire dominating over a much-reduced Mexico.

The European settlers in North America were not kind to the Native American population. The West and Southward territorial expansion of the United States frequently led them into conflict with the Native American tribes. The tribes were poorly armed compared to their European enemies. They did not have metal tools at the time of the European arrival. They wanted to trade with the Europeans grains in exchange for metal tools. However, the tribes had very little understanding of European institutions such as private property rights and land tenure. The European settlers could easily deceive the tribes into agreeing transfer of land rights in return for perishable goods of little value. In many instances, the tribes and their chiefs failed to understand the long-term consequences of such exchanges. Violent raids by settlers into Indian land in search of food and other provisions ultimately triggered violent reactions. For example, the settlers in the seventeenth-century English settlement of Virginia often relied on the native Powhatan tribes for provisions. The Powhatans in exchange appreciated English metal tools. However, the English settlers constantly expanded into Powhatan land to support their growing tobacco plantations and trade. This led them directly into conflict with the tribes. Moreover, settlers resorted to looting Powhatan villages when they ran low on provisions. These practices provoked a violent reaction from the Powhatans in 1622 when they attacked the settlers and massacred many.

Cruelty was also common as the European colonisers bestowed pathogen-infested blankets upon the tribes in order to trigger epidemics of deadly diseases such as smallpox. For example, the British as part of their war effort against the Native Americans of the Ohio Country in 1763 gave them items from a smallpox infirmary with the hope of triggering an epidemic. In addition to deception and cruelty, disproportionate violence and mass execution were also common. With the settlers claiming more and more land, the native population declined significantly since the arrival of the European settlers.

In 1812, the Indian tribes in the Midwest and South formed a military coalition against the United States government and the colonial settlers. The tribes allied with Britain and fought against the United States. However, they lost. This was perhaps the first major organised war effort by the Indian tribes against the settlers and the United States government. Following the defeat of 1812, more humiliation of the native population followed with the Indian Removal Act of 1830. This effectively legalised colonial land grab east of the Mississippi River and west of Oklahoma. Humiliated and dispossessed, Native American population's power and influence declined significantly over the next 100 years.

With large new territories joining the American Union, the terms of the Union were called into question. Especially, the status of the institution of slavery within the Union became a major issue of contention. The factor endowments and the structure of the economies in the north and south of the Union were very different. The south had a flourishing plantation economy erected on the sweat and blood of the African slave labour. The southern economy heavily relied on exports of raw materials such as king cotton, tobacco, sugarcane to the old world. Therefore, the political economy interests of the southern plantation owning elite was low tariffs and the continuation of the institution of slavery. Even though the unit cost of a slave increased significantly over time, it was still profitable to run plantations using slave labour. The production technology used in the plantations were labour and land intensive. The plantation owners were looking to expand into the new territories in the west and south that joined the union in the 1820s.

In contrast, the north was experiencing rapid industrialisation. The scale economies of industrialisation received a 'big push' during the years of the War of Independence against Imperial Britain as military production gained strength. The war effort against Mexico further bolstered the 'military industrial complex'. As a rising empire, the northern elite could foresee the necessity of rapid industrialisation in order to defend the Union and compete against the old world empires. They were largely in favour of using tariff protection as an instrument to compete against the cheaper British goods and industrialise. Trade protectionism and self-reliance also sat well with the largely isolationist (from the old world) and independent worldview of the founding fathers in general and James Monroe in particular. James Monroe called for carving out America's own sphere of influence independent of the European empires.

Even though the factories in the north were more capital intensive compared to the southern plantations, they still needed access to cheap labour in order to expand. Therefore, they were in favour of abolition of slavery to free up surplus African labour in the plantation economies of the south. They were also opposed to the expansion of slavery into the new western territories of the Union. Moreover, there was a moral imperative. Many in the north and the northern elite perceived the institution of slavery to be immoral and contrary to the republican spirit of the United States constitution. The political philosophy of modern republicanism, which guaranteed 'liberty' and 'inalienable individual rights' were the guiding principle of the United States constitution.

These inherent contradictions between the north and south of the Union came to a head in 1861 following the election of Abraham Lincoln, the first Republican Party President of the United States. The slave owning democrats of the south were bitterly opposed to Lincoln's leadership even though his initial position on slavery was ambivalent. Lincoln perceived slavery to be divisive issue for the union. He made it clear in his inaugural speech that he did not wish to intervene in the slave owning southern states as he viewed it as a matter outside the jurisdiction of the federal government. As a pragmatic man, Lincoln understood the risk of civil war associated with the institution of slavery which he wanted to avoid.

The slave owning southern states were unwilling to trust Lincoln's words. They viewed his election as a significant increase in power of the industrial elites of the north. In February 1861, seven slave owning southern states seceded from the Union of 32 states and formed the Confederacy. The Confederacy justified their secession by claiming that they had a right to do so within a flexible Union. The civil war formally broke out when the Confederacy forces attacked Fort Sumter in South Carolina. During the early years of the conflict, the Confederacy grew to 11 states all of which had representations in the Confederacy Congress. However, on the face of a restrictive naval blockade instituted by the Union navy sustaining the war effort became increasingly difficult for the Confederacy. On the western territories, the union forces expanded rapidly and made significant permanent gains. In contrast, progress was slow in the north and the east. Robert E. Lee, the commander of the Confederate forces made some initial gains in the north. However, his northern war efforts ended with the defeat in the pivotal Battle of Gettysburg. Casualties were high on both sides but the victory in Gettysburg turned the tide in favour of the Union forces. Union forces also destroyed the Confederate river navy, which rendered the Union instituted naval blockade impenetrable. The war formally ended in 1865 with Robert E Lee surrendering to the forces of Union commander Ulysses Grant.

The Confederacy never received formal recognition from the European Imperial States. None of the European Imperial States entered the conflict. Their reluctance is perhaps understandable at the back of another expensive imperial war in Crimea in 1855–1856. Moreover, the European states were reluctant to side with the Confederacy since they perceived revolutions, uprisings, and secessions as a threat to their own power.

The United States territorially expanded even further in 1867 with the purchase of Alaska from the Russian Empire. This added the vast Alaskan timber, fisheries, fur, and other resources to the United States resource base. In 1898, guided by the foreign policy principles of the Monroe Doctrine and a desire to acquire Cuba, Americans decided to intervene in the Spanish Cuban conflict. This culminated into the Spanish American war. The proximate cause of the conflict was an explosion in an American warship in Havana but the broader context cannot be ignored. The Americans prevailed in this conflict even though they failed to acquire Cuba. As a part of the settlement, they acquired Spanish imperial possessions in the Caribbean (Puerto Rico) and the Pacific (The Philippines, and Guam). With large territory, flourishing economy, powerful navy, and powerful army, the United States became the uncontested imperial power in the western hemisphere at the dawn of the twentieth century industrial age.

The Spanish possessions in South America did gain independence from Imperial Spain around early nineteenth century. They also attempted to unify under the leadership of General Simone Bolivar. However, their unification attempts fell short. Therefore, these territories never achieved the scale economies and the level of industrialisation required to seriously challenge the economic and military might of the United States in the western hemisphere. Furthermore, there were geographical barriers to unification in the form of the Andes and the Amazon, which turned out to be insurmountable.

6.2 Expansion in Australia

Spanish and Dutch explorers reached the Australian northern shores in the early seventeenth century. In particular, Spanish and Dutch explorers traced the Cape York Peninsula and Torres Strait Island coastline as early as 1606. However, none of the explorers expressed any interest in establishing a colony. In mid-seventeenth century, the Dutch explorer Abel Tasman reached Tasmania. He named it as Van Diemen's Land after the Dutch Governor General of East Indies Anthony van Diemen. Other explorers followed but it is only in late eighteenth century, the British explorer Captain James Cook charted the east coast of the continent and docked at Botany Bay, Sydney. Cook was very optimistic about the prospect of setting up a colony in New South Wales. Based on Cook's rave review and 10 years after his maiden voyage, the first British fleet arrived in Botany Bay with the specific aim of setting up a penal colony. The fleet carried provisions and convicts who were estimated to be over 1000 individuals.

The timing was important here. Following British defeat in the American War of Independence in 1783, the newly established United States (formerly Thirteen Colonies of North America) refused to accept any further British convicts. London was desperate to find an alternative as the English prison population exploded. They decided to establish a penal colony on the land claimed by Captain Cook in New South Wales, Australia. Subsequently, a further penal colony was established in Tasmania. Over time, more colonies were formed in Western Australia, South Australia, Victoria, Queensland, and New Zealand.

The resource endowment of Australia during the early part of colonisation in the 1820s and 1830s was similar to the American colonies. It was land abundant with a very small native population and a minuscule European population consisting of convicts, ex-military service members, and the military. Governor General Lachlan Macquarie transformed New South Wales from a penal colony to a free state by instituting some major reforms. British experience in the American colonies made the colonisers very aware of the adverse consequences of harsh treatment of the convicts and settlers. Macquarie arrived in Australia at the back of disorderly and lawless behaviour in the New South Wales colony. His mission was to institute order but not through repression. That trend in the governance of the colony continued following Macquarie. By 1840, the British colonisers moved towards granting self-government to Australia. This step by the colonial rulers was perhaps motivated by the earlier loss of the American colonies and also trouble in Upper and Lower Canada. The decision of not granting self-rule and more representation in the North American colonies cost the British dearly. Therefore, they did not want to repeat the same mistakes in Australia. Furthermore, the political trends in Britain also influenced this decision.

Given the resource endowment of the continent, a flourishing pastoral economy evolved. Australia quickly integrated itself into the trading network and supply chain of Imperial Britain. Australia exported wool, cotton, minerals, livestock, and grains to the imperial core while importing tea, coffee, textile, and other manufactured goods. The colonies also had a flourishing settler economy, which made generous profits from transporting free settlers to Australia from Britain and other parts of Western Europe.

With the advent of the steam engine, production technology underwent significant changes in the nineteenth century. Production became more energy and capital intensive. Steam engines made maritime navigation even more reliable significantly cutting transport time and cost. On land, railways could haul more goods at a fraction of the cost. Transporting goods and particularly minerals from inland to the seaport became more cost effective with the advent of railways. Declining transport cost and the advent of the industrial age unleashed new set of opportunities for Australia. Now Australian cotton could compete with cotton from the American south. Demand for Australian cotton increased in the mills of Manchester and Liverpool. Australian anthracite coal supported the coal-fired mills in Northern England. Australian bauxite supported the steel factories in the imperial core.

The Australian elite benefited immensely from scale economies and trade with the imperial core. However, it remained responsive to the distributive demand of the free settlers. All throughout, Australia remained egalitarian as documented by Atkinson and Leigh (2007) (see Fig. 6.1). Note that unlike the elite in the Thirteen Colonies of North America, the Australian elite stayed loyal to the British Crown. The Australian elite did not have an independent security architecture and relied entirely on London for the same. The British navy provided security along the maritime trade route. British navy and army were also responsible for addressing any security threat emerging from Australia's immediate neighbourhood. As trade and commerce flourished, the colonies of New South Wales, Victoria, Queensland, South Australia, and Western Australia formed a federation in 1901. There were other political motives but the scale economy advantages of a federation cannot be underestimated. A federation offered scale economy benefits from an integrated tax and administrative system. However, federation did not lead to Australia charting an independent course from Britain.

Australia also remained ethnically homogeneous as the White Australia Policy was instituted in 1901. The aim of the policy was to forbid non-European migration

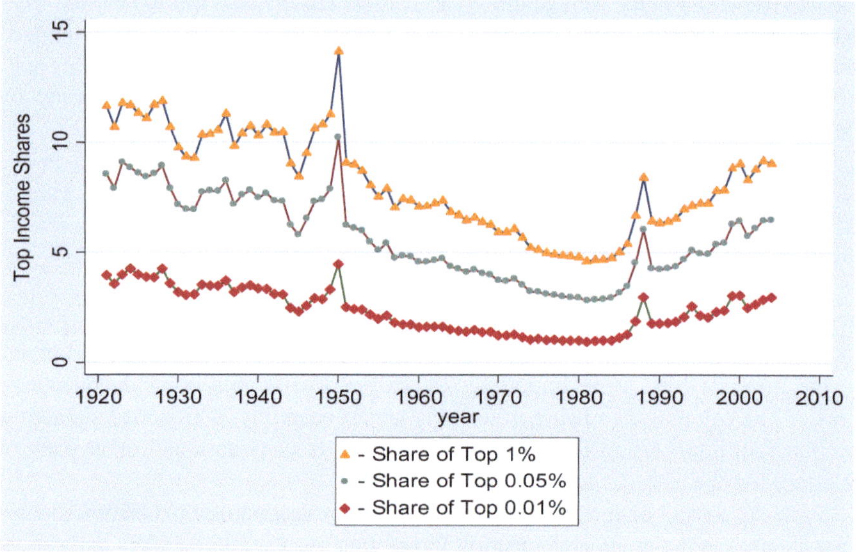

Fig. 6.1 Income share of the top 1%, 0.05% and 0.01% from 1921 to 2004. Source: Author's plot using Atkinson and Leigh (2007) data

to Australia. This came at the back of the xenophobic Chinese Exclusion Act instituted in the United States in the late nineteenth century.

Similar to North America, the European settlers in Australia were not kind to the native aboriginal population. They perished in large numbers with the arrival of the Europeans. European expansion threatened aboriginal traditional way of life. They became dispossessed in their own land and their culture threatened. During the first half of the twentieth century, the Australian government also instituted a policy of taking away aboriginal children from their families with the aim of forcibly assimilating them into the white European society. The victims of this practice are commonly referred to as the Stolen Generation.

Following federation, Australian economy steadily expanded. Bhattacharyya and Williamson (2011) document that as a raw materials exporter, Australian economy experienced frequent adverse terms of trade and real exchange rate shocks. These shocks were at times much more severe than other raw material exporting economies of that time (Bhattacharyya and Williamson 2016). However, Australia did remarkably well compared to the other comparable raw materials exporting economies. This among other reasons were due to the trusted relationship that Australian colonial elite had with the imperial core in London. The special relationship guaranteed unfettered access to the credit markets in London. In return, the investors in the imperial core viewed Australia as creditworthy and Australian assets valuable. Representative political institutions in Australia ensured a fairer distributive outcome for all free settlers as demonstrated by the very low levels of inequality

(Atkinson and Leigh 2007). Australia remained a loyal outpost of Britain leading up to World War I.

The tragic events of Gallipoli during World War I aroused national conscience in Australia. The desire to chart an independent course from Britain became real even though not as radical as the North American colonies a century earlier. During the Second World War, Australians fought alongside the United States and Britain to ward off Japanese aggression. By the conclusion of the Second World War and the War in the Pacific, Britain's power as a global empire was very much diminished. United States emerged as the global leader in commerce and military power. Australia increasingly aligned with the United States reoriented its economy as a supplier of raw materials and services to the far greater United States led alliance. The positive terms of trade shocks during the Korean and Vietnam wars were immense and the Australian economy expanded (Bhattacharyya and Williamson 2011). Exports of wool, minerals, livestock, and grains all expanded during the wartime. The economy also benefited from post-war industrialisation of South Korea, Japan, and later on China. However, Australia remains a staunch ally of the United States and heavily dependent on its security architecture in the Asia Pacific.

Bibliography

Atkinson, A., & Leigh, A. (2007). The distribution of top incomes in Australia. *The Economic Record, 83*(262), 247–261.

Bhattacharyya, S., & Williamson, J. (2011). Commodity price shocks and the Australian economy since federation. *Australian Economic History Review, 51*(2), 150–177.

Bhattacharyya, S., & Williamson, J. (2016). Distributional consequences of commodity price shocks: Australia over a century. *Review of Income and Wealth, 62*(2), 223–244.

Chapter 7
Expansionism, Russian Revolution, and the Two World Wars

Abstract The collapse of the international system (the concert of Europe) that managed competing European imperial interests ushered in an era of uncertainty and extremely violent imperial conflicts. This had catastrophic consequences for both elites and non-elites in Europe and the rest of the world. This chapter is broadly divided into three parts. The first part deals with the period leading up to World War I. This is followed by a discussion of the Bolshevik Revolution and the formation of the Soviet Union. Finally, the chapter ends with the audit of the World War II history (which is effectively a continuation of World War I). Key military and political events leading up to World War II are analysed. The toxic ethno-nationalist ideology of German exceptionalism as promoted by the National Socialists is examined. Key economic events such as the great depression and the role of the financial elites are also discussed in this context.

7.1 First Wave of Globalisation

The industrial age ushered in by coal and steam power and the use of iron and steel witnessed significant decline in transport cost during late nineteenth century. Production increasingly became energy and capital intensive. The internal combustion engine made energy use even more efficient as the amount of energy lost in previous versions of steam engine reduced dramatically. Railways expanded all across the globe. Railroad expansion in the resource-rich colonies meant that the colonisers could connect inland resources with seaports and transport resources at a fraction of the cost and time. It also made deployment of troops easier in areas of trouble and strategic importance. The shortening of transport time-integrated distant supply chain, which was previously rendered infeasible. The scale economies associated with declining transport cost reduced the unit cost of production significantly and thereby increased rent manyfold.

During late nineteenth century, trade and commerce flourished as the overall levels of tariff protection declined. Declining transport costs and declining trade costs in terms of tariff unleashed gains from trade unprecedented in human history. Continental Europe industrialised rapidly with railroad expansion in France and

S. Bhattacharyya, *A History of Global Capitalism*, Frontiers in Economic History,
https://doi.org/10.1007/978-3-030-58736-9_7

Germany. Russian Empire was the last to join the railroad revolution. Railroad expansion accelerated towards the end of the nineteenth century.

Germany experienced rapid industrialisation. This was also a time of relative peace. Europe did not experience any major conflict since the conclusion of the costly Crimean War. The dividends from prolonged peace and international trade were immense as it improved living standards across the board. Economic historians commonly refer to this period as the First Wave of Globalisation.

In addition to the disruptive technologies and revolutionary transport, the distributional consequences of international trade were also profound. With continual improvements in the total factor productivity of the non-farm and manufacturing sectors, the income of the workers increased relative to that of the landowners (Lindert and Williamson 2003). The landowners increasingly lobbied for tariff protection of the agricultural sector. Tariffs were instituted for both agriculture and industry in Germany, France, Italy, and Sweden during the late nineteenth century. Facing the adverse distributional consequences of trade and increasing pressure from unbalanced rural–urban migration, city, and national authorities embarked on erecting tariff barriers in order to slow down this deluge.

As Germany industrialised, its power and influence grew. Soon the German elites were laying claims to Africa and the Middle East to extend its colonial interest. The British and the French incumbents who had vast colonial interests in Africa, the Middle East, and Asia were unwilling to concede to the Germans. Relatively more agrarian Russia in the east was also catching up fast with rapid industrialisation and steady economic growth. The rapid industrialisation and urbanisation gave rise to a new threat for the incumbent elites. The threat of labour unions and revolutions. With countries increasingly resorting to the instrument of tariff protection, the international order based on peace, goodwill, and international trade started to unravel. Rival imperial interest re-emerged and the history of violent conflict reared its ugly head again.

7.2 Expansionism in the Far East and the Russo-Japanese War of 1905

As the Russian Empire industrialised, its imperial ambitions manifested itself in the Far East. Following the Meiji Restoration of 1868, the Japanese Empire rapidly industrialised and modernised its state. By the end of the nineteenth century, Japan was a modern industrialised state seeking to carve out its sphere of influence in the immediate neighbourhood. The Russian Empire also wanted to expand into the warm waters of the Pacific and Yellow Sea. The Russians had Vladivostok as their gateway to the Pacific but it was barely operational during the long winter months. They leased the Chinese naval base of Port Arthur on the Liaodong province and aspired for permanent access. They also sought exclusive access to the waters around the Korean Peninsula and Manchuria. The Japanese perceived this as a threat and had their own imperial ambitions. The Japanese offered Manchuria to Russia in return for Russian recognition of their domination over the Korean Peninsula. The Russians refused and demanded a buffer zone between Imperial Japan and Russia in the Korean Peninsula.

The negotiations failed and the Japanese mounted a surprise attack on the Russian base in Port Arthur in 1905. Russian losses were catastrophic and the Japanese offered further negotiations through the Court of Arbitration in the Hague. However, Tsar Nicholas II refused. Confident of the strength of his navy and army, he strongly believed that his men would prevail over the Japanese. Therefore, he doggedly pursued war which ended in 1906 with the conclusion of the Treaty of Portsmouth and total victory of the Japanese.

The Russo-Japanese War was the first victory of an Asian power over a mechanised European force. Therefore, undoubtedly it had military significance. Furthermore, the war was also a testament of catastrophic logistical failures as the Russians failed to bring reinforcements to the Far East on time.

The Russian defeat in the Russo-Japanese War was chaotic and this morphed into the failed revolution of 1905. Living standards for newly emancipated serfs were abject. The rank and file of the military lacked discipline due to high levels of corruption. The chain of command within the imperial power structure was increasingly dysfunctional. Worker unrest and strikes were common due to poor working conditions and very low wages. Very high levels of government debt following the defeat also triggered a hyperinflationary spiral, which made a bad situation worse.

The Monarchy survived the 1905 revolution. However, a state parliament was instituted along with a constitution and a multiparty political system. Cracks emerged continually into state power structure, which ultimately manifested itself in the form of the Russian Revolution two decades later. More on this later.

7.3 A War to End All Wars: World War I

War is a mere continuation of policy by other means. Carl von Clausewitz, Prussian General and Military Theorist, 1832

As the nineteenth century came towards its conclusion, the international system that dictated trade and security started to unravel. Disruptive technological change and rural–urban migration unleashed forces within empires that unsettled the existing social order. Revolutions and general strikes followed. The incumbent elite could not offer a way out and restore order. The unravelling of the international system and increasing use of tariff barriers brought back bitter memories of rivalry and violent conflict between different European empires.

The immediate trigger of the conflict was the assassination of Austro-Hungarian crown prince Archduke Franz Ferdinand in Sarajevo, Bosnia at the hands of a Yugoslav nationalist in 1914. This elicited a strong reaction from the Austro-Hungarians who issued an ultimatum to Serbia. Serbia replied but it failed to satisfy the Austro-Hungarians. The Austro-Hungarians declared war on Serbia. The Austro-Hungarians swiftly mobilised and started shelling Belgrade.

Different European states at that time were locked into multiple layers of military alliances which proved to be extremely dangerous. With the shelling of Belgrade, the Russian Empire felt the need to support its ally Serbia. The Russians mobilised swiftly and moved in to protect Belgrade. Therefore, de facto the Russians entered the conflict. Germany perceived Russian manoeuvres to be threatening to its own national security interest and that of its ally Austria and Hungary. Germany issued an ultimatum to the Russians and demanded that it withdraw within 12 h. The Russians were unmoved by this German ultimatum and did not withdraw. As a response, the Germans declared war against the Russians in support of its ally Austria Hungary. Following German entry into the conflict, the French joined in to support Russia against Germany. War against France and Russia meant that the Germans were fighting both on the Western and Eastern fronts. Germany formally declared war against France in August 1914 and invaded Belgium. The German military strategy was to invoke a swift defeat on the French first and then mobilise against the Russians in the East.

Facing the German invasion, Belgium invoked the Treaty of London with Britain. Britain under the said Treaty was Belgium's security guarantor in continental Europe if the latter were to be attacked by its larger European neighbours. The occupation of Belgium by Germany dragged Britain into the conflict. Britain mobilised and joined France on the Western Front. Subsequently, Ottoman Turkey also joined the conflict on the side of the Germans and the Austro-Hungarians. It mobilised against Russia in the Caucasus and against France and Britain in Mesopotamia and Egypt, respectively. A political assassination in the Balkans snowballed into a global conflict due to interlocking military alliances of the European imperial powers.

The proximate cause of the conflict is obviously the political assassination and the interlocking alliances. However, the root causes ran much deeper. As the Industrial Revolution arrived in continental Europe in the early to mid-nineteenth century, Germany and Austria-Hungary rapidly industrialised. Shipbuilding, automotive, and machine tools industries thrived. The rapidly expanding economic might of Germany meant that its imperial interests grew. Increasingly, it demanded its own sphere of influence in order to exploit the scale economies associated with expansion.

Britain and France dominated the international system in Europe and the colonies after the conclusion of the Crimean War. Despite some initial losses, Russia maintained its sphere of influence in the Black Sea region, the Caucasus, and the Baltics. Even though not as spectacular as Germany and Austria-Hungary, the Russian economy was also steadily modernising during the second half of the nineteenth century. Therefore, Germany was squeezed between two big neighbours, France in the West and Russia in the East. Increasingly Germany expanded into Africa and the Middle East. The Berlin Conference of 1884 is a testament to this expansion effort where the colonial powers of Europe decided to carve up Africa. Note that Africa and the Middle East were traditionally colonial strongholds of Britain and France. Other minor players such as the Kingdom of Belgium, and the Dutch Empire also had colonial interests in Africa but not as widespread as Britain and France. The Principle of Effective Occupation was used to carve up Africa, which meant that any of the colonial powers with a physical presence on the ground had legal right to claim that land as their colony. Germany and Austria-Hungary were also competing with Russia for influence over the Balkans. Britain, France, and Russia, the three great powers of Europe were unwilling to give way.

As major raw materials supplier to the German and Austro-Hungarian industries, Russia was reluctant to enter into direct conflict with Germany. However, trade protectionism by Germany during the late nineteenth century and early twentieth century may have tipped the balance. The disastrous Russo-Japanese war of 1905 was also a deterrent for the Russians. However, the Russians saw a moral imperative. The Tsar as the head of state perceived himself to be the protector of the Orthodox faith and the Eastern Slavs. Therefore, invasion of his close ally Serbia forced his hand into intervening.

The diplomatic stalemate for Germany in terms of carving out its own sizeable sphere of influence meant that the powder keg of conflict was already in place waiting for a spark. The political assassination in Sarajevo convinced the Germans to settle this out on the battlefield rather than in the corridors of diplomacy.

The conflict had disastrous consequences for all the parties. Germany's quest for a rapid victory over France on the Western front turned out to be elusive. Germany, France, and Britain were bogged down into a long drawn out trench warfare on the fields of Somme and elsewhere. The casualty numbers were unprecedented. Approximately 13 million lives were lost on the battlefield alone. In addition, the pandemic of Spanish influenza killed many more. The damages were such that the military industrial positions of all the European great powers were permanently damaged.

After Germany entered the war in support of their Austro-Hungarian ally, the main actors on the Eastern front were Germany and Russia. Turkey and Bulgaria sided with the German alliance while Romania fought alongside the Russian Empire. The battleline stretched from the Black Sea in the South to the Baltics in the North. Similar to the Western Front, the parties engaged into a long drawn out trench warfare. It was one of the first highly mechanised conflict in the history of conflicts. Given the high levels of mechanisation, the casualty numbers were unusually high. Almost 16 million combatants perished during the conflict on the Eastern front alone.

The financial and the human pressure of the conflict were such that many states could not survive the conflict. The Ottoman Turkish state disintegrated. Similar was the fate of the Russian Empire. Under the pressure of conflict, the Russian army started disintegrating. Such dire were the conditions at the frontline, many Russian military units refused to fight. The general lack of discipline and order in the Russian army rank and file following the 1905 defeat to Japan became exposed again under much greater pressure from the combined forces of Austria, Germany, and Turkey. The German alliance nominally prevailed on the Eastern front but in reality, it was largely a stalemate with huge human and material costs on both sides. The Russian defeat quickly degenerated into desertions, chaos, and rebellions. The Rebellions eventually morphed into the Russian Revolution.

Russian participation in the war ended with the Brest-Litovsk Treaty whereby Russia made substantial territorial concessions to Germany. However, these German gains were short-lived as the Treaty was nullified following the German defeat on the Western front against Britain and France.

As Russia suffered defeat on the frontline, at home the situation became dire for the government. The Russian army, one of the institutional pillars of the Russian state started disintegrating. This made the state and the Tsar vulnerable to internal challenges. The loyal Russian forces were still away from home battling on the frontline. The disloyal and disaffected former soldiers joined the unruly mob on the streets of St. Petersburg mobilising against the Tsarist government. Food shortage and dire economic conditions contributed to the general feeling of injustice among workers and citizens (Moore 1966).

The war implied mobilising men who would otherwise work the fields to deliver a good harvest. Such displacement of agricultural workers had a negative impact on harvest. In addition, the war required sending provisions from the warehouses to supply the army. Grain storage ran precariously low leading up to the war. The war tipped the balance and food shortages followed. Shortage of grains in general and bread in particular meant that the state had to introduce deeply unpopular bread rations. The rations were only partially successful in managing demand as the shadow economy thrived.

The Russian Imperial Government was running a huge budget deficit due to the war. The desperate need of war financing meant that the government increasingly resorted to monetising its debt. Large budget deficits were financed by printing new money. This invariably led to the collapse of purchasing power of the Rouble and hyperinflation. On average, the monthly inflation rate during that time reached over 50%. Hyperinflation turned a bad situation with food shortages into worse.

Popular discontent, hunger, and general lawlessness morphed into the February 1917 revolution. The Russian Empire disintegrated with the Tsar Nicholas II forced to abdicate. The Russian parliament took control of the newly formed republic. It launched another offensive against the advancing German forces but it ended in an abject humiliating failure.

The Republican government could not survive as it failed to address the underlying socioeconomic issues that brought it to power. Another armed revolution took place in St. Petersburg in October 1917, this time led by the Bolshevik party. The Bolsheviks stormed the Winter Palace in St. Petersburg and dislodged the city authorities from power. They transferred the capital to Moscow. They also ended Russia's participation in World War I by signing the Brest-Litovsk Treaty with Germany and allied powers.

Following the coup in St. Petersburg, Russia descended into a civil war between the Bolsheviks (the Reds) and the Republicans (the Whites). The civil war finally ended with the victory of the Bolsheviks in 1923 when they established the Union of Soviet Socialist Republics (USSR). The Ukrainian Soviet Socialist Republic was created by combining Russian territories from the Black Sea region with territories of Galicia, which were controlled by the Austro-Hungarians. Over time, the newly independent republics of Armenia, Azerbaijan, Belarus, and Georgia also joined the USSR.

7.4 Interwar Malaise and the End of Pre-war Globalisation

The interwar period witnessed the unravelling of the international system that governed international commerce and politics. The Treaty of Versailles in 1919 brought an end to the hostilities between Germany and the Allied powers. However, it was far from normalising relations between the belligerents. The inadequacy of the Treaty meant that the underlying geopolitical tensions continued to simmer for the next two decades. The immediate consequence was a precipitous decline in international trade. The challenges were so deep rooted that peace did not guarantee a return to normalcy in terms of international trade and commerce. Here I highlight some of the key factors that may have contributed to the decline in trade during the interwar period.

World War I was primarily a European imperial war fought on the European continent. War created additional demand for raw materials and commodities especially among the imperial belligerents, which led to a positive supply response from the commodity-exporting periphery. For example, as a legacy of the war economy wheat acreage increased substantially in Australia during the interwar period from 8.9 million in 1919–1924 to 11.97 million in 1924–1929 (Malenbaum 1953). Canada and the United States also experienced similar expansion with the latter experiencing expansion in wheat acreage by more than threefold (Eichengreen 1992). Within the Spanish colonial sphere, wheat acreage in Argentina increased from 16.02 million to 19.94 million during the interwar period (Malenbaum 1953). These positive supply responses were partially offset by declining production in continental Europe from traditional wheat exporting geographies such as Poland, Hungary, and the Russian Empire (USSR after the war).

It was not just grains, other primary commodities also experienced a positive supply response during the interwar period as a legacy of the war economy. Meat exports by the United States increased tenfold (Eichengreen 1992). Sugar exports from Cuba and Java (Indonesia) also increased manyfold (Aldcroft 1977). All the while European production experienced decline sometimes by two-thirds due to a serious decline in wartime production capacity.

The overall increase in production from the periphery meant that there was a supply glut in the world market putting downward pressure on prices. This decline in price did not lead to an increase in demand in the European colonial core as war damage significantly reduced purchasing power. Unemployment was high with endemic structural problems in the product and labour markets.

It was not just the raw materials and primary commodities market that experienced expansion during the wartime. European industries also expanded rapidly during the wartime to support the war economy (Findlay and O'Rourke 2007). However, as peace ensued, these industries were faced with a supply overhang and substantial excess capacity. For example, steel production in Britain increased manyfold during the war but it hit excess capacity following the war (Broadberry and Howlett 2005). Similar trends were observed all across continental Europe in the heavy industries of shipbuilding, iron and steel, machine tools, and engineering. The additional government demand generated by the war elicited a supply response. New factories were built in order to expand production capacity to support the expanding demand. Such rapid demand growth was not sustainable during peacetime as firms had to cut back production on the face of weak demand. This meant many of the production facilities remained idle adding to overall excess capacity. The excess capacity problem was further exacerbated in continental Europe with the restoration and upgrade of some of the war damaged factories. Excess capacity meant that unemployment and underemployment of labour were high.

The war economy necessitated European colonial powers to encourage industrialisation in the otherwise peripheral economies of the United States, Australia, Japan, South Africa, and India. Industrialisation in the United States was spectacular as it benefitted from its proximity to the war theatre in continental Europe. The United States stayed neutral for most of the war and supplied vital industrial goods to the belligerents. The United States financial markets also benefited from the war via expanding credit to all the belligerents during the war. Cotton textile production increased in Japan and India in order to mainly supply the local Indian market (Tomlinson 1993). As supply from British textile mills were redirected to continental Europe to support the war effort, the vacant Indian market left a golden opportunity for the Indian and Japanese textile industries to fill the void. Tata Iron and Steel in India also expanded supply to cater for the local market left vacant by the redirected British supply. The industrial expansion in India was significant but was not as spectacular as the United States. The scope for industrialisation in a non-sovereign colony was limited relative to a sovereign and increasingly powerful continent-sized economy such as the United States.

The political economy of Europe following the war was also unstable. With industrial excess capacity, high unemployment, and high underemployment, the redistributive demands were strong. Politics all across continental Europe took a turn towards socialism. Labour unions became increasingly militant and the workforce became highly unionised on the face of high unemployment. A rigid labour market increased the unit cost of production for the firms further exacerbating the problems of excess capacity and unemployment. Falling living standards for the masses meant that labour unions demanded more political representation for the average citizens. The European colonial power increasingly moved towards universal suffrage at least in the colonial core. Representative politics and a fast-changing political spectrum implied stronger redistributive demands from the voters in the form of welfare states. Weaker economic conditions meant that these redistributive demands were more often than not difficult to meet. Government and politics in continental Europe became more unstable compared to the pre-War era.

7.5 Policy Response

The policy response to the interwar twin malaise of falling prices and excess capacity was trade protectionism. Tariffs and quantitative restrictions to trade increased across the board. The psychological scar of the war left the legacy of deep-rooted mistrust among the former belligerents. This atmosphere of mistrust was impossible to overcome during the interwar period. Mistrust and lack of security meant that the European imperial elites anticipated another conflict down the line. Therefore, all the parties were extremely reluctant to engage in trade and weaken their industrial capacity. Rather the focus was on rebuilding industry using trade protection as a tool. The colonial powers also pursued supply chain independence so as not to rely on potentially hostile power's supply chain in the event of a conflict breaking out again. Neutral countries such as the United States benefitted immensely from this mindset as it integrated its economy with all the parties.

The protectionist policy response also had its political economy roots. A unionised workforce and a socialist turn of politics turned trade policy in general and protectionism in particular into a political weapon. It was increasingly difficult for the European imperial states to pursue deflationary policies as unemployment became politically costly. With high unemployment, persistent excess capacity, and falling prices, cheaper imported goods became a scapegoat. All European states including traditionally liberal Britain imposed high tariff protection during the interwar period. The prevalent belief was that tariff protection would protect jobs. Furthermore, it was perceived that protectionism and reliance on an autarkic model would reverse the secular decline in prices that in fact had deeper structural roots from the demand and supply sides. In addition to higher import tariffs, many countries also resorted to prohibition of imports of several commodities.

With the increase in acreage in the non-European periphery, prices of agricultural commodities also fell. This had an adverse impact not only on the commodity markets but also on the financial markets. The agricultural farm owners, especially in Germany and France, were heavily indebted. Therefore, falling prices meant that these farms were on the verge of a default. In order to reverse this deflationary trend and stave off widespread default, European policymakers resorted to agricultural protection which was largely unsuccessful.

The results of the interwar protectionist policies were significantly different from what was envisaged by its protagonists. Protectionism failed to reverse the deflationary trends in the global economy. On the contrary, it accelerated the deflationary tendencies. The lack of market access and the lack of expansion opportunities jeopardised economic growth. Rigidities in the factor markets imposed by unionisation of the labour force and government regulation made firms less flexible in an environment that desperately needed adjustments and reforms. As a result, firms in continental Europe became uncompetitive in the face of growing competition from the rapidly industrialising United States. Higher regulatory and factor market costs meant that the firms are unable to expand perpetuating the vicious cycle of unemployment, stagnation, and deflation.

Tariff protection also failed to address the twin deficit problems in many of the belligerent European colonial economies. Import substitution through tariff protection was meant to facilitate industrial expansion and exports, which in turn were expected to reverse the growing tides of trade and fiscal deficits. Protectionist policies however delivered exactly the opposite effect. Trade protectionism limited firms from exploiting agglomeration effects. It also made firms rigid and uncompetitive ultimately resulting into economic stagnation. Stagnating economy meant declining government revenue and declining exports perpetuating the challenges of twin deficit.

Overall trade declined and discriminatory trade policies proliferated all across the globe. Even though the League of Nations guaranteed non-discriminatory trade policies for all participating imperial powers, the practicality of international relations meant that this was largely ignored by all at that time. For example, being a neutral power the United States enjoyed relatively easy access to the markets of all European colonial powers and their respective imperial customs unions. Therefore, the United States could sign favourable bilateral trade agreements outside the purview of the League of Nations. However, the colonial powers protected each other's imperial domains with high tariff barriers. For instance, Germany protected her heavy industries with tariffs but allowed import of agricultural commodities from southern Europe in order to meet supply shortfall in agricultural commodities.

The League of Nations was an attempt to return the international system of commerce, politics, and security to the pre-war period. However, it proved elusive. The challenges were too complex and the mistrust too deep rooted for relations to return anywhere near normalcy. The attempt to return to the pre-war fixed exchange rate system based on the gold standard turned out to be unsuccessful (Eichengreen 1992). Towards the end of the 1920s leading up to the Great Depression, economic challenges became more acute. The policymakers increasingly abandoned the gold standard.

7.6 Debts, War Reparations, and Hyperinflation

War mobilisation in continental Europe also had a financial angle. The allies borrowed heavily mostly from the United States and Britain leading up to the war in order to mobilise resources. This amounted to approximately 26.5 billion US dollars. France was the largest debtor (Findlay and O'Rourke 2007). The largest creditor, the United States demanded payment in full from the debtors. This magnified the risk of currency crisis. Moreover, it also increased tensions between the United States and its former allies. Furthermore, the 1921 Reparation Commission levied a reparation bill of 33 billion US dollars on Germany alone. The claimants were primarily Britain and France but it also included other allied powers such as Belgium. These claims increased tensions between Germany and the allies that led to the invasion of Ruhr in 1923 by France and Belgium.

Germany's war financing strategy was based entirely on debt. In contrast, France relied on taxes to finance its war effort. The debt-based war financing strategy exposed Germany to currency risks during the interwar period. The German authorities were less concerned about such risk at the start of the conflict as they counted on post-war annexation of new industrial territories from the West and the East. They anticipated that a victorious Germany would easily be able to service these debts with a larger economy (including the annexed territories) and reparation payments from the defeated allied powers. The German debt servicing plan turned out to be illusory as Germany succumbed to a defeat at the hands of the allied powers.

With large debts owed to the United States and Britain and a stagnating economy plagued by excess capacity, the debt servicing challenges for Germany magnified. With a large trade deficit (predominantly with the United States) and a budget deficit, the German mark was under constant pressure from the dollar. The Mark steadily depreciated against the US dollar during the war years, which was a precursor to the hyperinflation and currency crisis that followed. Following the conclusion of the war and the German revolution of 1919, the post-war Weimar Republic was under serious threat of default. Even though its industrial capacity remained largely intact at least compared to France and Belgium in the West and Russia in the East, its resources were very much limited compared to the enormity of the debt burden.

On top of the debt burden, the Treaty of Versailles and the 1921 Reparation Commission levied a further 33 billion US dollars reparation bill on Germany. Initially, the Germans resisted the reparation claims but they agreed under the threat of British and French trade embargo. The Weimar Republic resorted to debt monetisation in order to keep up with the debt and reparation payments. Increasing the supply of paper Marks in order to purchase physical gold and US dollars meant that the Mark devalued rapidly. By August 1921, the German currency was under free fall against the US dollar. Debt repayment became impossible as the Weimar currency lost value.

Cost of imports increased astronomically. Germany was unable to import gold using its currency in order to pay the creditors. At the home front, currency collapse translated into hyperinflation. Investment and consumption demand collapsed accelerating economic contraction. In 1922, Germany defaulted on its debt to France as it was no longer able to buy precious metals or foreign exchange in the open market using the Mark. France responded by sending in troops to occupy the Ruhr industrial region so that the debt is paid for in industrial goods such as coal and steel rather than fiat currency.

Following the currency collapse, hyperinflation and general humiliation of the early 1920s, German monetary policy turned to the other extreme. In 1928–1929 leading up to the great depression, Germany moved towards a tight monetary policy regime. The intended objective of this policy was financial stability and less exposure to volatility in the stock market by caving in on wasteful speculative activities. The realised effect was opposite to what was intended. Very high-interest rate weighed in on the stock market with equity price collapse. It also had a negative effect on the real economy with credit crunch and low investments. Temin (1971) documents a continuous fall in investments in Weimar Germany over the period 1927–1931.

7.7 Financial Crisis and the Great Depression

The United States monetary policies during the 1920s were stable. The Federal Reserve discount rate was around 4–5% during the early half of the 1920s following the conclusion of World War I. In spite of a neutral discount rate, the stock market experienced continued expansion based on the strength of the American economy. American manufacturing gained immensely from the war economy. The initial neutral position of America helped in terms of market access to Europe encompassing all sides of the Great War. Steel, engineering, machine tools, automobile, and shipbuilding expanded during the early part of the 1920s. It was not just manufacturing, the agricultural sector expanded too. Acreage in wheat production increased manyfold boosting wheat and grain exports. Supply weakness and fall in acreage in the Eastern European grain belt (Poland, Hungary, and Russia) worked in America's advantage. American exports mitigated the Eastern European supply shortfall.

The post-war European economies were struggling to return back to normalcy with excess capacity in the manufacturing sector and supply weakness in agriculture. Moreover, high level of indebtedness in both public and private sectors spilled over to the financial sector with frequent bank failures, hyperinflation, and stock market crashes. In contrast, the American economy was stable and American dollar denominated assets offering a steady yield to the investors. The stock market and investment in the United States continued to increase until 1929. As a result, capital from Europe flowed into the United States in search of higher yield and steady returns. This continually made the dollar stronger.

Due to the high levels of optimism associated with the economy, speculative bubbles were forming in the financial and asset markets even with a neutral Federal Reserve discount rate. Galbraith (1955) documents the Florida property bubble of the 1920s as the start of trouble in the stock market. Powered by the common belief that the American middle class are chosen by the divine to be rich, the speculative bubble in the stock market gained strength. All throughout the late 1920s, year on year the stock market reached new highs breaking previous records. The speculative bubble was fuelled even further by the Federal Reserve cutting the discount rate from 4 to 3.5% in 1927. The intention was to discourage capital inflow into the United States and capital outflow from Europe. However, this had little effect in stemming the capital inflow as gold from all over the world converged into the United States in search of higher yield. The additional inflow of gold was used to expand credit in the form of broker loans which further inflated the stock market. In October 1929, it all unravelled as the stock market crashed. The market lost 11% of its value following the opening bell.

The financial crash of 1929 triggered a cycle of economic contraction all across the globe that was unprecedented in the economic history of capitalism. The underlying structural weaknesses in the world economy were exposed by the financial crisis. The overcapacity in the European economies following the war created deflationary pressures in the economy. This was further exacerbated by production expansion in the United States. Interwar production expansion, capital inflow, and investment growth in the United States guided the stock markets to an all-time high creating the right conditions for speculative bubbles to emerge. On the back of a stock market boom, banks expanded credit further inflating the stock market speculative bubble. In 1929, the disconnect between the real and the financial sectors of the economy came to a head. The lack of demand and excess capacity in the real sector of the economy was exposed. A massive correction took place in the share markets as the credit-driven speculative bubble collapsed.

Economic contraction over the period 1929–1932 witnessed a collapse in world trade, industrial production, and wholesale prices. Unemployment in America and all the European economies went sky high. The stage was set for further international great power conflicts. The economic hardship brought radical nationalist forces to power all across Europe. The European polity changed fundamentally. Politics moved away from the centre with radical left and right wing forces gaining strength.

7.8 The Rise of the Nazis and the Chaos Leading to the Second World War

Following the collapse of the German economy during the Weimar Republic, German politics also took a turn towards totalitarianism. German economy was plagued by hyperinflation during the late 1920s leading up to the Great Depression. Great Depression also accelerated the process of output collapse, high unemployment, and precipitous decline in living standards. The American stock market collapse of 1929 also triggered a series of bank collapse in Germany. The dire socioeconomic conditions created the right environment for radical political forces to thrive.

The National Socialist German Worker's Party (or the Nazi Party) was founded in 1920. It was the successor party of the German Workers Party founded a year earlier. The party subscribed to radical right-wing ideology. It rejected the terms of the Treaty of Versailles. It aspired for more European living space for the German people. It believed in racial superiority of the German race. Therefore, it aspired to create a state based on racial purity with the exclusion of all other races. It was opposed to the Weimar Republic and a proponent of ethnic cleansing of Jews, Slavs, Romanians, and other ethnic minorities. The Nazi party was viscerally anti-communists. The deep-rooted anti-Semitism of the Nazi party worked in tandem with its anti-communism, as majority of the prominent communist leaders in Europe at that time were also Jewish.

The economic and social collapse in Germany following the Great Depression catapulted this dangerously anti-Semitic and racist far right political machine to power. In 1932 Federal elections, the Nazi party won the largest share of popular votes but did not attain outright majority. Consequently, Adolf Hitler, the leader of the Nazi party led two short-lived coalition governments in 1932. In 1933, the German President Paul von Hindenburg appointed Adolf Hitler as the Chancellor of Germany. A month later the German parliament Reichstag was set on fire with Hitler and the Nazis accusing the communists of the crime. A massive crackdown on communists ensued with Hitler usurping power using the Reichstag arson as an excuse. Communists were found guilty of starting the fire as part of a broader conspiracy to overthrow the government. Hitler assumed emergency powers and his police was given unlimited powers to detain suspects. Criticism of the government in the popular press was outlawed effectively ending free press. Over 4000 communist party members were arrested as part of the conspiracy. Persecution of the Jews started at the earnest. In March 1933, the German parliament passed the Enabling Act with a large majority. This Act allowed Hitler to set aside the Weimar Constitution. Subsequent laws were passed, which were directly contrary to the Constitution. Other political parties such as the communists, social democrats, and the national people's party were outlawed. By July 1933, Germany became a single-party dictatorship under Adolf Hitler. A year later, Hitler formally assumed dictatorial powers and declared himself the Fuhrer.

The situation in continental Europe outside of Germany was similar. Economic collapse and high unemployment following the Great Depression created fertile grounds for radical political forces. Far right anti-Semitic governments emerged in Italy, Spain, and Poland. Territorial expansion and recouping lost national pride was once again at the top of the agenda of the radical right-wing governments in Europe.

Germany initiated troop mobilisation and rearmament programme. Civil war broke out in Spain between the Republicans and the nationalists. Ideological battle lines were drawn again in Europe. The Republicans were in alliance with the left-leaning Spanish Second Republic. The Spanish communists also ably supported them. Internationally, the Republicans received the backing of the USSR which supplied troops and mercenaries to fight alongside the Republicans.

On the opposing side were the Nationalists. The Nationalists were a coalition of monarchists, conservatives, Catholics, and far right militant groups. General Francisco Franco rapidly gained prominence among the Nationalists. Internationally, Nazi Germany backed the Nationalists. They also received support from anti-communist far right governments in Italy and Poland. After 3 years of conflict from 1936 to 1939, the Nationalists were victorious and Spain went down the path of a military dictatorship under General Francisco Franco. The Nazi support for Franco during the civil war meant that Franco's Spain was also in alliance with Germany during the Second World War.

With Germany rapidly rearming and the belligerent expansionist rhetoric coming out of Berlin, tensions were very high in Europe. All parties understood that the likelihood of a major European war breaking out is very high. Germany made territorial claims on all of its neighbours and especially Czechoslovakia, an ally of the USSR. Leaders of Britain, France, and Italy descended on Munich in September 1938 and concluded the Munich Agreement. The Munich Agreement allowed for the dismemberment of Czechoslovakia. Germany annexed large portions of western Czechoslovakia using the protection of German minority residing on that territory as a pretext. Poland an ally of Germany at the time also annexed North Eastern Czechoslovakia using the protection of Polish minority as a pretext. The USSR, an ally of France and Czechoslovakia requested troop passage via Poland in order to protect Czechoslovakia from German aggression. Poland refused access to the Soviet troops and Czechoslovakia capitulated effectively without any resistance.

The Polish ambassador to Berlin Joseph Lipski signed a Non-aggression Treaty with Nazi Germany in January 1934 in Berlin. The Treaty stipulated peaceful resolution of disputes between the parties including mutual territorial claims. This Treaty temporarily ended Polish–German territorial claims and led to normalisation of relations. The tension was de-escalated and the existing borders were made legitimate. Poland also withdrew claims on some German territory that it was supposed to receive under the Treaty of Versailles.

Following Munich and the dismemberment of Czechoslovakia, the battlelines were drawn. A big war was on the cards. Soviet Union anticipated a Nazi attack. The Western European powers were also weary of a resurgent Germany. With the memory of World War I being fresh, all the parties were desperate to avoid a direct military confrontation with Germany. Given that visceral anti-Semitism and anti-communism was the ideological foundation of the Nazi Party, it is unsurprising that Nazi German foreign policy was to seek a grand alliance against the USSR. The Soviets were acutely aware of this danger and sought a grand alliance against the Nazis instead. Poland under Josef Pilsudsky was bitterly opposed to this idea and its foreign minister Josef Beck lobbied heavily against it with France and Britain. France and Britain also had the Treaty obligation to protect Poland in the event of a military aggression. With international diplomacy breaking down, European powers were scrambling for a buffer zone in order to protect themselves from the Nazi invasion.

After coming to the realisation that a grand alliance against Nazi Germany is infeasible, the Soviets entered into a non-aggression pact (The Molotov-Ribbentrop Pact) with Nazi Germany in August 1939. Along with non-aggression, the protocol associated with the pact stipulated Soviet and German zones of influence. Soviets considered eastern Baltics (Estonia, Lithuania, and Latvia) in the North and the Black Sea regions of Bessarabia in the south as their legitimate zones of influence. The Germans considered Western Poland and associated territories as their zones of influence.

The Molotov-Ribbentrop non-aggression pact between Soviet Union and Nazi Germany did not prevent a great war in Europe. On 1 September 1939, Germany invaded Poland from the west. After a brief period of resistance, Poland succumbed to Nazi German aggression. The Polish government went into exile and later fled to London. Following the Nazi invasion from the west, the Soviet Union invaded Poland from the East and took control of territories stipulated as buffer zone in the Molotov-Ribbentrop Pact protocol. The Soviets justified their aggressive action by claiming that they had the right to do so under the non-aggression pact and safeguard their national security. Moreover, they also claimed that the Polish government seized to exist following the Nazi invasion.

Britain and France declared war on Germany following the invasion of Poland. German troops marched eastwards. The Soviets in response initiated a war against Finland in 1939. The Soviets accused Finland of conspiring with the Germans to lodge an invasion of Leningrad (now St. Petersburg). The Finns resisted for 3 months following which they capitulated to the Soviets. In the west during the 1940s, Germany rapidly took control of Belgium, the Netherlands, Luxembourg, Denmark, Norway, and France. These countries offered very little resistance. In June 1941, Germany along with Italy and Romania lodged the Operation Barbarossa and invaded Soviet Union. A bloody and protracted war ensued on the eastern front.

In the Far East, tensions were simmering in the 1930s with expansionist Imperial Japan becoming increasingly assertive. In July 1937, a war between Imperial Japan and the Republic of China started following a military incident. China was supported by the Soviet Union and the United States. However, the conflict with Japan did not become global until 1941 when Japan entered into direct military confrontation with the United States following the attack on Pearl Harbour.

Militaristic expansionist policies of Imperial Japan perhaps traces back to 1931 with the Japanese invasion of Manchuria. Japan defeated the Chinese republican forces and occupied Manchuria. Following the occupation, Japan installed a puppet government in Manchuria. Following victory in Manchuria, Japanese policy was to expand north. This brought imperial Japan into direct conflict with the Soviet Union and its communist ally Mongolia. Border skirmishes followed throughout the decade but it all came to a head in September 1939. The Japanese Sixth Army and its Manchurian ally entered into a battle with the Soviet Union and Mongolia at Khalkin Gol and lost. Marshal Georgy Zhukov was an architect of the Soviet victory. Japan signed a peace treaty with the Soviet Union, which gave the Soviets much needed breathing space to concentrate its war effort on the Western flank against Nazi Germany.

German troops made rapid progress during the initial months of Operation Barbarossa. The Red Army offered fierce resistance in defence of the Brest Fortress (Belarussian Soviet Socialist Republic) and elsewhere but the German advance seemed unstoppable. The combined might of the German mechanised units and the German Luftwaffe (air force) was overpowering for the Red Army during the initial months of the engagement. The Nazi German forces took control of one town after another in Belarus and Ukraine Soviet Socialist Republics (SSRs) while the Red Army retreated. By the end of 1941, the Nazis took control of most of the Soviet western territories and surrounded Leningrad launching a siege. The Nazi forces also reached as far as Moscow taking control of the outskirts.

In Ukraine, Baltics, and the Balkans, local Nazi collaborators ably supported the invading Nazi German forces. The Organisation of Ukrainian Nationalists (OUN) and its successor the Ukrainian Insurgent Army (UPA) committed genocide and war crime against ethnic Jews, Poles, and Russians on the occupied territories ably supported by Nazi German paramilitary organisations such as the Schutzstaffel (or commonly known as the SS). In the Baltic states of Estonia, Latvia, and Lithuania the Nazis set up Divisions of the Waffen SS staffed by local Nazi collaborators who actively engaged in genocide against Jews, Poles, and Russians. Similar mass murders were also committed in the Balkans by the Ustase, a Croatian fascist organisation ably supported by the German Nazis. The common ideological thread that connected these radical fascist organisations is their deep-rooted anti-Semitism and anti-communism. Moreover, all of them also subscribed to the obnoxious ideology of racial supremacy. They regularly conducted mass execution of ethnic minorities on the Nazi German-occupied territories in central and Eastern Europe. This mass murdering machine was later formalised by the Nazis in the form of concentration camps on these territories. The Nazis on the occupied territories of Poland and the Baltics set up concentration camps such as the Auschwitz, Betzec, Chelmno, Majdanek, Sobibor, Treblinka, Salaspil, Kaiserwald, Junfernhof, and several others. Over six million Jews, Russians, Ukrainians, Poles, and Soviet Prisoners of War lost their lives in these camps. This monumental tragedy of human history is collectively remembered as the Holocaust.

Now firmly in control of the Black Sea and Baltic regions, the Nazi German forces went for the Soviet strategic energy assets in the Caspian. The Germans understood that taking control of the petroleum assets in Baku and the Caspian would deliver a death blow to the Soviet war fighting capabilities. A highly mechanised war such as the World War II cannot be fought without petroleum. The Nazi Germans advanced on the key strategic city of Stalingrad. Stalingrad is strategically located on the river Volga, which connects central Russian military-industrial towns of Samara and Nizhny Novgorod (then Gorky) with petroleum assets on the Caspian. Fall of Stalingrad to the Nazis would have meant these important industrial towns would be completely cut off from the strategic asset of petroleum.

The Red Army fought back fiercely and the tide of the battle turned. The battle lasted for 5 months between August 1942 and February 1943 and it remains one of the bloodiest battles in the history of warfare with nearly 2.2 million combat deaths. The German army had some initial success in pushing the Red Army to the other bank of the Volga, but they were quickly encircled. After 5 months of intense battle, the encircled German forces ran out of ammunition and supply and capitulated. The German losses were heavy and they had to bring in reinforcements from the West in order to hold the line. The Red Army losses were significant but the victory in Stalingrad had a profound psychological effect. The invading Nazi German forces were no longer invincible. The Red Army regained self-belief that they can defeat the Nazis.

With increased morale, the Red Army defeated the Germans in Moscow and broke the siege of Leningrad. The Red Army destroyed the Nazi tank army in Kursk, which remains one of the largest tank battles in history. Intense firefight continued mainly on the Russian and Ukrainian SSR territories. The Red Army liberated Voronezh, Kharkov, Sevastopol, Kiev, and Dnipropetrovsk and continued marching forward. By December 1944, the Red Army liberated most of the occupied Soviet territories and continued engaging the Nazis on the territories of Poland and

Hungary. The Nazi war machine was fatally wounded in Stalingrad and it all went downhill for them from that point onwards. They continually retreated, as they could not match the firepower of the advancing Red Army. In 1945, the Red Army liberated the Nazi death camps on the territories of Poland and the Baltics. The Soviet Red Army liberated the infamous Auschwitz death camp in January 1945. Budapest, Prague, and other Nazi-occupied cities in central Europe also fell to the advancing Red Army. By April 1945, the German defence collapsed and the Red Army stood on the outskirts of Berlin. The final battle for Berlin began. It lasted for 2 weeks and the Germans capitulated. The First Belarussian Front of the Red Army raised the Soviet Red Flag on the Third Reich following German capitulation. This spelled the end of the Third Reich and Nazi Germany, one of the darkest chapters in human history.

On the Western front following the fall of France to Nazi Germany in 1940, around 300,000 British and Allied troops were trapped in France. The Allied soldiers retreated to the Northern French shores of Dunkirk against an advancing German army. In order to keep Britain's defensive capabilities potent, Prime Minister Winston Churchill decided to lodge a rescue operation and evacuate the stranded allied troops. The evacuation was a success even though there were significant losses of troops and equipment on the allied side.

In the summer of 1940, Nazi Germany launched air raids into Britain. The air raids were unsuccessful as the Royal air force ably defended Britain with British made Spitfire and Hurricane fighter planes. Nevertheless, the Germans continued their bombing raids. The city of Coventry experienced maximum damage from the bombings. London and especially East London also bore the brunt of the German blitz. The Germans wanted to invade Britain but they wanted to control the British airspace before launching a ground invasion. Britain held on without allowing the Germans air supremacy. The German military losses on the Eastern front against the Red Army meant that their ability to launch the invasion was limited. In June 1944, the Allied forces decided to launch a ground offensive against Germany on the Western front. Now the Allies ably supported by the Americans landed in Normandy to overpower the Germans. Intense fighting followed but the Germans succumbed to pressure from both the Red Army in the east and the Allies in the West. The Allies comprehensively defeated Nazi Germany in May 1945 and converged on Berlin. On 9 May 1945, the Nazi German Army (Wehrmacht) signed the surrender document in Berlin. The Allied Force and the Red Army also signed the document with the Americans and the French acting as witnesses. Adolf Hitler committed suicide to evade capture.

7.9 War in the Pacific

The war in the Pacific started with the Second Sino-Japanese War over the Marco Polo bridge incident in 1937. However, it quickly morphed into a global conflict as Imperial Japan allied with the Axis (Nazi Germany, Italy, and others) attached

British imperial interests in Asia. The Japanese took control of the strategically important port city of Singapore from the British and advanced in Burma. By 1941, the Japanese took full control of Burma threatening to enter India. In December 1941, the Japanese attacked Pearl Harbour, an important American naval base in the Pacific. This brought them into direct confrontation with the Americans. The Americans entered the war in the Pacific following the Pearl Harbour incident. The Japanese army also expanded south taking control of Indonesia and the islands of Papua. Indonesian islands gave the advancing Japanese troops a vantage point into northern Australia. In February 1942, the Japanese air force launched a bombing raid into the strategically important Australian port city of Darwin. It was a surprise raid and the losses for the Allied forces were significant. At the peak of the struggle, the Japanese army occupied Korea, Thailand, Malaya, the Philippines, and large parts of China.

With American entry into the war in the Pacific, the balance of power shifted again. The Americans mobilised and inflicted major defeats on the Japanese navy liberating Singapore, and large swathes of South East Asia. Following the victory over Nazi Germany in Europe marked by the 9 May 1945 surrender, the Red Army mobilised and concentrated its efforts in the East. The Soviet Union entered the land war with Japan in August 1945. The Japanese were no match to the combined firepower of the Red Army and the American forces. Within 3 weeks, the Red Army and its Chinese and Mongolian allies liberated Manchuria, Northern Korea, and Inner Mongolia. The Red Army also pushed the Japanese back along the Kuril Islands taking control of military strategic assets along the northern Sea of Japan. On 6th and 9th of August, the Americans dropped two nuclear bombs on the Japanese cities of Hiroshima and Nagasaki, which led to the instant deaths of over 300,000 people (mainly civilians). The use of nuclear weapons had long-lasting effects on the population, which manifested in the form of birth defects and malignancy. This remains the only use of nuclear weapons in combat. The use of nuclear weapons ended the war in the Pacific with Japanese surrender. The Red Army suspended its planned attack on the island of Hokkaido. The war finally ended with the sacrifice of an estimated 70–80 million lives of which the largest loss of life was in the Soviet Union (around 27 million) followed by China (around 20 million).

Bibliography

Aldcroft, D. (1977). *From Versailles to Wall Street 1919–1929*. London: Allen Lane.

Broadberry, S., & Howlett, P. (2005). The United Kingdom during world war I: Business and usual? In S. Broadberry & M. Harrison (Eds.), *The economics of world war I*. Cambridge: Cambridge University Press.

Eichengreen, B. (1992). *Golden fetters: The gold standard and the great depression 1919–1939*. Oxford: Oxford University Press.

Findlay, R., & O'Rourke, K. (2007). *Power and plenty: Trade, war, and the world economy in the second millennium*. Princeton, NJ: Princeton University Press.

Galbraith, J. (1955). *The great crash 1929*. London: Allen Lane.

Lindert, P., & Williamson, J. (2003). Does globalisation make the world more unequal? In M. Bordo, A. Taylor, & J. Williamson (Eds.), *Globalisation in historical perspective*. Chicago: University of Chicago Press.

Malenbaum, W. (1953). *The world wheat economy 1885–1953*. Cambridge, MA: Harvard University Press.

Moore, B. (1966). *Injustice: The social bases of obedience and revolt*. New York: White Plains.

Temin, P. (1971). The beginning of the depression in Germany. *The Economic History Review, 24*, 240–248.

Tomlinson, B. (1993). *The economy of Modern India 1860–1970*. Cambridge: Cambridge University Press.

Part III
The Post War Period

Chapter 8
Cold War Rivalry in a Bipolar World

Abstract This chapter covers the history of the cold war. It starts from the events such as the fall of Berlin and subsequent division of Berlin as the genesis of the cold war. It examines the Bretton Woods system, reconstruction of post-war Europe (predominantly Britain, Germany, and France), and the usage of the dollar as the currency for international commerce and maintaining reserves. This chapter examines the economic benefits accruing to the American financial elites under this new system. It also examines to what extent USSR's refusal to participate in the Bretton Woods financial and economic system transpired into the cold war. The Cuban Missile crisis, Soviet invasion of Czechoslovakia and Afghanistan, the Vietnam War, the Korean War, Sino-Soviet Split, the Oil Standard, and Sino-American Rapprochement are also analysed.

8.1 Genesis of the Cold War

As World War II approached its conclusion, the allies understood the need for another Vienna Conference to redefine security in Europe. This time the key stakeholders were the United States, the USSR, and the United Kingdom. In February 1945, Franklin Delano Roosevelt, Winston Churchill, and Joseph Stalin the leaders of the United States, United Kingdom, and USSR, respectively, met in Yalta, Crimea to discuss post-war security architecture in Europe. The Westphalian system of buffer zones that served well for European security following the defeat of Napoleonic France was again back on the agenda. The leaders understood that security underpins trade and commerce. Therefore, without a viable security architecture an economic system based on the capitalist mode of production would not be sustainable. The parties agreed on undivided security for the European continent. It also emphasized the right to self-determination of the liberated territories and people.

On paper, the Yalta declaration implied great power cooperation. However, underlying tensions due to fundamental differences remained. The United States, USSR, and Britain, the three Great Powers united in their quest of defeating Nazi Germany had obvious competing interests in a post-war Europe. All three powers were expansionist empires, albeit under different ideological banner. The United

S. Bhattacharyya, *A History of Global Capitalism*, Frontiers in Economic History,
https://doi.org/10.1007/978-3-030-58736-9_8

States and Britain viewed themselves as free trading internationalist empires and therefore ideological flagbearers of free-market economy and liberal democracy. The underlying modes of production in the United States and Britain were capitalist in nature. Rent generated due to market imperfections and excess supply of labour, were mainly appropriated by the owners of capital. The owners of capital collectively formed the imperial elite in these two countries. Therefore, protection and expansion of this rent was the key underlying economic motive of these elites. As I have demonstrated in Chap. 2, the objective of rent protection and growth can only be achieved through the control of international security architecture underpinning commerce. The United States was a rising empire with its industrial capacity largely intact. Britain was a declining empire heavily indebted and badly damaged by the war. The United States considered itself as the rightful heir of the British Empire given the close interconnections between the two elites. The United States elite understood very well that the eighteenth- and nineteenth-century European imperial model was becoming redundant. Modernising the model with indirect control was an objective of the American elite. I will return to this again later in the chapter.

In contrast, the USSR perceived itself as the flagbearer of socialism and communism. The key differences between a market-based system (the United States and Britain) and a socialist command and control system (USSR) was twofold. First, the difference associated with the adjustment mechanism and second, the difference associated with distribution. In a capitalist system, individual producers have property rights over their capital and land. They make factor payments to the owners of other inputs that they use in production but do not own. If the producers do not own an input, then they have to make payments at the margin to cover the user cost of that input. Any mismatch between supply and demand is adjusted through prices. Factor and product market imperfections are reflected through rent (i.e. the difference between price and marginal cost). In a capital and skill intensive production system with increasing returns, the rental payment to capital and skills could be significantly higher than payments to labour. This could be a source of inequality. The model followed by the United States and Britain would resort to limited intervention via the tax and redistribution system to correct such inequality.

In a socialist system, the model of production is capitalist but production is based on need. Need is estimated through demand projections. See Kalecki (1990, 1992, 1993) for a full account of the socialist economic system. Any demand and supply mismatch is adjusted not through price but quantity. All factors of production are owned by the state and therefore the state appropriates all the rent generated from the production process. Rent is generated due to imperfections or increasing returns. The state then equitably distributes this rent to the citizens based on their needs. In practice, this implies that the state and the communist party is the sole owner of all income generating assets and thus appropriator of rent.

Therefore, both systems would need to expand in order for them to be sustainable. Expansion could be in the form of new territories and new markets. It could also be in terms of innovations which significantly reduces the unit cost of production given a market size. With significant residual military potential, it was unsurprising that the United States and USSR led imperial systems would collide at some point. The

Soviet–American 'Thucydides' Trap' was always on the cards. Note that regardless of the ideological colour, the USSR was a successor of the Russian empire.

The underlying contradictions in imperial interests came to a head in Berlin after 9 May 1945. The two camps clashed over the status of Berlin and unification of Germany. The British, French, and the Americans demanded that the Soviets hand back control of the entire German territory to be incorporated into an American led system. The Soviets refused to concede. Berlin was divided along the contact line between the USSR and Allied forces. The contradictions sharpened to such an extent that the British Prime Minister Winston Churchill asked his war cabinet to draw up plans to lodge a surprise attack on the USSR to impose British and American will. These unrealised war plans are collectively known as the 'Operation Unthinkable'. The recently acquired nuclear first-strike capabilities by the United States perhaps influenced Churchill's belligerence. The Soviet Union acquired the nuclear bomb in 1949, successfully testing it in Kazakhstan and thereby restoring parity. The cold war ensued.

An iron curtain was enforced in Berlin. Europe was divided into two camps. Most of Berlin, East Germany, Poland, and Eastern Europe were absorbed into the Soviet-led camp. West Germany, Britain, France, the Netherlands, Belgium, Italy, Spain, and Portugal were absorbed into an American-led camp. The Yalta ambition of undivided security in Europe proved illusory as the American led alliance created its own collective security alliance in the form of the North Atlantic Treaty Organisation (NATO) in 1949. In response, the Soviet Union created the Warsaw Pact in 1955, a collective security organisation of the Soviet-led Eastern European countries. Confrontation rather than cooperation became the norm.

At the international level, the United Nations (UN) replaced the now defunct League of Nations. In April 1945, 50 government representatives converged in San Francisco and started work on the United Nations Charter. The Charter was adopted in October 1945 and the UN started operation. The UN charter stipulated the inviolability of international borders and the right to self-determination. It also declared that no territorial claims could be made by the defeated countries against the victors. The territorial boundaries set by the Allied powers after the conclusion of the war was final. The Security Council was created as the ultimate arbiter in international affairs and decisions related to war and peace. The allied powers of the United States, USSR, Britain, China, and France became the five permanent members of the UN Security Council with each having a veto over decisions. The veto power was granted as a device to encourage consensus among the great powers on matters relating to war and peace. As I will describe in the following chapters, this institutional structure proved to be extremely effective over the next 75 years in preventing great power conflict.

Cold war battlelines were drawn. Containment of the USSR and China were the official policy of the United States-led Western bloc. Thwarting the containment policy and challenging American interest in every corner of the globe became official Soviet policy. China, now under communist party rule and the leadership of Mao Zedong aligned with the USSR.

8.2 Post-war Reconstruction and Financial Architecture

Post-war reconstruction required financing and planning. All 44 allied nations including the United States, United Kingdom, USSR, and China (also known as the big four) converged on Bretton Woods, New Hampshire in 1944 to decide on post-war reconstruction and the financial architecture. America, largely unscathed from the ill effects of the war were the most powerful economy in the world. Its industrial base expanded significantly and did not suffer from the direct effects of the war. It also had the largest gold reserve as most allied European nations deposited their gold to the United States either as collateral for a loan or for safekeeping during the war. Unsurprisingly the United States pushed for a gold and dollar-based financial system given its large gold reserves and economic might. The Allied nations deliberated for 3 weeks at the Mount Washington Hotel in New Hampshire and signed the Bretton Woods agreement on 22 July 1944. A whole raft of new institutions were created in order to regulate the international monetary system and balance of payment imbalances. The International Monetary Fund (IMF) and the International Bank of Reconstruction and Development (IBRD) were established. The latter now is a part of the World Bank Group. The USSR participated in the conference but did not ratify the Agreement. Cold war tensions prevented cooperation.

The economics of the Bretton Woods international monetary system was the following. At the base of the system was the value of gold. Dollar as a fiat currency would be the means of international commerce whereby commodities would be priced in dollars. However, dollar would be fully convertible to gold. The key participating countries and American cold war allies (Britain, France, Germany, and Japan) would also have their currencies tied to the dollar and gold. For example, if France were exporting wine to America then the French producers would accept payments in dollars. However, they would have the full right to convert their dollars into gold. Through this mechanism, the value of the allied currencies (Pound Sterling, Franc, Deutschmark, and Yen) would be pegged to the dollar within a 1% window of variation. The International Monetary Fund (IMF) would bridge any temporary balance of payments gap. Trade settlement between the non-American allies could be either in national currencies or in dollars. Increasingly, the dollar dominated international commerce in strategic raw materials such as petroleum and metals. London, Paris, Frankfurt, and Tokyo all created institutions to support dollar-based financing in addition to New York. The City of London in a post-war environment became the centre of dollar-based financing in Europe and former British colonies. The Pound Sterling, Franc, Deutschmark, and Yen were also included into the IMF basket of reserve currencies.

The dollar-based system rendered some advantage to America as it could print dollars and control the asset value of the participating nations. However, money and credit creation was constrained by the dollar's peg to gold. Expansionary monetary policy in the United States would depress the dollar and could potentially make American exports cheaper. However, this could imply that the participating economies demanding more gold requiring matched increase in supply of a scarce precious metal. Given the finite supply of gold, this would put upward pressure on gold prices effectively breaking the peg. As a result, competitive devaluation of national currencies was prohibited under the Bretton Woods mechanism.

The International Bank of Reconstruction and Development (IBRD) and its European branch, the European Bank of Reconstruction and Development (EBRD) took charge of reconstruction in Europe. Following the conclusion of the war, American financial system was flush with capital as most of the globes (predominantly European) wealthy parked their savings in America. America also held two-thirds of the world's gold. Therefore, American financial system was in an ideal position to finance reconstruction in Europe and elsewhere. Due to the destruction of physical capital and infrastructure in Europe during the war, the returns to capital were high.

In spite of the economic merit of financing reconstruction, it is also important to analyse the political economy. Post-war reconstruction had two aspects, civilian and military. Military industrial production increased significantly during wartime in the United States (and to a much lesser extent in Britain). With the conclusion of war and the expected decline in demand for military equipment, industrial production in the United States could have followed the same path as interwar Europe. Excess capacity and deflation could have been a challenge in peacetime. Therefore, generating additional external demand was essential to avoid deflationary tendencies leading to a similar fate as interwar Europe. Post-war reconstruction of civilian infrastructure in Germany, France, Britain, and Japan provided an excellent opportunity to expand demand for industrial equipment. After 1945 with the division of Berlin cold war tensions intensified. This also offered an expansion opportunity for the market in military equipment. The Americans created the North Atlantic Treaty Organisation (NATO) in 1949 to ensure collective security. Membership of the NATO mandated that the allies integrate their military infrastructure and supplies. In practice, this offered scale economies to the American military industries as the allies signed up to buy American military supplies. It also gave the American military industries access to the local supply chain.

These arrangements also required financing. Under the Bretton Woods system, this meant dollar-based financing. Therefore, the reconstruction efforts offered enormous scale economies and expansion opportunities to the large Wall Street and City of London banks strategically aligned to the Americans. The large Wall Street and City of London banks were Goldman-Sachs, Lehman Brothers, JP Morgan, Rothschild & Co, and others. The mechanism of financing was broadly as follows. The IBRD created its initial capital pool by issuing shares (or equity) to its members. The American government held the majority of the shares. In addition, the IBRD issued bonds in the international financial markets (i.e. New York and London) to raise capital for specific reconstruction projects. These bonds in return were held by the large Wall Street and City of London banks who unsurprisingly owned most of the capital. The investment banks in return received coupon payments on their investment. The capital raised was then directed towards large American corporations participating in the reconstruction effort in the form of credit.

Initially, this was a credit to support essential imports from American corporations as post-war Europe hardly had any foreign exchange reserves. However, over time credit was directed to local firms under the Marshall Plan (or the European Recovery Programme) as the large American corporations developed their local supply chain.

Under Franklin D Roosevelt, the Anglo-American plan was deindustrialisation of Germany and Japan in order to eliminate the risk of a future great power conflict. To this effect, the Roosevelt administration adopted the Morgenthau Plan severely limiting steel and coal production in Germany and Japan. However, with the cold war intensifying and Harry Truman administration assuming power the situation reversed drastically. The Marshall Plan was adopted in 1948, which called for reindustrialisation of Germany and Japan. Soviet military threat in Europe and elsewhere was the pretext behind the change of course. The Marshall Plan was developed by the United States State Department under the leadership of William Clayton and George Kennan and the Brookings Institution.

Factors associated personality undoubtedly played a role but one cannot downplay the role of underlying economic and political factors. As the reconstruction process gained momentum, the financial and military industrial elite in the United States became even more powerful. It was in the interest of the big Wall Street banks to continue credit expansion and exploit scale economies. It directly contributed to the expansion of their economic rent. Similarly, expansion was also in the interest of the large corporations and military industries in order to benefit from agglomeration economies in the form of expanding economic rent. A cap on steel and coal production in Germany and Japan under the Morgenthau Plan acted as a constraint. Disarmament and arms embargo on Germany and Japan was also a constraint for the military industries. The collective economic and political power of the financial and military industrial elite overpowered any resistance to their plan (now called the Marshall Plan) of rearmament and reindustrialisation under the pretext of a Soviet military threat.

8.3 European Coal and Steel Community and the European Union

The continental European countries including West Germany formed the European Coal and Steel Community (ECSC) under the Treaty of Paris in 1951. The parties were France, Belgium, the Netherlands, Luxembourg, Italy, and West Germany. The treaty was designed to promote cooperation and regulate European industrial production. It also had a political dimension. It was aimed to appease French suspicion of Germany's industrialisation under the Marshall Plan. The French elite envisaged that they could control the rate of growth of West German industrialisation by imposing centralised institutional control over access to raw materials such as coal from continental Europe. The Americans viewed it as a minor concession in return for French support of the Marshall Plan. The ECSC offered agglomeration economies to the participating countries. It also created jobs for the working class in high unemployment post-war Europe. Furthermore, cooperation had peace dividends for all the participating countries. Peace was of prime importance in post-war Europe. Therefore, it had broad-based support from both the elites and the average citizens.

The Anglo-American interests were not threatened by the ECSC. It promoted peace and harmony among American allies which furthered American foreign policy interests in Europe. The Americans were firmly entrenched in Western Europe as they controlled the security architecture through NATO. Britain, increasingly a junior partner of the Americans also had its security interests in continental Europe protected via NATO. Both Britain and America had troops stationed in West Germany. In addition, the Americans indirectly controlled the economy of these allied countries through the dollar-based international monetary system under the Bretton Woods agreement. Therefore, ECSC was viewed as a benign non-military alliance by the Americans.

The ECSC evolved into the European Economic Community (EEC) following the Treaty of Brussels in 1967. The Treaty of Maastricht in 1993 led to the establishment of the European Union and European citizenship. The Maastricht Treaty added a political dimension to the EEC which was essentially a loose customs union. It set in motion a quest for political union between the participating nations. Due to the legacy of two German initiated great wars, Britain was a reluctant supporter. The European Union did not challenge American security interests in Europe. The EU does not have its own army or security agencies. For security, it is entirely reliant on American led NATO. Therefore, the Americans were not opposed to the creation of the EU. In fact, the EU and its predecessors furthered American foreign policy interests by showcasing American led success stories in Western Europe. It displayed the success of liberal democracy and market economy to the rival Soviet led Eastern Bloc.

8.4 Standard Oil, Saudi Arabia, and America

Energy is a key input in industrial production. In the late nineteenth and early twentieth century, coal played a major role as the raw material of choice for energy. However, the industrial input mix changed rapidly in the early twentieth century. Industries increasingly substituted coal with petroleum as the key energy input. With the advent of automobiles and the internal combustion engine, the demand for oil and related products soared. As petroleum became the input of choice for industrial production, the competition among great powers to secure strategically important petroleum resources intensified.

Standard Oil, the American oil monopoly was established in 1870 in Ohio as a corporation. It was the largest oil monopoly during the late nineteenth and early twentieth century. It not only produced oil, it also had monopoly over refining, transportation, and marketing. In 1911, the monopoly was dismantled as the United

States Supreme Court in a landmark antitrust determination ruled Standard Oil to be an illegal monopoly. With the dissolution of Standard Oil, it was divided into 34 smaller companies. One of them was Standard Oil California which in 1931 received oil exploration permits in the eastern al-Hassa province of Saudi Arabia. The Saudi Royal family had existing strong relationship with Britain as the latter protected the former from the Ottoman Turks. However, over time and especially during the interwar period Saudi Arabia established even stronger relationships with America. This alliance was solidified in 1945 during the meeting between Saudi King Ibn Saud and American President Franklin D. Roosevelt on board USS Quincy. The relationship had two key aspects. First, the strategic location of Saudi Arabia provided the Americans an important base overlooking the strategically important sea route of the Persian Gulf and the Strait of Hormuz. In return, American presence guaranteed security of the Saudi Royal family. Second, the Saudi petroleum assets gave American corporations and by extension the American state significant leverage over the international market for this strategically important raw material.

Furthermore, the post-war dollar-based financial architecture was also underpinned by control over strategic petroleum assets. During the 1945 meeting with Roosevelt, the Saudi Royals agreed to sell and price oil in US dollars. They also agreed to invest all the surplus generated from the oil sales into dollar denominated assets. This ensured the depth and breadth of dollar required to be a global reserve currency. Dollar captured a significant proportion of transactions in international trade and commerce. The demand for dollars increased manyfold. Dollar being tied to the steadily growing demand for a strategic industrial resource was less volatile as a currency.

8.5 Imperial Ambitions of Britain and the Suez Crisis

Even though nominally victorious against the Axis, Britain was a reduced power following the conclusion of the Second World War. The war significantly damaged British industrial capacity and waned its colonial influence around the world. In contrast, American power was rising. Its industrial capacity and economic prowess were unmatched during the post-war period. It accounted for more than half of the world's gold reserve. America did not fight the war on its home turf. The war took place in Europe and Asia. Therefore, its industrial capacity remained unscathed. The military losses in terms of combatants and equipment were also limited compared to other allied powers as America entered the war very late.

Given its economic and military might, the American elite perceived themselves as the rightful heir of the British and European imperial possessions. Perhaps they worked on the assumption that this is a fair price to ask in return for the financial help with post-war reconstruction. However, old imperial habits die-hard. In spite of its reduced capabilities, Britain still perceived itself as a global empire. The Suez crisis of 1956 is a case in point where Britain and France were competing with the United

States in their last gasp attempt to remain relevant in a region that used to be their imperial backyard. Note that Britain and France were allies of the United States. However, they were more than willing to compete against it when it came to defending their imperial interest. This episode demonstrates that the expansionist nature of the underlying economic system provokes confrontation even among allies.

In 1956, the president of newly independent Egypt Gamal Abdel Nasser nationalised the strategically important Suez Canal. In the 1950s, Arab nationalism was sweeping through the Middle East as more and more territories gained independence from their European colonial masters. Nasser as a nationalist decided to nationalise the canal so that Egyptians can benefit from its rent.

The canal's history goes back to 1869 when it was inaugurated after 10 years of construction using both Egyptian and French government finance. Egypt was ruled by the Muhammad Ali dynasty at that time. Muhammad Ali was of Albanian descent. The United Company of the Suez Maritime Canal operated the canal. It immediately became an important strategic asset as it significantly reduced the maritime route connecting Western Europe and the Far East. The scramble over control of this important strategic asset began at the earnest amongst the European colonial powers. In 1875, Britain became the near majority shareholder of the canal as Egypt sold its shares following a sovereign debt crisis. The majority shareholders were French private investors. In 1882, Britain invaded Egypt and defeated the Egyptian army at the Battle of Tel-el-Kebir. Egypt became a British protectorate or effectively a British colony. With the fall of Egypt to Britain, the canal effectively came under British control. Even though free passage was guaranteed under the 1888 Convention of Constantinople, in practice it was subject to British discretion. For example, during the Russo-Japanese War of 1905, Britain denied Russian naval access to the canal. This turned out to be decisive as Russian reinforcements to the Far East was delayed by several weeks. On the face of persistent Japanese onslaught, Russian supply line was seriously challenged and key battles lost.

The canal stayed in British hands till 1952 when British advisors were expelled from Egypt following a revolution. Therefore, a British reaction to reinforce its claims over this strategic asset was all but expected. Britain under Prime Minister Anthony Eden conspired with Israel and France to invade Egypt and take control of the canal. Israel invaded the Egyptian Sinai peninsula while Britain and France landed paratroopers along the Suez Canal. The Egyptians were defeated but they still managed to block the canal to all international shipping. The two military heavyweights, the United States and the USSR intervened. The United States made it clear to its Western European allies that it will not tolerate any European imperial expansion. Under heavy pressure from the United States and the USSR, Britain and France promptly withdrew. It was effectively the end of Britain's colonial ambitions.

8.6 Unravelling of the Soviet-American Wartime Alliance and the Inevitability of the Cold War

So far, we have seen how expansionism and imperial ambitions bring even allies and ideological partners into conflict. Next, we ask the questions, why the Soviet-American wartime Alliance unravelled during peacetime and why the cold war was inevitable.

World War II in Europe started with the German invasion of Poland in 1939. Initially, the Americans were reluctant to enter the war in Europe. They were also ambivalent to German or Soviet losses, as they perceived both to be ideological enemies. They supplied equipment to both Germany and the USSR. However, with the German aggression against Britain and the war against Japan in the Pacific, the American attitude to the war and the USSR shifted. The Americans entered the war in the Pacific after the Japanese bombing of Pearl Harbour on 7 December 1941. Japan was allied with Nazi Germany. Therefore, declaring war against Japan meant also declaring war against Germany. The Americans understood very well that the Anglo-American alliance alone are not in a position to confront Germany in Europe. Therefore, they entered into a tactical alliance with the Soviet Union. The alliance had a narrow short-term military objective of defeating Germany in Europe and defeating Japan in the Far East.

Once the wartime goals were achieved, the alliance unravelled during peacetime. Many scholarly works focus on the personality clash between President Harry Truman and Soviet leader Joseph Stalin as the genesis of the cold war (Cohen 2011). They also lament that many cooperation opportunities were lost between these two powers. This may very well be true. However, there are far deeper political economy factors that made the cold war inevitable.

Following the conclusion of the war, the United States was by far the strongest economic and military power in the world. It had the largest gold reserve. Its production capacity increased manyfold to service the war economy. It also had a food surplus, as its agricultural land assets remained unaffected by the war. Militarily, it was a superpower. Its military losses were limited compared to other allied powers and especially the Soviet Union. It was also the sole nuclear power following the nuclear attacks on Hiroshima and Nagasaki. Therefore, US elite considered themselves on the driving seat in terms of shaping the post-war politico-economic order.

In contrast, the Western European allies of the United States were all reduced powers. Britain barely managed to defend itself against Germany. France capitulated to Germany and the French elite had to flee to London. Therefore, their military power was limited. Both Britain and France were heavily indebted. Therefore, their economic influence was also limited. The defeated Axis powers such as Germany and Italy were completely destroyed and could barely stand on their own feet.

The Soviet Union, undoubtedly far weaker than the United States were not a reduced power. It almost singlehandedly defeated Nazi Germany in Europe. It also routed the Imperial Japanese Army in Khalkin Gol and beyond in the Far East. It payed enormous price in the process but its industrial and military capacity was by far the strongest in the Eurasian continent. In spite of heavy combatant and civilian losses during the war, it was by far the largest country in Europe. It also had a long and proud military and imperial history.

In terms of factor endowments and structure of the economy, it was similar to the United States. It was land abundant and labour scarce society after the war. It was also abundant in vital industrial raw materials such as coal, petroleum, iron ore, copper, and freshwater. It industrialised rapidly during the 1930s to prepare for the war. Therefore, it had a strong base of skilled labour force. Traditionally it was also a large producer of wheat and other agricultural products. Therefore, it was competing with the United States on the global market for agricultural commodities. War mobilisation meant that the Soviet Union possessed a vibrant military industrial complex, which produced automobiles, battle tanks, battleships, missiles, and aircrafts. Therefore, the endowments and the economic structures were such that they were more likely to be competitors rather than partners. After all, like poles repel each other.

This is exactly how it played out during the post-war era. Initially, the Soviet Union participated in the American led Bretton Woods conference. The American plan was to be the sole hegemon in a post-war dollar-based financial and economic system. Yes, there were other players such as Britain and France but their role was minor. Integrating with such a system would have meant compromising the Soviet military industrial capacity. The Soviet leadership correctly perceived this as a threat to national security. As a victorious power with glorious military imperial history, it was expected that the Soviet leadership would not settle for a junior role in an American led system. Furthermore, there were also ideological differences but the gap in economic interests were such that a confrontation was inevitable.

The Soviets never ratified the Bretton Woods Agreement. Once the confrontation over Berlin intensified, the wartime alliance fell apart. The American elites were confident of their military supremacy as the sole nuclear power on the planet. However, they were unaware of the rapidly developing Soviet nuclear programme, which led to the first successful testing in 1949. The Americans were also rightfully confident of their economic supremacy. Therefore, they were unwilling to make any concessions to the Soviet elites.

Once the wheels of confrontation was set in motion, it suited the military industrial complex of both nations. The cold war arms race meant that the peacetime excess capacity of military industries were no longer a problem. The military industries and special interests could continue to produce taxpayer-funded armaments under the pretext of an imminent military threat. Collective security organisations such as the NATO perfectly suited this agenda. In response, the Soviet Union created its own bloc comprising of allied Eastern European nations. It created the collective security organisation the Warsaw Pact in 1955. This was in response to the NATO integration of West Germany in 1954.

8.7 Post-war Economic Expansion of the USSR

In Chap. 2, we describe the capitalist economic system in non-socialist countries including Western countries. In such a system, the model of production is capitalist and price signals broadly dictate resource allocation. The owners of capital (or the capitalists) who are a small minority holds disproportionate power over the system and appropriate most of the rent from production. The capitalists, using their appropriated rent typically capture the political system. This enables them to protect their future rent and wield disproportionate political power.

In contrast, a socialist or a communist economic system uses the capitalist mode of production but a non-market-based mechanism of allocation of resources, output, and rent. I would call this system state capitalism. Under state capitalism, the allocation of production inputs (raw materials) and outputs take place not through price signals in a market but via central planning. Furthermore, any surplus (or rent) generated during production are socially appropriated rather than appropriated by the owners of capital. Soviet Union adopted this model of capitalism where the economy was run by command, control, and centralised five-year planning.

During the post-war period, the Soviet Union faced massive reconstruction challenges. The war in Europe was fought mainly on its soil and therefore the war damages were significant. The loss of an estimated 29 million people meant severe labour shortages. Nevertheless, the Soviet Union organised its reconstruction based on five-year plans. The plan was based on adding industrial capacity on top of the traditional industrial base in the Urals and the Volga. New ambitious industrial plan embarked on industrialisation of the territory along the Don and Dnieper rivers. These geographies were ideally suited for exploiting agglomeration effects with their access to the seafaring waterways and access to warm water ports on the Black Sea. They also had abundant reserves of industrial raw materials such as coal, iron ore, and freshwater. In the hinterland, these areas were endowed with fertile soil to keep food supply steady and effective grain wages low. Furthermore, they were very well networked to the supply chains of a continental sized economy with unlimited reserves of all the key industrial inputs.

Given the different structure of the Soviet economy, it is challenging to accurately measure Soviet GDP that could be compared with a market-based economy, Nevertheless, we can draw upon some numbers from the CIA World Fact Book. The CIA estimates that the Soviet GDP rose close to a trillion dollars in 1977 and to 2.7 trillion dollars in 1989. The CIA estimates that the Soviet Union experienced steady growth during the post-war period continually improved living standards. The post-war excess capacity in the economy was addressed by creating internal demand as well as demand from its allies. Due to the perceived threat of war, the Soviet Union never really transformed itself from a war economy to a civilian one. It had to rely on imports from its allies in Eastern Europe for goods associated with the civilian economy.

8.8 Cuban Revolution

Once the Soviet Union became a nuclear power in 1949, the cost of direct military confrontation between the United States and the Soviet Union increased manyfold. Therefore, direct military confrontation became increasingly infeasible. However, the cold war tensions were high and many indirect conflicts and proxy wars followed. There are many episodes of escalations between the two rivals during the cold war. However, no other event is perhaps more significant during the cold war than the Cuban Revolution in 1953–1959.

The Cuban Revolution was a momentous event in the history of the cold war as a group of youth led by the revolutionary Fidel Castro ousted the American backed military dictatorship of Fulgencio Batista in 1959. American investors mainly owned the sugarcane plantation and tourism assets of Cuba at that time. Their economic interests were heavily damaged following the revolution as Castro nationalised the economy and established a revolutionary socialist state. In the 1960s, Castro turned communist and established a one-party communist rule. The socialist revolution and subsequent events made Cuba a mortal enemy of the United States and an ally of the Soviet Union. Cuban revolutionaries led by Ernesto 'che' Guevara participated in cold war military conflicts in Africa, Southeast Asia, Latin America, and the Middle East against American interests and in favour of Soviet interests.

8.9 Cold War Flashpoints: Cuban Missile Crisis, Invasion of Czechoslovakia, Vietnam, Korean War

The Cold War history is riddled with confrontations and escalation flashpoints. Understandably I will not cover all of them here. However, here I will focus on some of the key flashpoints that I think significantly influenced Cold War history. I will start with the Cuban Missile crisis following which I will discuss the Soviet invasion of Czechoslovakia. I will also discuss the Vietnam and Korean wars.

8.9.1 Cuban Missile Crisis

Unimpressed by the 1959 socialist revolution in Cuba, an American backed group mainly consisting of Cuban exiles opposed to Fidel Castro invaded the Bay of Pigs located on the south-western coast of Cuba. The groups' military operation was directed by American security agencies. The invasion began with the US Air Force bombing of the Cuban airfields on 17 April 1961. The operation lasted for 4 days with the decisive victory of the Cuban Revolutionary Armed Forces.

The failed Bay of Pigs invasion was a precursor to a larger Cuban Missile Crisis. Bay of Pigs was a catastrophic foreign policy failure by the United States. It pushed

Cuba closer to the Soviet Union. Following the failed Bay of Pigs invasion, Fidel Castro approached the Soviet leader Nikita Khrushchev for security guarantees. Khrushchev agreed to secretly deploy Soviet short- and medium-range ballistic missiles in Cuba to deter further attacks by the United States. In 1962, the Soviet Red Army secretly started deploying in Cuba and building missile launch facilities.

In October 1962, the American spy planes took pictures of the Soviet deployment and raised alarm. The Soviet leadership considered this deployment as a justified response to the deployment of American short- and medium-range ballistic missiles in Turkey and Italy. Following the discovery of Soviet missiles, the Americans instituted a naval blockade on Cuba to stop further Soviet missiles from reaching the island nation. The Americans demanded a complete withdrawal of Soviet missiles from Cuba. Intense negotiations followed between the Soviet leader Nikita Khrushchev and American president John F. Kennedy.

After several days of negotiation, the Soviet Union agreed to a United Nations supervised withdrawal of missiles from Cuba. In return, the United States made a public declaration and signed an agreement providing security guarantees to Cuba. Further invasions were officially off the table at least for the time being. The United States not so publicly agreed to dismantle all the medium-range ballistic missiles deployed in Turkey.

Historians consider the Cuban Missile Crisis as the closest to a direct nuclear exchange during the cold war. Direct dialogue between the leaders of the two cold war adversaries prevented disaster. Important lessons were learnt. A hotline was established between the leaders of the two states. A series of agreements were reached between the adversaries broadly outlining the informal rules of the cold war. The agreements were based on mutual recognition (at least at an informal level) of spheres of influence. These agreements temporarily reduced tensions but did not prevent the arms race.

8.9.2 Soviet Invasion of Czechoslovakia

In January 1968, the First Secretary of the Czechoslovakian Communist Party Alexander Dubcek initiated a reform movement based on the agenda of partial decentralisation of the economy, federalisation, media deregulation, and democratisation. In doing so, he crossed a Soviet red line as the Soviet Union heavily disapproved of these reforms. The Soviet leadership in Moscow considered the Eastern and Central European countries East of Berlin as their zone of influence. Therefore, democratisation and media deregulation in, however, limited form posed an existential threat to Soviet hegemony over these territories. Furthermore, it also posed the additional risk of contagion to other territories within the Eastern Bloc and perhaps the Soviet Union itself.

In August 1968, the Soviet Union along with its Warsaw Pact allies decided to militarily impose bloc discipline on Czechoslovakia by invading the country. A total of approximately half a million Soviet and allied troops entered Czechoslovakia in

August. The majority were Soviet troops but they were ably supported by Poland, Bulgaria, and Hungary. The East German troops were mobilised but they stayed on the border and did not enter the Czechoslovakian territory. Not all countries within the Warsaw Pact supported the invasion. Romania and Albania refused to participate. Czechoslovakia also received diplomatic support from China as the Sino-Soviet relationship at that time was hostile.

Czechoslovakia did not offer any military resistance. Secretary Dubcek resigned and Gustav Husak who was loyal to the Soviet Union replaced him. Even though the military operation was swiftly over, civil disobedience continued for another 9 months. Nevertheless, Moscow was able to impose its will on Czechoslovakia by permanently stationing troops on its territory. Western powers lodged diplomatic protests in support of Czechoslovakia but beyond that there was very little else they could do short of declaring war on the Warsaw Pact.

8.9.3 Vietnam War

The genesis of the Vietnam War goes back to November 1955 with the Vietnamese struggle for independence from imperial France. Territories in modern day Cambodia, Laos, and Vietnam were part of French Indochina at that time and were colonial possessions of France. Initially, American involvement in the conflict zone was limited in the form of a handful of advisors. However, over time their involvement grew. The conflict turned into a full-scale cold war proxy conflict in August 1964 with the Gulf of Tonkin incident.

The National Security Agency (NSA) of the United States claimed that on 2 August 1964, the US Navy destroyer USS Maddox was attacked by North Vietnamese torpedo patrol boats while conducting a signal intelligence mission at the Gulf of Tonkin. The 2 August incident did take place but pentagon papers and later NSA publications revealed that the US Government misrepresented the facts. There were no casualties on the American side and USS Maddox sustained only a minor bullet hole from the North Vietnamese machine gunfire. Later on, the US Government also claimed an exchange on 4 August that never took place. This supposed incident gave the US Government a pretext to declare war against North Vietnam. A long-standing proxy war turned into a direct hot war.

The war continued till 1973 with significant civilian losses due to indiscriminate bombing campaign by the US Air Force. Despite civilian losses and destruction, the American ground forces did not make any progress. The Soviet Union and the People's Liberation Army (PLA) of China supported the North Vietnamese forces. Over time, American combatant losses and injuries grew. War fatigue set in and civilian pressure forced the American Government to withdraw from Vietnam in 1973. The Paris Peace Accord of 1973 allowed the Americans an exit from Vietnam. The Accord was immediately broken and fighting began between the North and the South Vietnam. The conflict ended with South Vietnam finally falling to the North in April 1975.

8.9.4 Korean War

The Korean peninsula was another cold war hotspot. Second World War was the genesis of the Korean dispute. Korea was under Japanese occupation during the major part of the Second World War. Soviet Union and the United States liberated Korea from the Japanese occupation in 1945. The Soviets approached Korea from the North while the Americans took on the Japanese from the South. After the Japanese surrender, Korea ended up into two zones of occupation with the Soviets occupying the territory north of the 38th Parallel while the Americans occupying the territory south of the same. The 38th Parallel became the de facto border with neither side recognising the legitimacy of the opposing side's territory.

The Soviets established a socialist state in the North under the leadership of Kim II Sung while the Americans established an anti-communist capitalist state in the South under the leadership of Syngman Rhee. It remained a frozen conflict until June 1950 when it restarted again with the North invading the South. Very rapidly, it turned into a cold war flashpoint with the Americans directly entering the war with a coalition of allies supporting the South. In response, China also entered the war in support of the North. Soviet Union did not enter the war directly but provided logistical and material support to the North Korean and Chinese forces. Soviet pilots also participated in combat with the North Korean and Chinese Air Force undercover. The conflict was largely a stalemate with neither side able to make progress in a vicious war of attrition. It lasted for 3 years until June 1953 when the guns fell silent with an Armistice Agreement.

Beyond the obvious ideological dimension of stopping communism, the American involvement in Korea had an obvious geopolitical dimension. The Korean peninsula is strategically located between China and Japan. The western coastline faces the Yellow Sea and China while the eastern coastline faces the Sea of Japan and Japan. Therefore, it is an important location to control the maritime traffic and institute containment of both China and the Soviet Union. The threat of dislodgement from a location of such strategic importance triggered American military response. On the Soviet and Chinese side, American military advantage from such a strategic location was well understood. Therefore, ending American military presence from the Korean peninsula was a worthy national security objective for them.

8.10 Sino-Soviet Border Conflict and Split

Soviet Union and the People's Republic of China were World War II allies and ideological siblings. Nevertheless, conflict broke out in the form of border skirmishes when ambitions collided. This conflict was similar in nature to the Anglo-American conflict over the Suez Canal. The latter did not turn into a hot war while the former did.

The Sino-Soviet relationship continually deteriorated following the death of Joseph Stalin. Joseph Stalin maintained a strong relationship with China and Chairman Mao Zedong while he was secretary of the Soviet communist party. However, that relationship broke down with the passing of Stalin and Nikita Khrushchev assuming power. Khrushchev publicly denounced Stalin during his speech at the 1956 20th Party Congress. Khrushchev and his administration adopted a De-Stalinisation policy to remove the effect of Stalin's personality cult from the Soviet Union. This was not well received by Mao Zedong in China as he viewed this as an indirect reference to his personality cult in China. The Sino-Soviet relationship soured progressively which is often referred to as the Sino-Soviet Split of 1956–1969.

Following the departure of Khrushchev in 1964, Leonid Brezhnev became the First Secretary of the Soviet Communist Party. The relationship soured even further culminating in a border conflict in 1969. Proximate causes of the Sino-Soviet split were ideological differences concerning the interpretation of Marxism–Leninism, de-Stalinization in the USSR, and Soviet doctrine of peaceful coexistence with the West. Far deeper cause was concerning the leadership of the communist bloc. China perceived itself as a major power and a sole arbiter in its immediate neighbourhood in Southeast Asia. Therefore, it was seeking to carve out its zone of influence in its neighbourhood, especially in North Korea, Vietnam, and Cambodia independent of the Soviet Union. Soviet elites were unwilling to grant that space to China and recognise it as a regional hegemon.

China rejected the role of a Soviet junior partner in international relations and wanted to teach Soviet Union a lesson for its apparent arrogance. This led to border clashes in Damansky Island and Manchuria in March 1969. There were military losses on both sides but it did not escalate into a full-scale war. Both sides refused to declare war but the skirmishes continued for a while. The conflict ended with a ceasefire and return to status quo but the territorial disputes remained. The territorial disputes were finally resolved following a series of treaties between the Russian Federation and China in 1991, 1994, and 2004.

This conflict is another testament to the expansionist ambitions inherent in a capitalist political-economic system irrespective of ideology. The mode of production in both countries was capitalist even though both claimed capital to be under social control rather than under private control.

8.11 US-China Rapprochement

The Sino-Soviet split and the border conflict of 1969 offered the United States a window of opportunity to mend its relationship with China. Following the humiliating defeat in Vietnam and the stalemate in Korea, the geopolitical strategists in America led by Henry Kissinger understood very well that America is far weaker than the combined political, economic, and military power of the Soviet Union and China especially on the Eurasian continent. Henry Kissinger, the principal architect of Richard Nixon administration's China policy secretly flew to Beijing in 1971 where he held several meetings with the Chinese leadership. This was a precursor to Richard Nixon's weeklong visit to China the following year. Nixon held several meetings with the Chinese leadership during his visit including meetings with Premier Zhou Enlai and Chairman Mao Zedong.

Prior to Richard Nixon's visit, there were no diplomatic relations between the People's Republic and the United States. During the Chinese civil war, the United States backed the nationalist and only recognised the Taiwanese administration as the legitimate government of China. However, the attitude changed following Richard Nixon's visit in 1972. Full diplomatic relations were established in 1979 and in return, China agreed to a political settlement of the Taiwan question.

Warming of relations with China also had a positive effect on Soviet–American relationship. Fearing a hostile China allied with the United States in its backyard, the Soviet leadership under Leonid Brezhnev also pursued détente with Richard Nixon's United States. This allowed the United States much need time to rebuild and regroup in this new Great Game following the debacle of Vietnam.

Richard Nixon inherited a weak American economy from Lyndon Johnson. The economy was plagued by high budget deficit, high unemployment, and high inflation. There were long-term structural challenges with the existing domestic production and investment-based model. It was yielding diminishing returns and low growth. Lack of pathbreaking innovations further intensified the diminishing returns challenge. After assuming office in 1969, Nixon followed conventional Republican macroeconomic policies of monetary and fiscal tightening to address long term structural challenges and control the budget deficit. It did not work as unemployment and inflation increased even further. In 1971, Nixon resorted to expansionary fiscal policy with the new Federal Reserve Chairman Arthur Burns simultaneously resorting to expansionary monetary policy. The economy grew and unemployment fell in the short term which helped Nixon win the 1972 election. However, in the long-term inflation plagued the economy and unemployment returned with the decline in investments and consumer spending. The 1973 oil price shock instituted by the Organisation of Arab Petroleum Producing Countries (a precursor to the modern Organisation of Petroleum Exporting Countries (OPEC)) against the supporters of Israel in the Yom Kippur War triggered another round of sharp economic contraction with high unemployment and high inflation. The American corporations suffered low profitability during this crisis and lobbied for structural solutions to the crisis.

The China opening offered an economic window of opportunity. With the death of Mao Zedong in 1974, the Chinese authorities were searching for an alternative model to stimulate the economy and improve living standards. They were eager to move away from the Soviet model of price controls and collectivisation. The search for profitability and higher investment returns by the American large corporations and the Chinese quest for industrialisation set the stage for a symbiotic relationship. With the passing of Mao, the ideological hurdles were relatively easy to overcome for the new generation of Chinese leaders. The Chinese authorities embarked on an ambitious economic reform programme.

The first wave of reforms involved de-collectivisation of agriculture, which increased food production reducing grain wages. This released surplus labour trapped into the unproductive agricultural sector. This was then duly followed by price deregulation, privatisation, and lowering of trade protection. More importantly, special economic zones were set up along the coastline to encourage foreign direct investments in order for foreign investors to benefit from the opening of China. The favourable political climate ushered in by the Sino-American détente meant that the American large corporations flocked in to invest in the special economic zones.

American corporations benefitted from offshoring their production activities to the Chinese special economic zones. Chinese cheap labour sharply reduced production costs and increased returns on investments for their shareholders. It reduced the price of gadgets and widgets for American consumers and thereby addressing inflation. As American corporations shed manufacturing jobs a new consumption-oriented economy emerged where retail and other associated services started playing an increasing role in the labour market. Former manufacturing workers switched to new albeit low payed retail and other service sector jobs. Consumer spending did not decline as a variety of cheaper consumer products emerged in the market. Profitable large corporations and a healthy equity market allowed American financial corporations to expand consumer credit. Fed switched to a loose monetary policy regime. The average household did not feel any consumption shortfall due to lower income as cheaper and widely available consumer credit more than compensated for the loss of income. Average household consumption remained steady even though inequality increased (Saez and Zucman 2019). The American economy underwent a structural change from manufacturing to services (Ford 2015). This new model delivered growth and higher tax revenue for the American Government. The American Government in return increased military spending to extend its hegemonic power all around the globe and counter the Soviet challenge. The American military industrial complex did not oppose this shift as they themselves also benefitted from this new supply chain. Furthermore, the military did not consider the military threat from China to be significant relative to the military threat that they were facing from the Soviet Union.

The Chinese state benefitted immensely from this symbiotic relationship. As American investments arrived, China industrialised rapidly. Even though China privatised and allowed private enterprise, it did not let go the crucial state monopolies. China effectively transformed from a socialist command and control economy to a state-led capitalist economy. With a bigger economy, the political power and influence of the Chinese state grew.

8.12 From Gold Standard to Oil standard

Under the Bretton Woods System, the participating nations were required to settle international trade accounts in dollars. In return, the United States had the obligation of making the dollar fully convertible to gold at a fixed exchange rate of 35 dollars per ounce. The participating nations also had the obligation of keeping the exchange rate within a 1% band. This system worked well during the post-war reconstruction period when all recovering economies in Europe and Japan required dollar in order to import capital goods and food from America. However, over time as the European and Japanese economies recovered, the external demand for dollars declined leading to accumulation of dollar reserves outside America. The dollar-based system offered America discretionary power over the creation of a fiat currency that controlled the value of other countries' reserves.

American industrial output progressively declined and trade deficit grew. Vietnam War further contributed to an already large public debt. Faster economic growth and growing trade surplus in West Germany and Japan increased claims on American gold reserves as these nations wanted to convert their dollar reserves for gold. By 1971, pressure was building up and the dollar fixed exchange rate to gold was becoming burdensome for the American economy. In August 1971, the Nixon administration unilaterally decided to suspend gold convertibility of the dollar. This effectively meant the demise of the Bretton Woods System. Dollar went into a free float.

Dollar was no longer backed by gold but it was now backed by oil. Following the oil shock of 1973, the Nixon administration went into an arrangement with the oil producing Arab economies. With falling domestic production, America agreed to import Middle Eastern oil while the Arab oil producers agreed to trade oil in dollars. This was an important anchor for the dollar in a post-Bretton Woods environment. The additional dollars that circulated outside America under the Bretton Woods System now found a new purpose in the global commodity trade. Over time, this new arrangement suited very well with the offshoring of manufacturing to China. The Sino-American trade was denominated in dollars. The Chinese producers and the state received dollars in return for producing manufactured goods as part of the American supply chain. China then used these dollars to import petroleum and other commodity inputs. A similar dollar-based trade triangle operated between America, the Middle East, and Korea-Japan. The new oil standard provided stability to the dollar, which helped ease inflationary pressures in the United States.

8.13 Soviet Invasion of Afghanistan

The Nixon administration pursued the policy of détente with both China and the Soviet Union. Reducing military tensions with the Soviet Union was a clear American strategic objective following setback in Vietnam. To this end, the Soviet Union and the United States concluded the Anti-Ballistic Missile (ABM) Treaty in 1973. Soviet Union in contrast were much more assertive with its military power.

On the economic front, Soviet Union was facing similar problems of weak economic growth and diminishing returns towards the end of Brezhnev's time in office. Therefore, expansion in Afghanistan offered a potential opportunity to turn the tide through boosting military production. Integrating Afghanistan into the

Soviet supply chain meant access to mineral resources. Controlling Afghanistan also had significant military strategic value as it is an important vantage point suitably located between China, Iran, and Pakistan.

In 1978, the Afghan Communist Party took power through a coup. However, instability followed and in December 1979, Leonid Brezhnev decided to directly intervene and deployed the Soviet Army. Soviet Army installed Barbak Karmal as the leader and a long insurgent war ensued. Soviet strategy was to stabilise the country by taking control of the cities and the roads. They failed in this objective as the more traditional rural communities opposed Soviet presence and resisted using guerrilla tactics. The insurgent groups collectively known as the Mujahedeen were supported by the United States, Pakistan, Saudi Arabia, and China. Afghanistan fell victim to another cold war era great power proxy war with more than two million lives lost over the course of the 9-year war. Soviet troops could not suppress the insurgency and withdrew in 1989. The civil war continued for another 3 years when the Mujahedeen achieved victory over the Soviet-backed government.

Bibliography

Cohen, S. (2011). *Soviet fates and lost alternatives: From Stalinism to the New Cold War*. New York: Columbia University Press.

Ford, M. (2015). *The rise of the Robots: Technology and the threat of a jobless future*. New York: Basic Books.

Kalecki, M. (1990). Political aspects of full employment. In M. Kalecki (Ed.), *Collected works of Michael Kalecki* (Vol. I). Oxford: Clarendon Press.

Kalecki, M. (1992). Central price determination. In M. Kalecki (Ed.), *Collected works of Michael Kalecki* (Vol. III). Oxford: Clarendon Press.

Kalecki, M. (1993). Introduction to the theory of growth in a socialist economy. In M. Kalecki (Ed.), *Collected works of Michael Kalecki* (Vol. III). Oxford: Clarendon Press.

Saez, E., & Zucman, G. (2019). *The Triumph of injustice: How the rich dodge taxes and how to make them pay*. New York: W.W. Norton.

Chapter 9
Dissolution of the USSR and Russian Decline in the 1990s

Abstract This chapter covers the episodes leading up to the dissolution of the USSR. In particular, it analyses the impact of political, economic, and social policies such as Perestroika and Glasnost. This is followed by analysis of events surrounding the unconstitutional dissolution of the USSR and the rise of Boris Yeltsin as the new leader. The chapter analyses foreign policy of the Yeltsin government in the 1990s along with domestic economic policies of privatization and liberalisation led by Yegor Gaidar and Anatoly Chubais. Special focus is given to the economic events leading up to the Russian Bond crisis and default in 1998.

9.1 Soviet Economic System and Structure

The Soviet economy industrialised in the 1930s. The industrialisation strategy was based on generating grain surplus to ensure a steady supply of grains to the growing industrial workforce (Allen 2003; Gerschenkron 1962). Collectivisation of farming reduced farming costs and offered scale economies. It also released surplus labour to be utilised in the urban industrial sector. Initially, collectivisation was implemented in the traditional 'black earth' (*Chernazom*) agricultural belt. However, it was gradually expanded to other areas. Collectivisation took the form of Kolkhoz (cooperatives) and Sovkhoz (state-owned farms).

Industrialisation focused on the development of heavy industries to service the Soviet military industrial complex (*Voennaya Promyeshnaya Komplex (VPK)*). Priority were given to the production of dual-use goods for both the military and the civilian sectors. For example, automobiles and aircrafts produced for the transportation sector were expected to be dual use. The constant threat of war and invasion from the western borders dictated the industrialisation priorities of the Soviet Union. Gerschenkron (1962) notes that the Soviet industrialisation strategy was dictated by its foreign and national security policies. During the post-war period, these priorities did not change as heightened military threats remained under the cold war paradigm.

S. Bhattacharyya, *A History of Global Capitalism*, Frontiers in Economic History,
https://doi.org/10.1007/978-3-030-58736-9_9

Soviet economy operated under autarky with the state having monopoly over exports and imports. It did trade with its socialist Eastern European allies through the Council of Mutual Economic Assistance (Comecon) arrangement. However, that trade was conducted using barter. The Comecon was created by the Soviet Union in 1949 for its socialist allies as an alternative to the American Marshall Plan. Even though the mode of production was capitalist, it was owned and controlled by the state on behalf of the society. The state appropriated any surplus and redistributed it among the citizens. The military industrial complex absorbed a significant proportion of the surplus (Clarke 2007). Resource allocation in the Soviet economy was based on central planning. The State Planning Commission or the *Gosplan* ran input–output planning operations every 5 years as a 5-year plan. The *Gosplan's* task was to anticipate effective demand based on need and purchasing power. Purchasing power in turn was a direct function of wages, which were also set by the *Gosplan*. Preferences did not play any major role in anticipating effective demand. On the supply side, the *Gosplan* set input costs including wages in order to reach the required level of output supply to meet demand. Any short-term demand–supply imbalance was managed through quantity adjustment and accumulation of inventory.

In summary, the fundamental idea behind socialist economic system was for people to work according to their abilities and earn according to their needs. This created inefficiencies in the allocation of resources which then stymied economic growth. Capital accumulation alone is not sufficient to grow the economy in the long run due to diminishing returns. Note that technological progress and productivity growth are the only two viable alternatives to achieve long-term growth. The production process in socialist economies nonetheless generates rent open for appropriation. Individuals with political power could then misuse their power and appropriate that rent. This in turn corrupts economic and political institutions. Competition for rent intensifies as diminishing returns set in and growth stagnates further eroding trust in institutions. Over time, we observe such trends in the post-war Soviet Union and other socialist economies.

9.2 Early Post-War Economic Expansion

The Soviet economy experienced rapid economic expansion during the early half of the post-war period. Living standards improved quite significantly over this period. Maddison (2004) estimates that the average growth rate in per capita GDP over the period 1950 to 1973 was 3.6 percent. During the post-war period, Khrushchev continued with the strategy of boosting agricultural productivity to facilitate industrialisation. To this end, he instituted colonisation of new lands for the purpose of agriculture. This less fertile land was supported by the use of fertilisers, irrigation canals, and drainage. Over time, surplus labours locked into the low productivity agriculture were absorbed by the industrial sector. Therefore, in the 1960s and beyond agriculture faced labour shortages and became more capital intensive

(Gaidar 2007). With increasing urbanisation and industrialisation, the demand for food was growing. Overall, the economy experienced productivity growth due to capital accumulation and structural change. Labour moved from low productivity agriculture to high productivity industry boosting overall productivity. Investments increased in both agriculture and industry. Therefore, capital accumulation driven growth was not limited to industry alone.

Production of producer goods received priority over the production of consumer goods (Grossman 1987). Producer goods serviced the military industrial complex. Moreover, Soviet planners believed that a strong base in producer goods is the necessary precondition for the development of consumer goods. Khrushchev in the 1960s emphasised the importance of increasing the share of consumer goods in industrial output. In spite of these efforts, the share of consumer goods in industrial production continued falling over the period 1950 to 1975 (Gaidar 2007).

9.3 Economic Slowdown and Structural Challenges Over the Period 1975 to 1985

The capital accumulation induced rapid growth ran its course over the period 1950 to 1975. During the late 1970s and beyond, growth became sluggish as diminishing returns to capital set in. Maddison (2004) estimates that the average growth rate in per capita GDP over the period 1974 to 1984 was 0.9 percent. The Soviet Union was facing several structural challenges. As population grew, so is the demand for food. Sluggish growth in agricultural output increasingly forced the Soviet Union to import grains from abroad (Gaidar 2007). Slowdown in industry also necessitated import of capital goods from the rival western economies, predominantly West Germany. Soviet trade deficit with the developed economies in terms of machinery and equipment grew significantly over the 1975 to 1985 period.

An autarkic economy is heavily reliant on investments to deliver growth needed a renewed growth strategy. There were no new and significant technological breakthroughs at that time to deliver scale economies. Efficiency gains could have been a potential pathway towards further growth. However, the command and control structure of the economy hindered the imposition of strict production discipline. Discipline was imposed using coercion during wartime and the early post-war years. This strategy became unviable over time as the demand for personal freedom increased among workers and citizens. Unlike a market-based system, there were no price signals in the Soviet economy to impose discipline. Inefficient use of inputs was a challenge and the Soviet Union hardly produced at the production frontier. Gaidar (2007) estimates that the Soviet Union used 2.1 times more energy and 1.6 times more raw materials than the United States to produce the same output during this period. Moreover, depreciation of fixed capital also contributed to production inefficiency as the average age of machinery were significantly higher in the Soviet Union compared to other advanced economies (Popov 2010).

With economic slowdown and détente with the United States, Soviet trade with the advanced OECD countries grew sharply. Unlike barter trade with Comecon, the trade with OECD was mainly denominated in dollars. Such trade triggered specialisation and altered the internal economic structures even further. Capital goods, consumer durables, and food imports from the Soviet Union's geopolitical adversaries increased while the Soviets increasingly specialised in the export of raw materials and energy. This made the Soviet economy exposed to adverse terms of trade shocks as the international price of energy and raw materials were far more volatile relative to high value-added manufactured goods.

In the short run, balance of payment challenges were manageable. Soviet Union received dollar liquidity in return for petroleum exports. It then used dollars to import grains, agricultural commodities, machinery, and consumer durables. However, over time due to perverse specialisation the trade deficit widened multiplying balance of payment challenges. Following the Soviet invasion of Afghanistan in 1979, the Saudi–American alliance engineered a negative oil price shock by increasing supply. The oil price declined sharply which triggered a balance of payments crisis. The Soviet Union did not have enough dollars to finance its food imports.

9.4 *Perestroika*, *Glasnost*, and Soviet Decline Over the Period 1985 to 1991

The power balance shifted within the Soviet political elite. A constituency demanding liberal economic and political reforms gained traction within the population. Mikhail Gorbachev assumed power and embarked on political and economic reform programmes namely *Perestroika* and *Glasnost*. The aim of *Perestroika* was to liberalise the economy and the aim of *Glasnost* was to liberalise the political system by encouraging freedom of expression and the right to protest. These reforms had sharp contractionary effects on the economy. Maddison (2004) estimates that the average growth rate in per capita GDP over the period 1985 to 1991 was −1.3 percent triggering a sharp decline in living standards. In what follows, I discuss some of the specific policies instituted under this reform package and their effects.

Glasnost was an attempt to introduce civil liberties and media freedom into the Soviet political system. Here I will discuss the economic consequences of *Glasnost*. It also had a broader political economy and foreign policy effects, which I will discuss later. The political culture in the Soviet Union and its predecessor the Russian Empire could be described as deferential. In contrast, *Glasnost* encouraged adversarial political culture. Sudden introduction of adversarial institutions had a profound destabilising impact on economic and social order within the Soviet society. For example, industrial relations in the Soviet Union was based on the local factory managers receiving orders through the chain of command all the way up to the Gosplan and the Central Committee of the Communist Party. Their task was to follow these orders and meet targets at the factory level by controlling the workers. Workers were supposed to follow orders that they received from their managers. Note that there were no price signals in the system. Only the chain of command ensured quantity produced. Therefore, the system relied heavily on the discipline of all members of this ecosystem from the Central Committee to the workers. This discipline was enforced by the threat of coercion but coercion was increasingly difficult to carry out during peacetime and under de-Stalinisation. Introduction of the new adversarial system under *Glasnost* meant that the workers were allowed to protest, demand higher wages, and better treatment from their managers. This led to the breakdown of factory discipline that was a prerequisite for the smooth functioning of the Soviet economic system. Industrial actions became commonplace reducing output. Under the new rules, the factory managers struggled to find an appropriate response, as they did not have the ability to hire and fire workers.

Perestroika introduced market-based reforms. It decentralised the economic command structure granting more independence to the local factory managers. Almost simultaneously, it also deregulated prices. In December 1987, the state reduced its procurement of all products (capital and consumer goods) from 100 percent to 50 percent effectively deregulating prices. The economic chain of command broke down and the shadow economy thrived. Local factory managers were no longer concerned about the target set by the *Gosplan*. They concentrated their efforts into maximising and appropriating rent by selling their surplus products into the black market. Flexible state procurement targets made it open to the interpretation of the local factory managers. This further exacerbated the problem of shadow economy. Markets became segmented as the same good sold for three different prices namely a state price, a free-market price, and a black market price. Over time, industrial output declined, scarcity increased, and the shadow economy thrived. Average workers also witnessed the benefit of colluding with their corrupt managers to cater for the shadow economy and receive a share of the rent. Corruption and lawlessness increased sharply and the social order broke down.

9.5 Gorbachev's Political Motivations Behind Reforms and His Foreign Policy Posture

Gorbachev's rise to power was largely due to the economic stagnation over the period 1975 to 1985. Following the demise of Brezhnev, power struggle within the Soviet elite intensified. Personal ambitions and factional politics dictated who would be elected as the General Secretary of the Communist Party of the Soviet Union. Seniority within the ranks also played a role but infighting was rife. As the economy stagnated, distributional conflict within the society sharpened intensifying internal power struggle. Yuri Andropov, Konstantin Chernenko, and others followed Brezhnev in their brief stints as the Soviet leader. None of them was in good health as they were all veterans within the party ranks.

Gorbachev was among the new generation of Soviet leaders who were expected to deliver economic growth and maintain peaceful coexistence with the West. However, he was not a favourite of the powerful Soviet Military Industrial Complex (VPK). In internal factional politics, Gorbachev represented the party bureaucrats (or *Apparatchiks*). In order to secure his position within the party, Gorbachev conveniently used deregulation of the economy and unilateral foreign policy concessions to the West as a battering ram to weaken the influence of the Military Industrial Complex. This made him deeply unpopular within the Soviet elite but the Soviet political structure endowed him and his Politburo with disproportionate political power. Therefore, he was largely immune to challenges.

In 1989, Gorbachev unilaterally withdrew from Afghanistan. This move was popular among the citizens and the regular soldiers but it was deeply unpopular among the Soviet military hierarchy and the VPK. Gorbachev also pursued détente with the Reagan Administration and offered unilateral arms reduction. Soviet economic malaise and confusion also spread over to its socialist allies in Eastern Europe. Protest movements broke out in Poland, East Germany, and elsewhere. The lack of moral leadership from the Soviet Union made the leadership in these allied countries disaffected and confused. The Berlin Wall collapsed in 1989 as the East German citizens demanded German unification. Following the collapse of the Berlin Wall, the entire Eastern Bloc was engulfed in a series of protest movements, which brought down the socialist governments in these countries. Soviet Union under Gorbachev did not intervene as political transition took place in Eastern Europe. In 1991, Gorbachev signed the Strategic Arms Reduction Treaty (START 1) with the George HW Bush Administration. He also agreed to the unification of Germany and its incorporation into NATO under the verbal promise from the then US Secretary of State James Baker that NATO will not move eastwards beyond the borders of an unified Germany.[1] Gorbachev also dissolved the Warsaw Pact and unilaterally withdrew all Soviet troops from Eastern Europe.

Understandably, all these moves made Gorbachev popular among the Western elites as they witnessed rapid weakening of their main geopolitical rival, the Soviet Union. However, with a failing economy and lawlessness he was deeply unpopular at home. The unilateral concessions also made him deeply unpopular among the Soviet elite and the military. The events that followed in Moscow was perhaps a testament to the challenges that he was facing at home.

[1]In February, Secretary of State James Baker offered the Soviet Foreign Minister Eduard Shevardnadze, 'iron-clad guarantees that NATO's jurisdiction or forces would not move eastward'. On the same day in Moscow, he famously told Gorbachev that the alliance would not move 'one inch to the east'. He argued that in a post-Cold War Europe NATO would be 'less of a military organization, much more of a political one, would have no need for independent capability'. See Savranskaya and Blanton (2017) for details on the archival records of these conversations.

9.6 The August 1991 Coup, Belovezha Accords and the Dissolution of the USSR

Collapse of the Eastern Bloc, lack of leadership in Moscow, and severe economic crisis ignited nationalist sentiments within the Soviet Union. Events in Eastern Europe discredited socialist ideology which now started infecting the Soviet Union. Socialism was the ideological glue that held the diverse country together. With that ideology under existential challenge, many in the constituent republics favoured strong national identity as the basis for nation building in a post-soviet era. National identity-based politics started gaining traction in all the constituent republics as the Soviet system failed to address the basic economic needs of citizens. By 1990, strong secessionist movements erupted in the Baltics and the Caucuses. Republics of Estonia, Lithuania, Latvia, Armenia, Georgia, and Azerbaijan declared quasi-independence from Moscow.

In this backdrop, Gorbachev proposed the New Union Treaty to preserve the union but under a much reformed format. The New Union Treaty envisaged a loose union with significant powers devolved to the constituent republics. A referendum was held on 17 March 1991 to decide on the future of the Soviet Union. The following question was on the ballot.

> Do you consider necessary the preservation of the USSR as a renewed federation of equal sovereign republics in which the rights and freedom of an individual of any ethnicity will be fully guaranteed?

This was the first and only referendum that took place in the USSR. Approximately 80 percent of the registered voters voted in the referendum with approximately 78 percent voting in favour of preserving the union.

The process of dismantling the USSR was already set in motion. Even under Gorbachev's New Union Treaty, the USSR would have ceased to exist. The proposal intensified power struggle within the politburo. A group of eight politburo members under the leadership of Gennady Yanayev organised a coup in August 1991 to take over power from Gorbachev while he was on holiday in Crimea. This group declared a national emergency and rolled out the army in Moscow and elsewhere. They called themselves the State Committee on the State of Emergency (GKChP). Yanayev was the nominal head of this group while the real mastermind was Vladimir Kryuchkov, the Head of Soviet Secret Service (KGB).

A group of officers from the Soviet Secret Police (KGB) arrived at Gorbachev's residence in Crimea with a declaration to relinquish power to the GKChP. They asked Gorbachev to sign this declaration and relinquish power citing health reasons. Gorbachev refused to sign this document. The GKChP did not have any constitutional authority to take over power. They hesitated and their coup attempt failed spectacularly. Gorbachev returned to Moscow but his administration was already discredited. He claimed to have the situation under control but he was a fallen leader with no authority. Chaos reigned on the streets of Moscow and other capitals of the constituent republics. Crowds opposed to the illegitimate coup government started gathering on the streets.

Ironically, the main beneficiary from this chaos was Boris Yeltsin who was the leader of the Russian Soviet Socialist Republic (RSSR). The coup plotters wanted to restore the USSR while Yeltsin wanted to dismantle it. Yeltsin positioned himself as the leader of the masses by mobilising street protests in Moscow. He delivered his speeches atop Soviet Army tanks. On 8 December 1991, Yeltsin conspired with Leonid Kravchuk, Stanislav Sushkevich, and others at the Belovezha forest's dacha in Belarus and declared the dissolution of the USSR. Leonid Kravchuk was the Ukrainian President while Stanislav Sushkevich was the Chairman of the Belarusian Parliament. This unconstitutional declaration is known as the Belovezha Accords. Gorbachev did not exercise his constitutional authority to stamp out this unconstitutional power grab. He later revealed that any intervention on his part would have triggered a civil war that he wanted to avoid. On 25 December 1991, Gorbachev resigned as the first and last President of the USSR. The mighty Soviet Union ceased to exist.

The United States and other Western powers did not oppose the Belovezha Accords and the unconstitutional seizure of power that followed. They were quick to diplomatically recognise all the constituent republics and Boris Yeltsin's government in Russia. The demise of their key geopolitical rival was favourable. Boris Yeltsin's pro-Western foreign policy position was convenient. As I discuss in the next section, Yeltsin's agenda of weakening Russia's military power also worked in favour of the Western hegemonic interests.

9.7 Russia Under Boris Yeltsin in the 1990s

In spite of the disorderly start in 1991, Russia embarked on a journey towards a market economy and democratic representative government. Boris Yeltsin assumed power following an election as the first President of the Russian Federation. Being the largest constituent republic of the USSR, the Russian Federation became its successor state. As the successor state, Russian Federation inherited all the debt obligations of the USSR allowing all the other post-soviet republics to walk away debt free. It remained a permanent member of the United Nations Security Council.

It also inherited all the nuclear weapons of the USSR. Soviet nuclear weapons were also stockpiled in now independent republics of Belarus, Kazakhstan, and Ukraine. These republics did not have operational control over these weapons but they had physical control. Operational control was with Russia under the Russian electronic command and control system. In December 1994 at the Organisation of Security and Cooperation in Europe (OSCE) conference in Budapest, Russian Federation, the United States, and the United Kingdom entered into three identical agreements with Belarus, Kazakhstan, and Ukraine to surrender physical control of their nuclear weapons to Russia in return for security guarantees. These agreements are known as the Budapest Memorandum, which offered security assurances to the three newly independent countries against military threats that could undermine their territorial integrity. The Memorandum also led to the accession of these three republics to the Nuclear Non-proliferation Treaty. From 1994 to 1996, all the stockpiles in Ukraine and elsewhere were physically removed back to Russia.

Arrangements over conventional forces were somewhat different. The Soviet Army and its stockpile of conventional weapon systems were largely distributed among the newly independent republics based on their location. For example, troops and hardware including aircrafts located in Ukraine remained in Ukraine. The situation with the navy was somewhat different. Majority of the Soviet ports and naval assets were located either in Russia or Ukraine. Sevastopol in Crimea was a major warm water port for the Soviet Navy. Crimea was now part of the Ukraine. Russian Federation signed a 25-year lease agreement with the Ukraine to keep the naval base in Sevastopol and all its assets. The other smaller ports of Odessa and Nikolayev stayed with Ukraine. Odessa and Nikolayev hosted the largest Soviet dry docks and shipyards capable of producing aircraft careers. The loss of these two facilities meant that Russia lost control over two Soviet strategic assets. To maintain access to these facilities, Russia entered into a Defence Cooperation Agreement with the Ukraine.

Because of the Soviet disintegration, the Russian Federation, its successor state was far weaker militarily. The Russian Federation lost more than one-third of its army personnel. It also lost approximately 40 percent of its military hardware. The Russian Federation was also a fragile state given the disorderly and unconstitutional nature of its creation. Approximately 25 million Soviet citizens of Russian origin found themselves outside the boundaries of the Russian Federation due to the break up. They faced intense economic hardship and loss of livelihood. Nationalist sentiments were high in all the post-soviet republics at that time. Therefore, many of them faced discrimination under the new authorities.

The Yeltsin administration embarked on economic reforms to transition Russia from a socialist to a market-based economy. He appointed Yegor Gaidar as his Minister of Finance and later as the Prime Minister. He also appointed Anatoly Chubais as the Deputy Prime Minister. Chubais and Gaidar took charge of economic reforms. They appointed an advisory group of foreign experts to advise them during the transition process. The group composed of distinguished economists Jeffrey Sachs, David Lipton, Andrei Shleifer, Anders Aslund, and others. The policy stance taken by the Ministers and their group of advisors is commonly known as 'shock therapy'.[2]

The primary task set by the 'shock therapists' was to privatise a vast array of Soviet industries, which were controlled by the state monopolies. The government distributed 10,000 roubles worth of vouchers to every Russian family. These were meant to be shares or claims of every household on the state-owned corporations. It

[2]Klein (2007) reviews application of the 'shock doctrine' in countries around the world including in Latin America.

was based on the then valuation of the entire state-owned monopolies. However, the valuation methodology used remains unclear.

All the while, the real economy was experiencing severe contraction. World Bank (2002) documents that the Russian economy experienced seven consecutive years of sharp economic contraction following the political transition in 1991. The contractionary shocks were from both the supply and the demand sides. Due to the breakdown of both input and output supply chains, industrial and agricultural production was falling rapidly. There were severe shortages of food and other essential commodities. Wages for workers remained unpaid for months. In many instances, workers' wages were paid in kind by the factory managers. For example, workers in a shoe factory would receive wages in shoes. Workers would also collect gadgets and equipment of value from the factory floor with the hope that they can exchange it for food or other essential commodities elsewhere. Workers in other sectors of the economy received no wages at all. Barter economy took hold. Shadow economy and lawlessness became commonplace. Lawlessness was further exacerbated by the non-payment of wages to frontline public sector workers in policing and law enforcement.

Non-payment of wages meant that the government was unable to collect taxes. Tax revenue collapsed while the government's external debt obligations cumulatively increased with borrowing from the International Monetary Fund (IMF) and other international organisations. Unsustainable fiscal deficit and large sovereign debt relative to GDP led to the collapse of the rouble, which triggered hyperinflation. Hyperinflation further eroded capital reserves of the firms. Workers on the factory floor grabbed whatever they could lay their hands on including machinery and scraps. Factories liquidated at a rapid pace with approximately 70,000 factories closing down over the 1991 to 1997 period (World Bank 2002). Removal of energy subsidies increased input costs for enterprises further squeezing them.

Facing hyperinflation, the economy team under Gaidar and Chubais sharply tightened money supply. This increased inflation even further as the source of hyperinflation was not overheating from the demand side but a collapse in output supply and tax revenue. Russian economy suffocated due to the lack of liquidity. This pushed more and more transactions into barter and the shadow economy magnifying the original problems with output supply and tax revenue.

Desperate citizens exchanged their vouchers for essentials such as a loaf of bread. Intermediaries lapped up these vouchers quickly for almost next to nothing. The state monopolies were up for auctions in due course. Severely battered by hyperinflation and capital erosion, they were heavily undervalued. The vouchers could now be used to bid for these state-owned enterprises. A handful of individuals with access to dollar and foreign currency denominated financing purchased a large number of vouchers. They used these vouchers to capture the undervalued state-owned monopolies. The government and the citizens made a net loss from the auctions while a handful of individuals benefited immensely from the botched privatisation. An oligarchy was born. Boris Berezovsky, Mikhail Khodorkovsky, Mikhail Friedman, Petr Aven, Vladimir Gusinsky, Vladimir Potanin, and Alexander Smolensky were some of the notable beneficiaries of this process.

Russia went into IMF programme and received its first tranche of 719 SDR (1 billion USD) in 1992 (Odling-Smee 2006). The conditionality of the programme included banking reforms (bankruptcy legislation, contract enforcement, bank supervision, creditor rights strengthening etc.); trade liberalisation; removal of energy subsidy; restructuring of natural monopolies in energy, telecom, and railways; privatization and introduction of user charge in education; partial privatisation of healthcare; and pension reform among others. The reforms were contractionary in the short run and therefore faced immense political opposition.

The beneficiaries (commonly known as oligarchs) of the botched privatisation process gained immense power and influence within the political system under Boris Yeltsin using their newfound wealth. With a weak President and a shaky government in power, the oligarchs reigned supreme. Political corruption ran amuck. In spite of single-digit approval ratings leading up to the 1996 presidential election, Yeltsin was re-elected amidst allegations of vote buying and fraud. His administration remained deeply unpopular.

Privatisation did not lead to investment growth. World Bank (2002) notes that Russia experienced modest or no growth in new enterprises following privatisation. The share of employment in new enterprises stayed at 20 percent while the share of value added stayed between 20 and 30 percent. The same applies to foreign direct investments (FDI) as Russia's FDI inflow was 0.3 percent of GDP over 1992–1995 and 0.7 percent of GDP over 1996–1999. Most of that investment occurred in the petroleum sector and did not spur growth in SMEs. The new owners of former state enterprises rapidly liquidated potentially income generating assets, converted them to foreign currency and deposited them in offshore bank accounts. Some of that deposit supported luxury spending abroad without any meaningful benefit to the Russian economy. As the existing Russian enterprises were stripped of potentially income generating assets, capital outflow remained a pervasive problem throughout the decade.

All the macroeconomic indicators during the 1990s were dismal. After seven consecutive years of economic contraction, the cumulative decline in Russia's GDP was more than 40 percent (World Bank 2002). This was far longer and deeper than the economic contraction experienced by the United States and the United Kingdom during the Great Depression. Cumulative GDP decline in the United States during the Great Depression was 27 percent with 4 consecutive years of contraction while for the United Kingdom the same was 6 percent and 2 consecutive years, respectively. Income inequality measured by Gini coefficient doubled during the early Yeltsin years. World Bank (2002) estimates that Gini over the period 1987—1990 was 0.26. It increased to 0.48 in 1993—1994. Poverty increased sharply with 1 in 20 individuals living in absolute poverty with income below 1 USD a day in 1993. In contrast, the same in 1988 was 1 in 60 individuals. The macroeconomic performance culminated to a sovereign default in 1998 which triggered another episode of hyperinflation.

The economic chaos was accompanied by underfunding of healthcare. Healthcare workers did not receive salaries for months. Health crisis ensued and epidemics of tuberculosis and HIV spread all across the country. Mortality rate increased sharply and male life expectancy declined to 57 years from the Soviet-era 65 years a decade earlier. Stuckler et al. (2009) estimate that the radical economic reform programmes of 'shock therapy' increased the average adult male mortality rate by 12.8 percent in a sample of post-communist economies. The effect for Russia is likely to be larger as it experienced a much sharper economic contraction compared to Poland or the Baltic Republics. Similarly, Rosefielde (2001) attributes 3.4 million Russian premature deaths over the period 1990 to 1998 to the 'shock therapy' economic reforms.

Yeltsin government systematically underfunded the military making the Russian military weak and vulnerable. The ruling faction under his leadership was extremely pro-Western in their foreign policy orientation. They were a strong believer in unilateral disarmament. This undoubtedly suited the Western hegemonic interests. However, these moves faced stiff opposition from within and led to immense power struggle throughout the decade. The power struggle was broadly between the ruling pro-Western factions and the opposition national security faction. Note that the national security faction in modern Russia is the successor of the once mighty VPK in the USSR. In 1999, the national security faction prevailed as Yeltsin appointed the head of Federal Security Service (FSB) Vladimir Putin as the Prime Minister. In early 2000, Boris Yeltsin departed from office citing ill health. He handed over power to the new President Vladimir Putin. I will return to this in more detail in Chap. 11.

Bibliography

Allen, R. (2003). *Farm to factory. A reinterpretation of the Soviet industrial revolution*. Princeton: Princeton University Press.

Clarke, S. (2007). *The development of capitalism in Russia*. London: Routledge.

Gaidar, Y. (2007). *Collapse of an Empire. Lessons for modern Russia*. Washington, DC: Brookings Institution Press.

Gerschenkron, A. (1962). *Economic backwardness in historical perspective, a book of essays*. Cambridge, MA: Harvard University Press.

Grossman, G. (1987). Command economy. In J. Eatwell, M. Milgate, & P. Newman (Eds.), *The New Palgrave dictionary of economics* (Vol. I, pp. 494–495). London: Macmillan.

Klein, N. (2007). *The shock doctrine: The rise of disaster capitalism*. Toronto: Knopf.

Maddison, A. (2004). *The world economy: Historical statistics*. Paris: OECD.

Odling-Smee, J. (2006). The IMF and Russia in the 1990s. *IMF Staff Papers, 53*(1), 151–194.

Popov, V. (2010). *Life cycle of the centrally planned economy: Why Soviet growth rates peaked in the 1950's*. CEFIR/NES working paper series. Working paper no 152.

Rosefielde, S. (2001). Premature deaths: Russia's radical economic transition in Soviet perspective. *Europe-Asia Studies, 53*(8), 1159–1176.

Savranskaya, S., & Blanton, T. (2017). *NATO expansion: What Gorbachev heard*. Briefing Book Number 613, National Security Archive, George Washington University, 12 December 2017. Accessed July 18, 2020, from https://nsarchive.gwu.edu/briefing-book/russia-programs/2017-12-12/nato-expansion-what-gorbachev-heard-western-leaders-early

Stuckler, D., King, L., & McKee, M. (2009). Mass privatisation and the post-communist mortality crisis: A cross-national analysis. *Lancet, 373*, 399–407.

World Bank. (2002). *Transition the first ten years: Analysis and lessons for Eastern Europe and the Former Soviet Union*. Washington, DC: The World Bank.

Chapter 10
End of History and Exceptionalism: International System After 1991

Abstract This chapter focuses on the events after 1991. The withdrawal of the USSR from Eastern Europe created enormous expansion opportunities for the American and Western hegemonic interests. This period oversaw economic and territorial expansions of the European Union. The financial, trade, and military architecture of this expansion is discussed in detail. The role of the dollar as the currency that underpins this system is explored. The role of monetary policy is discussed in conjunction with trade and security policies. I show how these policies ran their course over the next three decades as diminishing returns set in. Excessive reliance on credit creation and service sector growth brought volatility and financial crisis of 2000, 2008, and beyond. The issue of offshoring jobs to China and the Asia Pacific and their subsequent impact on the American labour market and income is discussed. The cold war origins of this policy is revisited along with internal political economy factors. The chapter covers the long-term consequences of replacing income with credit in order to support consumption. In other words, it entertains the thesis how excessive reliance on the monetary policy credit channel leads to asset price bubbles. On the national security side, special attention is given to conflicts in the Middle East (Iraq, Libya, Syria, Afghanistan), and Yugoslavia. Attention is given to tensions in the South China Sea and the Korean Peninsula. Ever expanding military and security budget, growing national debt, and the stability of the national currency is analysed.

"We're an empire now, and when we act, we create our own reality. And while you're studying that reality—judiciously, as you will—we'll act again, creating other new realities, which you can study too, and that's how things will sort out. We're history's actors … and you, all of you, will be left to just study what we do." Karl Rove, Senior Advisor and White House Deputy Chief of Staff, President George W. Bush Administration.

10.1 End of History and Expansion in Eastern Europe

The dissolution of the USSR was perceived as the end of great power geopolitical competition and the start of United States led unipolar hegemony. United States as the sole superpower on the planet was perfectly placed to be the hyperpower

S. Bhattacharyya, *A History of Global Capitalism*, Frontiers in Economic History,
https://doi.org/10.1007/978-3-030-58736-9_10

hegemon. The expectation was that the sole superpower would end the historical role of great power spheres of influence in maintaining international order. Therefore, there would be no need for a Vienna Congress or a Yalta in the future.

In the 1990s, this indeed appeared to be the case. However, the euphoria was short lived as great power geopolitics slowly caught up with the international system. The retreat of the USSR and subsequent disintegration created much needed space for the Western alliance in Eastern Europe. The cold war arms race was economically debilitating for both sides as it degenerated into a war of attrition. The American economy coming out of the cold war during the Reagan Presidency was in recession.

The new Eastern European elites were willing actors eager to integrate into the American led Atlantic economic and security system that was initiated after the Second World War through the Marshall Plan. They also had strong support from the majority of citizens. The iron curtain descended and a new wave of euphoria swept across the European continent. The prospect of migrating to the high wage economies of Western Europe was a real sweetener for the young working age population in Eastern Europe.

The economic transition process in Poland and the Czech Republic was swift and successful (World Bank 2002). This offered a strong foundation for integration into the Atlantic system. Recessions were relatively shallow and short lived in Central and Southern Europe and the Baltics. GDP contraction was not as sharp as the Russian Federation. By 1993, most of Central and Southern European economies returned to growth. The growth of the private sector and exports were also impressive. For example, in the Czech Republic the private sector's share of GDP was 65 percent by 1994 and it increased to 80 percent by 1999 (World Bank 2002). Real export growth in Poland over the period 1993–1998 was approximately 13 percent. These economies also kept inequality under control avoiding major social disharmony during the transition process. For example, income inequality measured by the Gini coefficient stayed at 0.28 in Poland before and after the transition only to increase to 0.33 over the period 1996–1998.

By the mid-1990s, all the former socialist countries of Southcentral Europe concluded free trade agreements with the European Union and by 1999, most of them have concluded their pre-accession agreements. These countries received major financial assistance packages to transform their markets. Their markets and supply chain were closely linked with the USSR and other Comecon member countries. As that network broke down following political transition in 1989–1991, they were ably assisted with financial packages from the EU and the European Bank of Reconstruction and Development (EBRD) to reorient their economic supply chain.

The economic and security architecture of the newly evolving 'Extended Atlantic System' was as follows. The new markets in Eastern Europe integrated with the Western European countries within the EU single market. The three key pillars of the EU single market were Germany, Britain, and France. All three of them were net contributors to the EU budget. Germany and France specialised in industry and agriculture. Germany's relative strength was more in industry while France specialised more in agriculture and food systems. The Southern European economies of Spain and Italy were also major food surplus countries within the common market. Britain in general and the City of London in particular specialised in financial services and especially in the US dollar-based transactions within the common market.

The opening of new markets in Eastern Europe offered scale economies to all three sectors. The EBRD is located in the City of London. It could make dollar-based investments in the form of loans in the private and public sectors in transitional economies. These investments offered good returns to its public sector shareholders. The EBRD shareholders are its member countries with a majority share with the United States. The EBRD lending activity was coordinated with the EU to select projects of common interest and maximise returns by exploiting scale economies. The transitional economies in Central Europe and the Baltics required transforming their industrial supply chain, food system, governance, public services, and transport among others. Therefore, the investment projects were not limited to one sector or the other. The field was wide open with a diversified portfolio to exploit scale economies and derive capital accumulation driven growth. Note that these economies were substituting their old capital stock with new Western sourced capital stock. Given the low initial levels of these types of capital, the returns were relatively high with no immediate challenge of diminishing returns. EBRD securitised some of these loans. These financial assets were also bought and sold in the wider capital markets thereby benefitting London, New York, and Frankfurt.

Western European food systems and retail chains received access to new markets in Eastern Europe. Again, this offered scale economies. It increased their profit margin as they could expand and increase their revenue. In addition, they could source cheaper raw materials for finished products from new locations.

Transforming the energy systems in Eastern Europe was complicated and expensive. The energy system was largely Soviet build and expensive to replace. Furthermore, there was no cheaper alternative source of energy in Western Europe, which could satisfy demand in the East. Oil and gas from the North Sea were finite and none of the major energy producers (Britain, the Netherlands, and Norway) were large surplus countries by the 1990s. Germany and Belgium had a functioning coal industry but its output was largely consumed internally. Polish coal was also not enough to transform the entire energy systems of Central Europe and the Baltics. Environmentalism in the 1990s meant that there was little appetite for new a coal-based energy system. Therefore, Russian energy was the only alternative. The energy system in these countries remained largely unchanged. I will return to this again in Chap. 11.

The surplus generated by the common market and especially by Britain, France, and Germany from expansion in agriculture, industry, and financial services helped finance further transfers into Eastern Europe from the EU budget. It also helped German integration by generating additional revenue for the unified German government.

The Baltic and Central European countries were gradually integrated into the 'Expanded Atlantic System' of trade and commerce. The real economy was integrated into the EU, a key component of the Atlantic System. The financial economy was integrated into the US dollar-based system. In 2004, all the Baltic and Central European countries acceded to the EU.

Following accession, a large number of young people of working age from these countries migrated to the high-wage economies of Western Europe making use of 'free movement' enshrined in EU Treaties. Britain alone received approximately 3 million citizens of Poland and the Baltics. The host countries benefited from this flow as it addressed labour shortages. It also offered a steady supply of cheap semi-skilled labour to businesses in the host countries. For the origin countries, outmigration released pressure on a tight labour market. Households in these countries benefited from the remittance flows.

Integrating these new EU countries into the Atlantic security system was challenging. The EU by design did not have its independent security architecture.[1] For national security, it was entirely dependent on NATO and by extension the United States. Given the verbal promise of James Baker and others to Mikhail Gorbachev regarding NATO expansion, the Western alliance needed to perform a delicate diplomatic manoeuvre not to look overtly hostile to Russia. Nevertheless, the Western Alliance perceived Russia to be too weak to respond back in the event of a NATO expansion eastwards. Czech Republic, Hungary, and Poland joined NATO in 1999 while the rest of the other Eastern European nations followed in 2004.

This offered immense expansion opportunities to the American and Western producers of armaments and weapon systems. Integrating into NATO implied that member countries exclusively use NATO (predominantly American) produced weapon systems. The American military industrial complex benefitted immensely from this expansion as it offered them scale economies. It also benefitted the financial sector as it could offer credit to potential buyers in the new member countries to acquire these systems. The American weapon producers are large corporations and have significant market power (close to monopoly power) over the type of systems that they produce. These are also publicly traded companies. Expansion opportunities in Eastern Europe offered a bonanza for the equity markets in New York and London.

10.2 Monetary Policy, Financial Crises, and the Dollar

With seemingly unlimited market in US dollar-based transactions in energy, raw materials, weapons, financial assets, and consumer durables, the conventional constraints on credit creation seemed to have been relaxed. A currency such as the US dollar so widely used no longer needed to be anchored in traditional stores of value such as precious metals or hard currency reserves. Trust in the currency from a large population of users were sufficient to support its value. The risk of inflation from

[1]See Chap. 8, for a discussion on European Coal and Steel Community and the European Union security architecture.

expanding the money base through credit creation was minimised. Financial innovations and the advent of Internet reduced money demand and the rate of circulation of money. Electronic money in the form of keyboard lending reduced the velocity of money as fewer and fewer individuals used cash transactions.

More and more countries including the United States opted for Central Bank independence. Central Banks could monitor credit creation and monetary policy independent of the political cycles. Credit creation could also smooth consumption, investments, and government expenditure over a long period. This led to a reduction in GDP volatility during the 1990s and the late 2000s. Business cycles appeared to be a thing of the past in an era of 'Great Moderation'. US Federal Reserve Funds rate progressively declined in the 1990s to around 5 percent from a 1980s average of 10 percent.

The political economy context behind a soft monetary policy was perhaps the US-China rapprochement concluded a decade earlier.[2] America was undergoing rapid structural transformation due to the new trade arrangements with China. Declining transport costs and growth in air travel made it increasingly cost effective for US-based corporations to ship relatively less skill-intensive tasks to China. As China industrialised, Chinese workers acquired more skills through 'learning by doing'. Progressively more and more skilled jobs also went to China. American corporations found it more profitable to ship their production operations to China and benefit from the relatively low labour cost and agglomeration economies. Offshoring and trade in parts and components flourished. It proliferated beyond China and to other economies of Southeast Asia such as Vietnam and to a lesser extent Thailand.

All the while, American corporations were able to offer healthy returns to their shareholders. US dollar-based equity and bond markets were flourishing. Investment banks in Wall Street made excellent returns by selling stocks and bonds to facilitate this trade. Industries related to national defence also followed the same path of offshoring.

The American economy and the labour market underwent profound changes as a result of this trade. Manufacturing sector workers lost their manufacturing jobs. However, these workers were absorbed into the service sector either as self-employed or as employee of large service sector corporations. This structural realignment in the labour market and the economy led to a decline in real income but it did not affect consumption. Ford (2015) documents the decline in real income and the increasing gap between productivity and real wages in post-war America. Household consumption remained stable due to the soft money policy pursued by the Fed. Consumer credit was easily available with financial innovations and the advent of credit card technology. Mortgage markets flourished because of low Fed Funds rate. Therefore, housing was not a problem for the average household in spite of the drop in real income. On the demand side, the economy underwent structural

[2]See discussion in Chap. 8.

change. It became heavily reliant on consumption spending and government expenditure as opposed to investments.

The soft money policy addressed the immediate challenge of consumer spending and government expenditure stability but it did not address the long-term structural challenges. The gap between productivity and real wages continued to widen (Ford 2015).

At the global level, the export-oriented economies of China, Japan, and Germany took Fed's lead and engaged in competitive devaluation by progressively cutting interest rates. The raw material exporters in the Middle East and Latin America also followed suit. This gave rise to global imbalance. Goods and raw materials flowed from the export-oriented economies to the United States. United States paid for these commodities in dollars and ran large trade deficits with the exporting countries. The exporting countries then used dollar liquidity to actively acquire US Treasury bonds. Bond prices soared while the bond rates collapsed making it cheaper for the US Government and corporations to borrow. US Government enjoyed significant fiscal space to run large budget deficits. In particular, it could afford large defence budgets that favoured the US defence industry and associated contractors.

Needless to say that this financial model was unsustainable. The low-interest rate environment that prevailed encouraged asset price bubbles. Even though the low-interest rates and credit expansion smoothed aggregate expenditure and reduced volatility in the short to medium run, it accumulated trouble in the long run. The relative calm in the short run meant sharp financial market corrections in the long run increasing systemic risks. The first such shock was in 1998 triggered by the collapse of the Hedge Fund Long Term Capital Management (LTCM). The Fed had to organise a private bailout involving other hedge funds to mitigate systemic risk. Fed's response was to cut the funds rate and increase leverage to stimulate the financial markets. The result was another tech company led asset price bubble and crisis in 2001 commonly known as the 'Dot Com Crisis'. The overvalued share prices of the tech companies collapsed and the Fed had to organise a bailout involving other investment banks to prevent systemic risk. Fed cut rates even further following the 'Dot Com Crisis' bringing it well below 2.5 percent. Asset prices soared again including house prices. The market for financial derivatives also expanded. This time bubble economy appeared in the housing market fuelled by reckless subprime lending. Subprime mortgages were relatively large and given to households with relatively high probability of default. Many of these households did not have a stable income to service their mortgage debts long term. The subprime lenders extended credit regardless as they believed that rapidly increasing house prices is a reliable hedge against default by high-risk lenders. Liberalisation of the derivatives market meant that the risky subprime mortgages could now be securitised and bundled with other assets. These securities were widely sold as safe assets and received strong ratings from the credit rating agencies.

Feeding frenzy in the market for subprime loans ended in late 2007 with a string of defaults by borrowers. The lenders were exposed and securitisation meant that the extent of contagion was unknown. The volume of losses were such that large Wall Street banks Bear Stearns and Lehman Brothers folded. The interconnected derivatives market quickly spread the banking crisis around the world. Banks appeared to be shaky and exposed in Europe. Northern Rock, Royal Bank of Scotland in the United Kingdom were in trouble. The same appeared to be the case in Ireland, Spain, and Portugal where housing market collapse triggered a banking crisis.

The troubled banks were systemically important. In order to prevent a systemic collapse, US and other Western European governments response to this crisis were to socialise the losses by offering large bailout packages to the troubled banks. This subsequently led to sovereign debt crisis in Europe but not in the United States. Deleveraging by the banks following the crisis triggered a credit crunch and a deep recession over the period 2008 to 2009. The US economy partially recovered in 2010 but then ran out of steam again.

The Fed viewed the economic crisis as a liquidity problem. To mitigate credit crunch, Fed engaged in Quantitative Easing (electronic money creation) and repeated asset purchase programmes. Quantitative Easing (QE) injected more liquidity into the banking system and Fed anticipated that some of that liquidity would trickle down to the real economy and stimulate activity. This policy restored financial stability, stimulated the asset markets, and kept inflation under control at least in the medium run. However, it largely failed to stimulate the real economy as real income declined, inequality increased, and living standards declined. The deep long-term structural inequality persisted. Saez and Zucman (2019) estimate that the income of top 1 percent grew five times faster than the bottom 90 percent since 1970. This trend continued to the extent that the top 1 percent now earns double the amount of income relative to the bottom 50 percent (approximately 160 million citizens). In the 1970s, the bottom 50 percent earned double that of the top 1 percent. Therefore, fortunes reversed. A large proportion of the top 1 percent income is capital gains as opposed to earnings. A similar pattern emerges with wealth distribution.

On the fiscal side, the US government increased leverage even further and did not follow austerity. Trade and budget deficits increased progressively since 2010. The national debt as a share of GDP increased to more than 100 percent. The US authorities did not perceive any threat to the stability of the dollar. Given the global reserve currency status of the dollar, policymakers viewed the level of leverage as sustainable and unlikely to jeopardise currency stability. I will return to this issue again in Chap. 12.

The other Western governments were not as fortunate as the United States. They did not have the luxury of a global reserve currency. The policy space available to them following the crisis was limited. Governments no longer had the pre-2008 fiscal space as they bailed out the banks. To put the fiscal house in order, governments in Europe had to rely on austerity policies and cut government spending. This had a long-lasting contractionary effect. The Central Banks mimicked the Fed and engaged in QE and asset purchases. They kept rates low and relied on the credit channel to stimulate the economy. The effects on the real economy and the financial markets were similar. The only difference is that the government balance sheet was marginally better in Europe relative to the United States.

10.3 National Security Policies of the Western Alliance Post 1991

10.3.1 Gulf War and War in Yugoslavia in the 1990s

The 1990s were a decade of consolidation for NATO. The Atlantic security architecture was mainly engaged in absorbing new potential members from Eastern Europe. The military industries in the United States and its Western European junior partners received new contracts. Force planning needed to be re-examined. New security challenges needed to be defined. There were no major combat operations for NATO in the 1990s except for the Gulf War and the war in Yugoslavia.

The Gulf War lasted from August 1990 to February 1991 and the mission was to remove the occupying Iraqi forces from Kuwait. This mission was successfully accomplished by the American and allied forces. Under the UN Security Council Resolution 678, the United States created a coalition of 35 countries including its NATO allies against Iraq.

The civil war in Yugoslavia started in 1991 with Slovenia seceding from the union. By 1990, the Federal communist authorities lost control of the country and it was slowly descending into chaos. Separatist movements erupted all across the country. The Federal authorities were also divided along ethnic lines. Separatism degenerated into a civil war along ethnic lines. Successive conflicts broke out in Slovenia, Croatia, and Bosnia during the first half of the 1990s. The Atlantic alliance led by the United States favoured the separatist forces. A large federation of multiple ethnicities were no longer viable in the Balkans. NATO did not have any involvement in direct combat in Slovenia and Croatia but backed the nationalist leaders diplomatically and logistically. However, in Bosnia NATO did intervene militarily on the side of the Bosnian and Croat forces. In 1995, NATO provided close air support to the Bosnian and Croat forces to push back the Bosnian Serb forces.

In 1998, another war broke out in the Yugoslav autonomous region of Kosovo. Kosovo wanted independence from Serbia after Serbia repealed the 1974 Yugoslav Constitution which granted autonomy to Kosovo. This time it degenerated into an ethnic conflict between the Serbs and the Kosovo Albanians. NATO directly intervened and sided with the Kosovo Albanian militia the Kosovo Liberation Army (KLA). The conflict lasted for a year with NATO bombing of Novi Sad and Belgrade. NATO prevailed in its mission. Kosovo became independent from Serbia even though the latter never recognised it.

In a surprise move, Russian peacekeeping forces stationed in Bosnia entered Kosovo and took control of the Pristina International Airport. Russian President Boris Yeltsin was under intense political pressure domestically to respond following NATO attack on a historic Russian ally. Earlier the Russian Prime Minister Yevgeny Primakov cancelled his trip to Washington in protest. He famously ordered the pilots to turn his aircraft back home halfway into the Atlantic after he learnt about the NATO strikes. President Clinton later negotiated with President Yeltsin for the

Russian forces to operate as a unit of Kosovo Force (KFOR) but not under the command of NATO.

10.3.2 September 11 and Wars in Afghanistan and Iraq

On 11 September 2001 during President George W. Bush's first term, Islamic terrorist group al-Qaeda conducted a large-scale coordinated terrorist attack on American soil. This was the first-ever terrorist attack conducted by an Islamic terror group on American soil. Nineteen al-Qaeda terrorists hijacked four civilian aircrafts from the United Airlines and the American Airlines. They crashed three of the aircrafts into the World Trade Centre in New York and the Pentagon in Washington D.C. The fourth aircraft approached Washington D.C. but crash landed in Pennsylvania. As a result of the attack, the twin towers at the World Trade Centre collapsed. Over 3000 individuals lost their lives and many more sustained life-threatening injuries.

This cataclysmic event completely changed the security posture of the United States. Islamic terrorist Osama bin Laden was the mastermind and American intelligence agencies identified Afghanistan as his location. The hunt for bin-Laden began at the earnest. The United States issued an ultimatum to the Taliban government in Afghanistan to surrender bin Laden which they refused. On 7 October 2001, the United States declared war on Afghanistan and began aerial bombing raids along with the British Royal Air Force. On 7 December 2001, Kandahar, the then capital of Afghanistan under Taliban fell. However, the war degenerated into a 19-year-long insurgency which is still continuing. Like the Soviets a decade earlier, the United States led forces are unable to take control of the whole of Afghanistan. In fact, at present the Taliban controls the majority of the country as successive US Administrations desperately look for an exit strategy.

Following the invasion of Afghanistan, the Bush Administration shifted its focus on Iraq. Saddam Hussain's Iraq had nothing to do with al-Qaeda or the September 11 terrorist attacks. Neither did he possess any weapons of mass destruction. Yet, a false and intense media campaign followed against Iraq claiming its involvement in the terrorist attacks and how its possession of Weapons of Mass Destruction (WMD) endangers American national security. The Secretary of State Colin Powell at the UN Security Council presented misleading evidence but the Council remained unconvinced. It did not authorise military action against Iraq. The Bush Administration went to war regardless cobbling together a coalition of willing. The coalition included Britain, Australia, and Poland (the only Eastern European nation to enthusiastically support American military intervention). Russia, France, Germany, and China opposed military intervention.

It took more than a year for the American forces to mobilise. On 19 March 2003, the American and British forces invaded Iraq with joint air raids. Ground invasion followed. The combat operations ended in May 2003 with President Bush declaring victory. Baghdad fell but the conflict degenerated into a vicious insurgency.

American troops failed to take control of the country and withdrew in 2011 only to return in 2015 to fight the Islamic terror group Islamic State (ISIS).

American troops are still in Iraq without the authorisation of the Iraqi government now battling Iran backed Iraqi Shia militia forces. The Shia Militia declared war on the US forces following the assassination of the Iranian Revolutionary Guard (IRGC) General Quasem Soleimani by the American forces on the Iraqi soil. The Iraqi government in response ordered all American and allied troops to leave the country as it deemed the assassination illegal. The current Trump Administration ignored the orders and American and allied troops continue to be stationed in Iraq.

The conflicts in Afghanistan and Iraq proved debilitating for America. The insurgency drained both financial and human resources. It has dented troop morale. At home, it led to war fatigue to the extent that successive American Administrations are reluctant to expose American troops to direct combat. They have adopted a more reductionist approach using American airpower including unmanned drones while on the battlefield using proxies instead of American troops. This has somewhat limited the political cost of these ongoing conflicts but the financial cost remains significant.

10.3.3 Conflicts in Libya and Syria

In 1969, Muammar Gaddafi assumed power in Libya through a military coup deposing the Western-backed Senussi Monarchy of Idris. As a revolutionary and an Arab nationalist, he was not the favoured ruler of Libya for the Western hegemonic interests. Over time, he transformed Libya into a socialist state nationalising the key oil sector. From 1977 onwards, Gaddafi pursued the agenda of transforming Libya into a Jamahiria (or a state of the masses). Jamahiria was a form of Islamic socialism practiced solely in Libya under Gaddafi.

Gaddafi's relations with the Western powers were not very congenial. The West accused him of funding rebel groups and exporting instability while he largely viewed the West as colonial powers. The West also held him responsible for organising the Lockerbie bombings in Scotland and imposed international sanctions on him.

As an Arab nationalist and socialist, Gaddafi's Libya was a natural ally of the Soviet Union. It had strong defence connections with the USSR and most of its military hardware were Soviet made. The USSR also maintained a military presence there with naval bases and signal intelligence facilities in Tripoli and Tobruk. Therefore, the USSR provided implicit security cover for Libya during its existence.

However, that security cover was no more following the dissolution of the USSR. Understanding the new realities, Libyan foreign policy shifted towards a détente with the Western alliance and especially America and Britain. In 2009, Libya offered to give up its missile and nuclear weapons programme in return for sanctions relief and normalisation of relations with the West. Indeed, in 2009–2010, Libya surrendered its weapons programme. However, the euphoria was short lived.

A decline in oil prices and a sharp increase in food prices in 2011 led to protests across the Middle East and North Africa region. Protests broke out mainly in eastern Libya over high unemployment and falling living standards. The government responded in a heavy-handed manner to these protests and as a result, the protests became increasingly violent. Armed rebel groups mobilised themselves in the eastern Libyan city of Benghazi against the government. The protests degenerated into a civil war.

Western governments sided with the rebels and Britain, France, and the United States started actively arming them. The Western Alliance expressed alarm that the government might use the air force against the Benghazi rebels to restore order and this might lead to unacceptable civilian casualties. On the initiative of Britain, France and Lebanon UN Security Council resolution 1973 was passed in 2011. Russia and China abstained during the vote and did not use their veto. The resolution demanded a ceasefire and the establishment of a 'no fly zone'.

Britain, France, and the United States used the establishment of a 'no fly zone' under resolution 1973 as a pretext to bomb Libya on the side of the rebels. Effectively these countries provided air cover for the rebels. Libyan air defence was too weak to respond and Libyan air force was not up to the task. The rebels advanced towards Tripoli and deposed the government. Subsequently, the rebels also captured and killed Muammar Gaddafi.

Libya descended into chaos. Civil war raged. Multiple factions, many of them Islamic radicals battled it out on the battlefield. The seemingly endless civil war is still ongoing. Marshal Khalifa Haftar led Libyan National Army (LNA) and allies currently controls approximately 90 percent of Libyan territory while the Tripoli based Government of National Accord (GNA) controls the remaining 10 percent.

The conflict in Libya damaged America's foreign policy reputation. However, the damage was much greater for Europe. It jeopardised Europe's national security by increasing the flow of illegal migrants (many of them Islamic radicals) across the Mediterranean. It also destabilised the Sahel with armed conflicts involving Islamic radical groups breaking out in Mali and elsewhere.

The Syrian conflict initiated in March 2011 as citizens gathered in Damascus and Aleppo to protest over rising food prices and unemployment. The protesters were inspired by the popular protests taking place all across the Arab world. Initially, the protests were peaceful but in some places they turned violent as a small group of protesters fired live ammunitions at the police force leading to casualties. The authorities responded in a heavy-handed manner to crackdown the protests. It had the opposite reaction as the protests turned increasingly violent.

Over time, the protests degenerated into a civil war with rebel groups emerging along sectarian lines. Many of the rebel groups were Islamic radicals and offshoots of outlawed terrorist groups on the UN Terror list. The rebel groups received supply of live ammunitions via Syria's border with Turkey and Iraq. The supplies were not difficult to organise from the burgeoning international black market for arms. Following the collapse of Libya, rebel groups received plentiful supply of ammunitions from the Libyan state arsenal. These ammunitions were channelled into Syria via the shadow economy.

In spite of some initial gains, the Syrian security forces struggled to prevail over the insurgency. Nor did the government manage to set the political process in motion with many of the Western- and Turkey-backed rebels demanding resignation of the government led by President Bashar al-Assad. The Obama Administration and its allies echoed these demands. In 2013, the Obama Administration and its European allies (Britain, France, and The EU) were accusing the Syrian government of using chemical weapons against its own population. There were calls in the media for the Obama Administration to authorise military action against Syria. However, there were also anti-war popular pressure on the Obama Administration from US citizens. The bitter experience of war in Libya was fresh in the minds of many American citizens. In September 2013, Russia brokered a deal with the Syrian government to surrender its chemical weapons stockpile and destroy them under United Nations supervision. The Syrian government agreed to enter into new international agreements. The inspection and destruction of stockpiles were carried out by the Organisation for the Prohibition of Chemical Weapons (OPCW), the UN watchdog on chemical and biological weapons. The OPCW inspection teams had significant Western representation. In January 2016, OPCW certified the destruction of Syria's entire chemical weapons stockpile catalogued by its inspectors under UN supervision. Note that the US Navy, Army, and associated contractors aboard the US Maritime Administration vessel *Cape Ray* carried out the actual destruction of the stockpiles.

Unfortunately, this did not end the conflict. In 2014, the notorious Islamic terrorist group ISIS emerged in Iraq and spread over to Syria taking control of vast swathes of territory. By late 2015, facing ISIS onslaught Syrian government lost control of almost 80 percent of the country's territory and was on the verge of collapse.

In a surprise move, Russia entered the conflict in September 2015 by deploying a small contingent of its air force in the Syrian Khmeimim airbase. The Russian contingent started assisting the Syrian army with close air support. In addition, the Syrian Army also received combatants from the Lebanese militia group Hezbollah and Iran. Russian assistance turned the tide of the Syrian war. Syrian army was able to take back control of all the major cities and approximately 70 percent of the country's territory.

The situation remains stable in most parts of Syria. However, the civil war continues in the rebel-held Idlib province. At present, the country is effectively carved up into three pieces. The government controls all the population centres and the major towns. Turkey backed rebels (many of them Islamic radicals) controls northern Idlib. In addition, Turkey also directly controls about a 30-kilometre stretch of Syria between the city of Aleppo and the province of Idlib. The Kurdish rebel groups (initially American backed) control the sparsely populated but oil-rich eastern Syria to the east of the Euphrates River. American troops directly control most of Syria's oil assets located in that region. In addition, American troops also control the al-Tanf crossing between Syria and Iraq and the surrounding territories. Al-Tanf is located in eastern Syria. Note that neither Turkey nor the United States has any legal authority under international or Syrian law to deploy troops on Syrian soil.

A civil war in Syria quickly morphed into a great power battlefront. For the Americans, the Syrian civil war was an opportunity to dislodge another hostile government in the Middle East and protect American hegemonic interests in the region. Syria is perceived to be hostile by the American elites because of its close alignment with Iran and Hezbollah. Syria is also hostile to Israel, another core foreign policy interest of America in a volatile region. For the Russians, the Syrian challenge was to pre-empt the threat of Islamic extremism spilling over from Syria into the North Caucuses. In addition, it was about maintaining a Russian military presence in the Eastern Mediterranean. Fall of Damascus to the extremists would have meant Russia losing control of its only Mediterranean naval base in Tartus.

Russian success in Syria increased its geopolitical influence in the region. Russian military assets are likely to stay in Syria over the long run. It has also increased Iranian influence. In contrast, the failure of American and Turkish proxies on the battlefield significantly reduced the influence of American led western alliance. Iraq is increasingly hostile to American military presence and American footprint in Syria is now extremely limited. Therefore, continued American presence in Syria and Iraq appears to be in jeopardy. However, Syria will remain a great power battlefront for some time to come.

10.3.4 Tensions in the South China Sea and the Korean Peninsula

In 2012, the Obama Administration embarked on a new foreign policy initiative dubbed ‘Pivot to Asia’. The stated goal of this initiative was to refocus American resources into the Asia-Pacific region and making it a foreign policy priority over traditionally overemphasised regions of Europe and the Middle East. In reality, this initiative was a continuation of the Clinton and Bush Administrations military deployment in Guam, Japan, and Singapore.

China viewed this new initiative as an escalation of the military containment strategy pursued earlier by the Clinton and Bush Administrations. American stated aim was the protection of all the East Asian waterways along the South China Sea and exercise freedom of navigation. China, with the second largest economy in the world and increasingly assertive military policies were not willing to give way. China relies heavily on these waterways for the import of raw materials and the export of finished goods. Therefore, it was not willing to surrender control of shipping lanes vital to its economy. American naval control over strategic choke points such as Singapore on the Straits of Malacca made the Chinese authorities vulnerable. China’s historical experience of European imperialism a century earlier did not reduce fears.

China in response embarked on a programme of creating artificial islands on the South China Sea and started placing its military and naval assets on them. Tensions flared in an otherwise peaceful region.

In 2016, the Obama Administration initiated the Trans Pacific Partnership (TPP) as the economic arm of its 'Pivot to Asia' initiative. The aim was to create a free trade area in the region with Australia, Brunei, Canada, Chile, Japan, Malaysia, Mexico, New Zealand, Peru, Singapore, and Vietnam. Notably, the initiative excluded China and Russia, the two key great power rivals of the United States in the region. This initiative collapsed following the election of Donald Trump in 2017 who broadly favoured protectionism over free trade. Nevertheless, containment remained the stated goal of American foreign policy towards China.

Trump Administration also chose the path of escalation in the long-standing dispute with North Korea. The Administration hoped escalation would yield more concessions from the North in terms of abandoning its nuclear programme. In spite of intense international pressure, the North acquired nuclear weapons and the capability to deliver them by missile. The escalation strategy also did not yield any meaningful concessions from the North. North demands removal of all American troops from the Korean peninsula. The situation currently remains a stalemate.

In conclusion, the economic and national security policies pursued by the American led western alliance did not end great power rivalry and elite feuds. It aggravated it. Great power rivalry returned with a vengeance in the naughties as the American led alliance increasingly appeared to be overstretched and exhausted. The cumulative resource base, economic power, and military strength of the Western Alliance are not sufficient to negate the same of the other rival great powers. Therefore, the resultant power balance three decades after the dissolution of the Soviet Union is not entirely unexpected.

Bibliography

Ford, M. (2015). *The rise of the Robots: Technology and the threat of a jobless future*. New York: Basic Books.

Saez, E., & Zucman, G. (2019). *The Triumph of injustice: How the rich dodge taxes and how to make them pay*. New York: W.W. Norton.

World Bank. (2002). *Transition the first ten years: Analysis and lessons for Eastern Europe and the Former Soviet Union*. Washington, DC: The World Bank.

Chapter 11
The Rise of China, India, and Russia: The Building Blocks of a New International System

Abstract This chapter analyses the spectacular rise of China as a global economic powerhouse. This narrative is entertained in conjunction with the rise of India, Russia, and the BRICS as a group. The chapter discusses ramifications of new international institutions such as the New Development Bank (BRICS Bank), Asian Infrastructure Investment and Development Bank (AIIDB), the Shanghai Cooperation Organisation (SCO), and the Eurasian Economic Union (EAEU). Infrastructure initiative such as the China led Belt and Road (OBOR or BRI) and the Russia–India–Iran North-South corridor is discussed. This analysis is undertaken in the backdrop of Asian Development Bank's estimate that Asia would need \$1.7 trillion annually to sustain its growth momentum.

The last three decades since the 1990s witnessed spectacular economic progress in China and to a lesser extent in India. After the lost decade of the 1990s, Russia eventually returned to growth in the naughties and started recovering rapidly. The result was an eastward shift in the economic gravity of the world. The emerging market economies of the east started growing much faster than the Western economies and the gap narrowed. Rising economic power translated into influence in international affairs for these nations. For Russia, it was rebuilding. Therefore, it implied a gradual return to its great power status. For China and India, it was a journey towards reclaiming their long lost pivotal position in international commerce and diplomacy. In what follows, I review the development trajectory of these nations since 1990 in turn.

11.1 Rise of China

Data from the World Bank's World Development Indicator indicates China's economy grew at an annual rate of approximately 9 percent over the three decades since 1990. Such spectacular economic expansion had a significant impact on every aspect of life in China and beyond. Rapid growth transformed China from a low-income

S. Bhattacharyya, *A History of Global Capitalism*, Frontiers in Economic History,
https://doi.org/10.1007/978-3-030-58736-9_11

country to a high middle-income country in terms of GDP per capita. Growth was accompanied by a remarkable decline in poverty. In 2010, China surpassed Japan in terms of GDP and firmly established itself as the second largest economy in the world only next to the United States.

China pursued investment and exports led growth strategy, relying heavily on both foreign direct investments (FDIs) as well as domestic investments. The economic geography of the growth strategy is also noteworthy. Export processing zones in the coastal areas attracted FDIs from multinationals while these high growth areas were networked with the inland to exploit spillovers and scale economies. As the economy expanded, government revenue increased. Government maintained trade and budget surplus while encouraging domestic investments. It maintained a large current account surplus with the rest of the world continually strengthening its net foreign assets position. China accumulated the largest foreign exchange reserve. It became one of the largest holders of US Treasury bonds.

In spite of being prudent, the Chinese authorities did expand and upgrade national infrastructure. China invested heavily in the development of an excellent fast train network and telecommunications. Transport and telecommunications undoubtedly delivered scale economies. Shorter journey times and better connectivity meant that former farmworkers inland could now easily commute to the coastal cities in search of work in the factories. A steady supply of cheap labour from inland helped maintain the profit margins of the coastal firms. In the rural areas, it released surplus labour from the inefficient farms raising farm productivity. It also ensured food security by increasing food supply. Remittance flow from the coastal factory workers to inland areas reduced poverty.

After three decades of this process, the economy not only specialised in low-skilled activities but also underwent significant skill upgrading through 'learning by doing'. Import of capital goods and technology from leading R&D intensive firms meant China also specialised in high-end R&D intensive products. The story of Apple and its effect on the manufacturing of handheld devices and laptops in China is widely known.

The structural policy of relying on exports to the Western markets and investments as the engine of growth ran its course for approximately three decades since the 1980s. It came to an abrupt end in 2008 with the Global Financial Crisis and subsequent Great Recession. Sharp macroeconomic contraction in the overleveraged economies of the West and especially the United States had adverse consequences for China. China responded by expanding private credit to boost domestic demand. However, this strategy was hardly successful as it fuelled a housing bubble and subsequent asset market volatility in 2011 and beyond.

In 2013, the Chinese authorities returned to its time tested economic expansion strategy of market integration. Chinese President Xi Jinping announced the ambitious 'Belt and Road Initiative' (BRI) during his official visit to Kazakhstan and Indonesia. The strategy aims at integrating markets in Eurasia and Africa through targeted investments into the development of transnational transport corridors. The initiative envisages connecting China and Russia via Mongolia using road, railways, and energy networks. It also aims to connect China with Western Europe using an integrated transport corridor via Kazakhstan and Russia. To the west, the plan is for a transport corridor to connect China to the Turkish ports on the Eastern Mediterranean via former Soviet republics of Central Asia. To the south, two transport corridors from China would connect Bangladesh, India, and Southeast Asia. An additional transport corridor will connect China and Pakistan. China will also connect with east Africa via a sea route traversing the South China Sea and the Indian Ocean.

Infrastructure investments of this scale would require financing. In 2013, China set aside to the tune of 100 billion US dollars as initial capital to realise these investments through the Asian Infrastructure Investment Bank (AIIB). The AIIB currently has 78 member countries with Russia and India as two founding members. Since its inception, the bank's capital base has increased with more member countries contributing. In 2014, President Xi Jinping added another 40 billion US dollars as development fund to support the 'Belt and Road Initiative'. The development fund would lend directly to businesses. It is a separate entity from the AIIB and other contributing banks.

In 2015, the integration process started between the BRI and the Russian led Eurasian Economic Union (EAEU). The EAEU is a much closer knit and integrated version of integration project within the post-Soviet space compared to the earlier Commonwealth of Independent States (CIS). The Treaty on the EAEU was signed on 29 May 2014 between Belarus, Russian Federation, and Kazakhstan and it came into effect on 1 January 2015. Armenia and the Kyrgyz Republic signed the Treaty in December 2014 and joined the union on 2 January 2015. Tajikistan, Uzbekistan, and Mongolia are three candidate member states with Tajikistan likely to join as a full member soon. Moldova currently has observer status. The Union has major free trade agreements with Vietnam, China, Iran, Serbia, Singapore, and Indonesia. It is currently negotiating a free trade agreement with India and Egypt.

The EAEU single market is large. It has a combined population size of 180 million people and a combined GDP of 5 trillion dollars (PPP). The integration process ensures free movement of goods and services by creating a customs union. It has an ongoing process of creating institutions to ensure common policy on macroeconomic management, transport, industry, agriculture, energy, trade, investment, telecommunications, anti-monopoly, and anti-trust laws. A single currency and greater political integration are also on the agenda.

The Supreme Eurasian Economic Council comprising of the heads of states is the main body of the Union. The second most important intergovernmental institution within the union is the Eurasian Intergovernmental Council comprising of the Heads of governments of the member states. The Eurasian Economic Commission runs the day-to-day affairs of the union and is located in the Belarusian capital Minsk. It also has a court system called the Court of the EAEU.

Following the free trade agreement with China in 2018, the EAEU agreed to closely coordinate its integration project with the BRI so that all the participants can exploit the maximum scale economies from the integration.

In addition to the EAEU integration project, integrating the BRI with the development of the Russian Arctic is also on the agenda. Russia has embarked on an ambitious plan of developing its segment of the Arctic. As the largest Arctic nation, it enjoys access to the biggest chunk of the Arctic sea shelf. The Arctic is rich in petroleum and other mineral resources. Harnessing these resources is on the agenda. Russian sovereign wealth fund, energy companies, and infrastructure companies have signed bilateral agreements with Chinese, Indian, and Vietnamese companies to harness resources in the Arctic. Cooperation is based on co-financing of projects and mutual development of technologies. Russian sovereign wealth fund along with its international partners created the initial capital base for financing of projects which is constantly replenished with new financing from additional participants.

Arctic sea is also a major transit route. With the rapid melting of the polar ice cap, the Arctic sea route is becoming more accessible. It is significantly shorter than the Indian Ocean route via Suez Canal. Russia is heavily investing in its fleet of icebreakers, the largest in the world. Chinese co-financing is involved. The northern sea route would cut journey time for sea cargo from China to European ports such as Amsterdam by up to 4 weeks. This will significantly reduce transport costs and unleash scale economy induced growth. Russia is positioning itself as a major transit hub in a Trans Eurasian trade while China is integrating the BRI with the northern sea route.

As I postulated in Chap. 2 while introducing my theoretical framework, any integration project would have to be underpinned by a security architecture. The Chinese BRI, the Russian EAEU, and their amalgam is no exception to this rule. The BRI and EAEU integration efforts are underpinned the common security architecture under the Shanghai Cooperation Organisation (SCO) and the Collective Security Treaty Organisation (CSTO). The SCO was formally established in June 2002 when the six founder members China, Russia, Kazakhstan, Kyrgyz Republic, Tajikistan, and Uzbekistan signed its charter. SCO currently has two more full members India and Pakistan making it the largest security alliance in the world in terms of population and territory. Afghanistan, Belarus, Iran, and Mongolia currently have observer status while Armenia, Azerbaijan, Cambodia, Nepal, Sri Lanka, and Turkey are dialogue partners.

The CSTO is Russian led with a fair bit of overlap with the SCO and the EAEU. Armenia, Belarus, Kazakhstan, Kyrgyz Republic, Russia, and Tajikistan are full members of the CSTO. On the territory of all the CSTO member countries, Russia has military presence. CSTO and particularly Russia ensures maritime security along the Arctic Sea route and has growing and significant military presence along the Arctic coastline on both land and sea. These supranational organisations are relatively recent and post-Soviet in nature. They are constantly evolving.

The membership and mandate of SCO and CSTO make it apparent that its primary objective is to ensure security along the transport corridors that are crucial for the Eurasian integration. Therefore, these arrangements are no exception to the theoretical postulates made in Chap. 2. Expansion to exploit scale economies is always accompanied by military expansion to ensure security.

11.2 The Rise of India

Before I write about the rise of India following the economic reforms of the 1990s, I will take a detour via Indian economic history, particularly post-independence India to put the reforms into perspective. I have not covered this material in Chap. 5.

During the eighteenth century, the Mughal Empire was on the decline which left a large vacuum in Indian polity. Regional powers scrambled to get a fair share of the vacant territory and confusion and chaos ensued. Already the effective tax rate under the Mughals was as high as 40 percent of the total farm produce. But amid this confusion and endemic local warfare, regional powers embarked into revenue farming and increased tax rate to 50 percent or more (Raychaudhuri 1983; Bayly 1983). The farmers were left with very little savings to invest in the next season and farm productivity declined. As a result, grain prices increased and grain wages declined throughout the eighteenth century (Mukherjee 1939; Broadberry and Gupta 2005). This had a devastating impact on manufacturing as the farming sector became more attractive for workers relative to manufacturing. This effect was further aggravated by frequent droughts.

During the nineteenth century, Indian manufacturing faced another major shock. Declining transport cost and productivity growth in British textile mills made it increasingly impossible for Indian textile to be competitive in the world market. Faced with higher labour cost[1] and lack of innovation, Indian manufacturing first surrendered its export markets to Britain and then the domestic market. The decline of the domestic market was further precipitated by the decline of royal courts who were major consumers of local goods. The high tax rate remained intact throughout this period. Feuding courts were so engaged in local warfare that they paid very little attention to infrastructure investments and technological progress which may have integrated the local markets better. Being a victim of revenue farming, individual artisans also had very little savings to invest in their machines to withstand British competition. The result was a steady decline of manufacturing over this century.

The practice of revenue farming persisted even after the British Crown formally took control of the British East India Company in 1858. Banerjee and Iyer (2005) show that in majority of areas the colonial administration handed over proprietary land rights to the landlords as opposed to the cultivators. This in effect made revenue farming legal under the colonial administration.[2] Furthermore, the absolutist nature of the colonial administration and no representation from the local farmers and artisans made it impossible to constrain the actions of the colonisers using established channels. Banerjee and Iyer (2005) find that the practice of revenue farming had long-term economic consequences. Areas with proprietary rights in land

[1]Measured using grain wage.

[2]This model goes back to the Permanent Settlement of Bengal between the East India Company (headed by Lord Cornwallis) and the Bengali landlords concluded in 1793. The agreement between the two parties was that the landlords would transfer a fixed magnitude of the revenue raised from land to the Company.

with the landlords produced significantly worse outcomes in terms of agricultural investments, productivity, health investments, and education investments relative to areas with proprietary rights in land with the cultivators.

In summary, Indian manufacturing suffered shocks from both within and without. They were political, climate, and globalisation shocks. The political shock followed from the decline of the Mughal Empire and British colonisation. The climate shock resulted from frequent droughts. The globalisation shock resulted from lower transport costs and European productivity growth. Indian manufacturing succumbed to these shocks because of military defeats to the British East India Company. It lost control of its supply chain, transport network, and markets to the British. Deindustrialisation ensued and the Indian economy experienced virtual stagnation during the eighteenth and nineteenth century.

Leading up to independence India and especially the provinces of Bengal and Punjab suffered catastrophic humanitarian crisis aided and abetted by the British Colonial Administration. Winston Churchill was the British Prime Minister at that time. During the period 1943 to 1944, the province of Bengal encountered a largely man-made famine. Approximatelyt two to three million people perished due to starvation and diseases. The famine was caused by the wartime procurement policies (particularly of rice) of the British Colonial Administration and its preferential distribution among the Civil Servants and the British Armed Forces. The procurement policies triggered food price inflation. The vast majority of subsistence farmers in an extremely poor country could not survive a sharp decline in grain wages.

Wartime Bengal famine was followed by loss of life during partition in 1947. British Parliament passed the Indian Independence Act in 1947 under the new Labour Prime Minister Clement Attlee. The Act stipulated partitioning India into two territories along ethnic and religious lines. This was the final price for independence. India was partitioned into two territories of India and Pakistan. The provinces of Bengal and Punjab were carved up in an arbitrary fashion displacing between 10 to 12 million people. Hindus residing in west Punjab and east Bengal were forced to migrate to the Indian territory while the Muslims residing in east Punjab and west Bengal were forced to migrate to Pakistan. Such forced displacement along religious lines triggered untold misery and violence with up to two million lives lost.

11.2.1 Post-Independence India

India's first Prime Minister Jawaharlal Nehru was a staunch critique of the colonial administration and held the view that deindustrialisation was a direct consequence of British colonial rule (Nehru 1947). Therefore, it was not surprising that he emphasized import substitution and planning led economic development after assuming power in 1947. Independent India pursued a mixed economy model with private property rights but a significant element of planning. The mixed economy model did not perform well as India experienced extremely slow growth over three decades following independence. India's growth rate in per capita income over the period

1950 to 1980 was as low as 1.7 percent (Rodrik and Subramanian 2004). This phenomenon is commonly known as the 'Hindu rate of growth'—a term coined by the eminent economist Raj Krishna.

What went wrong? The answer may lie in the quality and nature of India's regulatory institutions. The import substitution led industrialisation strategy relied on high tariff and quota restrictions to prevent imports. This was to protect domestic investments from foreign competition. Furthermore, private sector investments were discouraged and the role of the public sector expanded.[3] Five-year plans akin to socialist economic systems and a tightly controlled regulatory system were adopted. Such a policy framework discouraged the development of the private sector by design. The shared belief amongst policymakers and politicians around that time were India is a capital scarce country and therefore capital needs to be conserved. The private sector and the market mechanism are not best to decide where and how scarce capital should be allocated. Private individuals are myopic and only care about short-term private benefits. They are not able to foresee the long-term positive externalities or social benefits of investments in infrastructure and human capital. Therefore, aggregating private benefits resulting from private investments will always be less than the net social benefit achievable in the presence of externalities. Social planners, the government, and the public sector have a longer time horizon. Therefore, they can minimise net social loss by directing capital to its highest-valued use over the long run. Private investments were subjected to rigorous scrutiny using a tedious process of licensing to prevent wastage of capital. Licensing led to a culture of widespread rent-seeking described in Bhagwati and Desai (1970) and Krueger (1974).

In summary, after independence India experienced sluggish economic growth largely due to weak regulatory institutions. The negative impact of excessive regulation on growth and investments far outweighed the positive effects of property rights and other market-friendly institutions. This is in line with the cross-national evidence reported by Bhattacharyya (2009a) where he shows that over regulation leads to slower growth in a country even if property rights and contracting institutions are favourable.

11.2.2 1980s Policy Shift and Turnaround

Indian economy experienced a turnaround in the 1980s. Growth in per capita income more than doubled from 1.7 percent in 1950 to 1980 to 3.8 percent from 1980 to 2000 (Rodrik and Subramanian 2004). De Long (2003) and Williamson and Zagha (2002) note that India's growth rate approximately doubled a full decade before the

[3]However, it is important to note that private sector was not entirely discouraged. In other words, India never completely went down the socialist path. The idea was to build a mixed economy with public sector as the main driver.

1991 reforms. In recent years, the Indian economy accelerated even further. What caused this turnaround? Many observers suggest that the 1990s reforms may have made the difference (Bajpai and Sachs 1999; Ahluwalia 2002; Srinivasan and Tendulkar 2003). However, 1980s growth cannot be explained by reforms of the 1990s. Rodrik and Subramanian (2004) argue that attitudinal change of the government towards business and industrial establishments initiated the growth process in the 1980s. To counter the electoral threat from the Janata Party and reclaim some of her lost ground during the 1977 elections, Indira Gandhi was actively trying to garner support from the business community (Kohli 1989). As a result, when she came back to power in 1980, her government took a more business-friendly stance without making any significant policy changes. Consequently, this small shift in attitude triggered a large productivity response which powered growth in the 1980s. More formal policy changes through economic liberalisation took place in 1988 and 1991 which boosted growth in the 1990s. However, not everyone agrees with the attitudinal change explanation. Ahluwalia (2002) and Srinivasan and Tendulkar (2003) argue that the 1980s growth was driven by fiscal expansion and was inherently unstable. Even though supported by data, this explanation ignores the potential productivity impact of fiscal expansion (Rodrik and Subramanian 2004). Indeed the data shows that the fiscal expansion and current account deficit was not a one for one relationship during the 1980s implying that an increase in demand may have played a role in boosting productivity.[4] Kotwal et al. (2009) present an excellent account of the literature on economic liberalisation and its impact on economic growth in India.

How and where institutions fit into this story? Attitudinal change in the 1980s may have brought about changes in informal institutions and business environment overall. This may have improved the quality of property rights and contracting institutions contributing to productivity growth even further. After the reforms of 1988 and 1991, the quality of regulatory institutions improved manyfold. Reforms also had an impact on the quality of property rights institutions. The International Country Risk Guide (ICRG) expropriation risk index which is a measure of property rights institutions jumped from 6 in 1982 to 10 in 1993 and thereafter. In fact, the effect of liberalisation on institutions is even more noticeable when one compares 1991 expropriation risk with that of 1992. The score jumps from 6.2 to 8.2. This is in line with cross-national results of Bhattacharyya (2009b). Bhattacharyya (2009b) shows that liberalisation leads to improvements in institutional quality. Therefore, in summary institutions improved both in the 1980s and in the 1990s. A part of it was due to a major policy shift. Attitudinal change also played a role. Improved regulatory institutions had a major impact on productivity growth since 1991.

[4]Rodrik and Subramanian (2004) show that this holds even after adjusting for capacity utilization.

11.2.3 India in the 2000s: Economy and Foreign Policy

Indian economy expanded at a steady pace in the 2000s. The annualised growth rate of GDP even exceeded 7 percent in the 2010s. The steady expansion made India the third largest economy in the world in terms of purchasing power parity (PPP). Economic expansion also affected India's foreign and security policy positions. India increasingly engaged with the other members of BRICS. It substantially increased trade with China. Trade with Russia also increased to an annual turnover of 25 billion dollars. India floated its own transport corridor, the North-South corridor in collaboration with Japan. The purpose of the corridor is to integrate with Russia and the EAEU via the Arabian Sea, Iran, and the Caspian. The projects are in their planning stages and there are issues concerning financing. India does not have the ability of mobilising finance on its own to the extent that China can.

On the security front, India's policy so far could be characterised as multi-vector. India and Russia are strategic partners in international affairs. India has a longstanding defence procurement relationship with Russia. Most of India's military hardware is either Soviet or Russian made. India remains the largest purchaser of Russian hardware till date. However, India is also diversifying its procurement and exploring other options with Israel, France, and the United States. India remains a member of the SCO and BRICS. It is currently negotiating a free trade deal with the EAEU. India is a founding member of the Chinese led AIIB. Nevertheless, it is also a member of the Quadrilateral Security Dialogue (QSD) along with Australia, Japan, and the United States.

So far, the Indian elites have not exhibited any grander vision in terms of expansion plans. Its foreign policy is still overwhelmingly concentrated in the immediate neighbourhood. However, this might change with further economic expansion. The Indian economy is likely to continue to grow as it allocates surplus labour from unproductive agriculture or informal sectors into the high productivity formal sectors. This process is likely to continue for at least another decade when India would need to confront some hard realities.

11.3 Return of Russia

11.3.1 Economy and Politics Since 1999–2000

Russia survived the onslaught of 'shock doctrine' in the 1990s and returned to growth in the 2000s. Data from the World Bank's World Development Indicator shows that the Russian economy grew on average at an annualised rate of 5 percent over the period 2000 to 2010. In 2014, Russia graduated as a High Income Country in terms of income per capita measured in PPP according to the World Bank. In 2020, the IMF and the World Bank estimates Russian economy to be the sixth largest in the world in terms of GDP measured in PPP only marginally behind Germany.

Russia rapidly modernised its economy over the two decades since 1999. Its investment climate improved remarkably as is reflected in the World Bank Doing Business Index. Russia currently occupies 31st position on the Doing Business League Table, which is significantly higher than other emerging market economies. It is also higher than in many EU member countries. In the 2010s, Russia digitised its economy and the tax system at a rapid pace. Digitisation of the tax system improved tax compliance delivering healthy revenue flow to the treasury. The government was able to maintain budget surplus throughout the 2010s except for the fiscal years 2015 and 2016. Russia underwent pension reforms in 2019 further stabilising the state of long-run public finances. Overall, Russian macroeconomic balance sheet is strong with both budget and trade surpluses and very low sovereign debt to GDP ratio (currently 19 percent). Very low proportion of Russia's sovereign debt is foreign currency denominated making it less susceptible to external shocks. Russian foreign currency denominated private (including corporate) debt is also one of the lowest in the world largely due to financial sanctions introduced by the United States and the EU in 2015.

Russia was on IMF programme throughout the 1990s and it borrowed 15.6 billion SDRs[5] (22.1 billion USD) in aggregate to manage its balance of payments and public finance (Odling-Smee 2006). It is noteworthy that the IMF disbursed large tranches in 1995, 1996, and 1998. Russian presidential election took place in 1996 and the large tranches in 1995 and 1996 helped the incumbent Boris Yeltsin. Russian parliamentary (or Duma) elections took place in 1999 and 1998 was the year of Russian Bond Crisis.

Russia made small repayments over the period 1996 to 1998 but started making large repayments in 1999 following the departure of Yeltsin's favoured cabinet. Yevgeny Primakov became the Prime Minister but the power struggle between pro-Western Presidential Administration and the Prime Minister continued. In August 1999, Vladimir Putin was appointed Prime Minister by Boris Yeltsin. On 31 December 1999, Boris Yeltsin resigned as President and Vladimir Putin took charge. In 2006, Russia repaid all its outstanding debts to the IMF and exited the programme.

By mid-2000s, the internal power struggle was well and truly over. The national security faction prevailed over the Yeltsin led pro-Western faction. Vladimir Putin with his background in the security services was hardly known. After the chaotic 1990s, the position of the President was weak. This started changing in the 2000s. Chain of command and vertical power structure was gradually restored offering efficiency in public service delivery and law enforcement. The Federal Government was broadly a coalition between the national security faction and the pro-Western faction. The national security faction occupied key ministries of defence, foreign affairs, internal affairs, and policing. The pro-Western faction occupied ministries of finance and the economy.

[5]SDRs are special drawing rights, which is IMF currency. The US dollar figure in the parentheses.

With an expanding economy, Russia embarked on integrating the former Soviet space into a common economic space. These efforts root back to the 1990s and the initiation of the Commonwealth of Independent States (CIS). These initial attempts were only partially successful. The more recent Eurasian Economic Union (EAEU) initiative is better resourced and well organised. I have already discussed this initiative in detail under the subsection 'Rise of China' (Chap. 11).

In addition to the EAEU and the China led OBOR, Russia is heavily investing in infrastructure projects for the development of the Arctic economic space and the Northern Sea Route. These projects come under the umbrella of the National Infrastructure Projects. Two noteworthy projects under this plan is the construction of a 300 billion Roubles (4 billion Dollars) deep-water year-round port in Indiga on the Russian Barents Sea coast in the Arkhangelsk region and the Belkomur Railway connecting northern ports with industrial regions of Siberia, Ural, Kazakhstan, and the Kyrgyz Republic. The Indiga port and the associated infrastructure will have the capacity to handle 80–200 million tons of cargo per year connecting shipping from Kazakhstan, Kyrgyz Republic, Japan, and China via the Northern Sea Route and Belkomur Railway. It is currently under construction and is expected to be fully operational in 2025. It will primarily handle shipments of coking coal, forestry products, minerals, chemicals (including petrochemicals), fertilizers, and paper. This will add significant capacity to the Northern Sea Route and allow for diversification away from St. Petersburg. The other major ports on the Northern Sea Route are Murmansk, Arkhangelsk, Belomorsk, and Sabetta. The Belkomur Railway network will reduce the distance for deliveries from Siberia and the Urals by 800 kilometre. Thus, it will significantly reduce transport costs and time. This new infrastructure will offer Russia economies of scale for the development of the Arctic.

11.3.2 Security Posture and NATO

Throughout the 1990s, Russia's conventional military power was in decline due to drastic funding cuts and corruption. Nevertheless, Russia's nuclear potential was maintained. Russian victory in the North Caucuses over the period 1999 to 2001 arrested territorial decline. Russian armed forces prevailed over Islamic insurgency in the North Caucuses during the second Chechen war. Following that hard-earned crucial victory, Russian national security posture shifted. The new Russian government embarked on a military reform programme to address the weaknesses that were exposed during the North Caucus campaign. New funding was approved and a major rearmament programme was initiated. Strategically important military industries were rejuvenated. They were integrated into the rearmament programme through state procurement. After the tumultuous decade of the 1990s, they received a lifeline.

NATO response throughout the 1990s and the 2000s were in line with the assessment that Russia is extremely weak. Therefore, it is not in a position to respond to NATO advances in Eastern Europe and elsewhere. The power structures of the Western/Atlantic Alliance expected diplomatic protests but nothing beyond that.

This assessment was correct at the time. Indeed, militarily Russia was only a shadow of the Soviet Union. However, it needs to be said that this assessment grossly underestimated Russian military potential going into the future. The chaos of the 1990s led Russia watchers and security strategists to assume that the subsequent decades would be a mirror image of the 1990s. With the benefit of hindsight, we can now conclude that such assessment was wrong.

The first signs of a NATO–Russia confrontation was during the formers Serbia campaign in 1998.[6] This was followed by NATO enlargement into Eastern Europe in 1999 with the Czech Republic, Hungary, and Poland were the first to join. The alliance expanded further to the east in 2004, now bringing in Bulgaria, Estonia, Latvia, Lithuania, Romania, Slovakia, and Slovenia. In 2009, Albania and Croatia were brought into the fold. Russian concerns were ignored. Assurances were given that the expansion is not targeted towards Russia and NATO do not perceive Russia as a hostile power. These assurances were hardly credible for the Russian security establishment, especially on the backdrop of earlier promises on NATO expansion made by Western leaders to Mikhail Gorbachev.[7] Russian trust in the Western alliance was broken.

At NATO Bucharest Summit on 3 April 2008, Ukraine and Georgia were invited. These countries were seeking a NATO Membership Action Plan (MAP). The summit declared that Ukraine and Georgia were potential candidates for NATO membership and would eventually join the alliance. This move threatened Russia's core national security interests in the Black Sea and Caucasus regions. It appears from the diplomatic cable sent by the then US Ambassador to Russia William J. Burns on 1 February 2008 that the Bush Administration was fully aware of the Russian position before issuing invitations to Ukraine and Georgia in Bucharest. Summarising his cable to the NATO Joint Chiefs of Staff, National Security Council, Secretary of State, and Secretary of Defense Ambassador Burns writes,

> Following a muted first reaction to Ukraine's intent to seek a NATO Membership Action Plan (MAP) at the Bucharest summit (ref A), Foreign Minister Lavrov and other senior officials have reiterated strong opposition, stressing that Russia would view further eastward expansion as a potential military threat. NATO enlargement, particularly to Ukraine, remains "an emotional and neuralgic" issue for Russia, but strategic policy considerations also underlie strong opposition to NATO membership for Ukraine and Georgia. In Ukraine, these include fears that the issue could potentially split the country in two, leading to violence or even, some claim, civil war, which would force Russia to decide whether to intervene. Additionally, the GOR[8] and experts continue to claim that Ukrainian NATO membership would have a major impact on Russia's defense industry, Russian-Ukrainian family connections, and bilateral relations generally. In Georgia, the GOR fears continued instability and "provocative acts" in the separatist regions (Source: WikiLeaks http://wikileaks.org/plusd/cables/08MOSCOW265_a.html)

---

[6]See Chap. 10 for a full discussion of this conflict.

[7]See discussion in Chap. 9.

[8]Government of Russia.

Therefore, it can be concluded that the actions of the Western Alliance were deliberate. The geopolitical motivation behind bringing Ukraine into the Atlantic Alliance's security orbit stems from Brzezinski (1997, 2004). Brzezinski (1997, 2004) posits that Russia would cease to be a great power without Ukraine in its orbit. Indeed, there is merit in this thesis as the Soviet and then Russian military industrial supply chain significantly depended on supplies from the industrial regions along the Dnieper and Don rivers. However, it significantly underestimates the ability of supply chains to adapt to new realities. It also overestimates the role of these two Ukrainian industrial regions.

Tension between the Atlantic Alliance and Russia escalated with the Russian–Georgian conflict. In a surprise move on 7 August 2008, the Mikhail Saakashvili led Georgian government initiated military action against the breakaway region of South Ossetia to the North of the country. UN Security Council approved Russian peacekeeping mission troops were stationed in Tskhinvali, the de facto capital of the breakaway region. On the night of 7 August, the Georgian troops initiated military action under the cover of heavy shelling. The Russian troops suffered casualties. Russia responded with combined firepower from Air Force, Navy, and Army. Georgian Army could not withstand the assault and withdrew from South Ossetia within 5 days. Russian Army did not advance beyond the borders of South Ossetia but Georgian Army losses were substantial.

Russia faced unanimous condemnation from the Atlantic Alliance but made it clear for the first time since 1991 that it would not hesitate to respond militarily if its core interests are threatened. We now know that the Georgian President Mikhail Saakashvili initiated the conflict by provoking Russia (European Union 2009). He strongly believed that he would have the military backing of NATO in the event of a Russian response. Therefore, he perceived the risk for his government was minimal. The EU Independent Fact Finding Mission Report headed by the Swiss diplomat Heidi Tagliavini later confirmed this run of events (European Union 2009). The EU Report apportions blame on Georgia and its then President Saakashvili as the initiator of the conflict.

Russia made its intentions clear but NATO did not retreat leaving the fight for another day. The Obama Administration initiated the much publicised 'Russia Reset' following his election in 2009. The Reset was meant to be a change of course for the United States' Russia Policy. There was optimism that Russia–US relations would improve under the new Russian President Dmitry Medvedev. In reality, the expectation was that the Obama Administration could now extract unilateral concessions from Russia under a new president without fundamentally changing its Russia policy. Without a fundamental shift in the US's Russia Policy, the outcome of the Reset was unsurprising. It failed.

On 13 December 2001, the Bush Administration notified Russia that it is unilaterally withdrawing from the Anti-Ballistic Missile (ABM) Treaty. The ABM Treaty was concluded between the United States and the USSR in 1972 limiting the use of anti-ballistic missile defence systems on each other's territory. This was a landmark arms control treaty ensuring nuclear strategic balance between the two nuclear superpowers. Russia responded by increasing its nuclear potential.[9] The Bush Administration concluded the Strategic Offensive Reductions Treaty (SORT) with Moscow in 2002, which mandated cuts to the deployed warheads but not to stockpiles. It also did not have any enforcement powers.

In the absence of ABM Treaty and the Obama Administrations' plan of deploying a ballistic missile defence system in Poland and Romania alarmed the Russians. Russia saw this as a threat to its nuclear strike capabilities. The Obama Administration cited ballistic missile threat from Iran as the reason behind these deployments in Eastern Europe. The Russians did not find this explanation credible. Iran did not possess ballistic missiles at that time. Tensions were rising, mutual trust was in short supply, and communication channels were breaking down. Ukraine became the new battleground between the American led Atlantic Alliance and Russia.

11.3.3 Battleground Ukraine

Before I discuss the current tensions in Ukraine, it is useful to take a detour into Russian–Ukrainian history to put the said into context. As noted in Chap. 4, majority of the territories in modern Ukraine, especially the eastern territories around the Black Sea basin, switched hands from the Ottoman Empire to the Russian Empire in the mid-1700s during the reign of Catherine the Great following successful military campaigns. In 1776, imperial Russia allied with the Austrians crushed the Ottoman backed Crimean Khanate and took direct control of Crimea. Since then most of what is now known as Ukraine stayed within the Russian Empire and its successor state the USSR. The only exception is during the Crimean War of 1853 to 1856 and the Second World War when Russia temporarily lost control of some of the territories. Chapters 4 and 7 offer more details.

Successive British, French, and Prussian Imperial administrations sided with the Ottomans against the Russians. The Western European Empires viewed Russian expansion into the Black Sea as a threat and therefore were prepared to use the Ottomans to contain Russia.

In 1919 following the Bolshevik Revolution, USSR was established as the union of 15 republics including the Ukrainian Soviet Socialist Republic (UkSSR). Following the establishment of USSR, Vladimir Lenin embarked on significant administrative changes. He lumped the Russian Imperial administrative division of *Malorossia* (or little Russia) which was part of the Russian SSR into the Ukrainian SSR. *Malorossia* was a territory around the Don and Dnieper river basins excluding Crimea. It is currently located in South-eastern Ukraine. It can be surmised that the main motivation behind this administrative change was to encourage the ideological union between the peasants from Central Ukraine (Kiev and hinterland) and the industrial workers from *Malorossia*.

---

[9] More on this under subsection New Arms Race. See below.

Following the Second World War, Joseph Stalin added further territories into the Ukrainian SSR. The Western territory of Galicia, which belonged to Poland prior to the war, was now part of the Ukrainian SSR. The city of Lvov (also known as Lemberg or Lviv) is the capital of Galicia.

Following Stalin's death in 1953, Nikita Khrushchev became the Soviet leader in 1954. He was Ukrainian and relied heavily on the support of the Ukrainian faction within the Soviet Communist Party to gain power. To please his Ukrainian supporters, Khrushchev unilaterally signed a decree in 1954 declaring Crimea to be a part of the Ukrainian SSR. This decree was in contravention to the Soviet Constitution but it remained unchallenged at that time. A change in administrative regions within a country was hardly viewed as contentious at that time. However, foundation of a future territorial dispute was already being laid. It became apparent following the dissolution of the USSR.

Following Belovezha Accords and dissolution of the USSR in 1991, Moscow and Kiev hastily worked out long-term arrangements for the Russian Navy to remain in Sevastopol, Crimea. A 20-year-lease agreement was signed to grant the Russian Navy user rights to the base. This agreement was extended in 2010 as the Russian Ukrainian Naval Base for Gas Treaty. The new agreement extended Russian Navy's lease of Sevastopol for another 25 years.

Ukraine's post-soviet history is unstable. Spatial heterogeneity in voting patterns across the country is noteworthy and perhaps is a symptom of inherent instability. Political preferences of voters in the West of the country appear to differ markedly from voters in the east and this difference persists over time. Such inherent structural imbalances deliver perpetually unstable political outcomes. Because of such political instability, Ukraine has suffered the worst decline in living standards in the post-soviet space. Ukraine was the wealthiest region in the USSR only to become one of the poorest in the post-soviet space. In 1991, Ukraine was the sixth largest economy in Europe in terms of GDP (PPP) whereas in 2020 it is one of the poorest. Data from the World Bank's World Development Indicator (WDI) indicates that Ukraine's GDP per capita (PPP) declined from 10, 464 International dollars in 1991 to 4797 International dollars in 2000. GDP per capita recovered somewhat in the subsequent decade reaching 7906 International dollars in 2017, still significantly lower than the 1991 level. Reliable GDP estimates are not available for the last three years but the expectation is that living standards declined significantly.

The geopolitical tug-of-war between Russia and the Atlantic Alliance in independent Ukraine led to the first disorderly transfer of power in 2005 following the Orange Revolution. This undoubtedly dampened trust in government even further. Traditionally more nationalist (and hence anti-Russian) Western Ukrainian political block took power. In 2010, the pendulum shifted again. Now the more pro-Russian Eastern Ukrainian political block assumed power. The power transfer this time was orderly through elections which were deemed free, fair, and legitimate by the EU and international observers. Victor Yanukovych became the President of Ukraine.

All the while, competition between the Western Alliance and Russia in Ukraine intensified. The external influence created perverse incentives for the Ukrainian ruling class. For example, Ukraine would receive economic transfers from the EU and other Western Aid agencies to institute pro-Western political reforms. US Assistant Secretary of State for European Affairs Victoria Nuland attests to such transfers and the underlying political agenda in a speech to the US-Ukraine Foundation in December 2013. She says, 'The United States has supported Ukraine's European aspirations. We have invested over 5 billion US dollars to assist Ukraine in these and other goals that will ensure a secure and prosperous and democratic Ukraine.'[10] Russia would respond to these transfers by offering Ukraine fuel (oil and gas) and other goods at a price significantly below the market. Transfers of this nature from both sides undoubtedly weakened government and politics in Ukraine. Western transfers meant Ukrainian politicians could now farm external revenue and neglect the national economy and falling living standards. Similarly, Russian fuel and other subsidies meant that Ukrainian politicians could now sell these goods to the European and international markets for a mark-up and appropriate the rent.

World Bank data indicates that the Ukrainian economy stagnated over the period 2010 to 2013. The persistent problem of rampant corruption intensified even further. Victor Yanukovych ran on the promise of seeking EU membership for Ukraine. This undoubtedly was popular with the young voters as EU membership offers the prospect of migrating to high wage economies of Western Europe. In late 2013, the EU offered an Association Agreement to Ukraine. This Agreement stipulated that Ukraine would have to enter into an exclusive Free Trade Agreement with the EU which would override pre-existing trade or customs agreements with other parties. The Ukrainian government estimated that the financial assistance package offered by the EU would not compensate for the economic losses that Ukraine would incur during the transition period. Yanukovych decided to delay the signing of the Agreement with the EU.

Ukraine was part of Russia led CIS Customs Union since the mid-1990s. It had multiple friendship agreements and an open border with Russia ensuring free movement of goods and labour. The EU Association Agreement would have meant imposition of a hard border with Russia, which had significant economic and political costs. For Russia, the EU Association Agreement meant a threat to its defence industry supply chain, which procured many of its vital intermediate goods from Ukraine. Moreover, it would have meant significant trade diversion. Cheaper EU goods could now enter Russian market tariff free via Ukraine while the converse may not have been true.

Ukraine was facing a balance of payments crisis at that time. Russia stepped in with a 17 billion US dollar assistance package spread over 5–7 years with an immediate disbursement of 3 billion US dollars. Yanukovych accepted this package and the first tranche of 3 billion US dollars as it offered friendlier terms. Street protests broke out in Kiev and it increasingly turned violent. There were fierce battles in Kiev's Maidan Square between 18 and 20 February 2014. Unidentified snipers indiscriminately fired at protesters and police from rooftops. The identity of these snipers and the planners remains unknown till date.

[10]Source https://www.youtube.com/watch?v=U2fYcHLouXY. Link accessed on 18 July 2020.

Under pressure from the EU and the United States, Yanukovych government decided to withdraw the security forces from the streets of Kiev and enter into EU brokered negotiations with the opposition. On 21 February 2014, the Yanukovych government entered into an agreement with the opposition entitled 'The Agreement on Settlement of Political Crisis in Ukraine'. The parties to the Agreement were Viktor Yanukovych (President of Ukraine) and the opposition represented by Vitali Klitschko (Ukrainian Democratic Alliance for Reform), Arseniy Yatsenyuk (All-Ukrainian Union 'Fatherland'), and Oleh Tyahnybok (Svoboda). The Agreement was also signed by Frank-Walter Steinmeier, Radoslaw Sikorski, and Eric Fournier the foreign ministers of Germany, Poland, and France respectively as witness. Vladimir Lukin, the Special Envoy of the President of the Russian Federation participated in the negotiations but did not sign the Agreement as witness. The Agreement stipulated early elections and power sharing with the opposition in the interim period.

The opposition did not honour the Agreement. Armed opposition groups took control of government buildings the next day now that they were unprotected following the withdrawal of police. The protesters called for the capture of President Yanukovych. Realising the threat to his life from the armed protesters, Yanukovych left Kiev for the eastern city of Kharkov. Soon Kharkov became unsafe as armed far right groups started taking over government buildings and establishing street checkpoints in the city. In the cover of darkness, Yanukovych left Kharkov for Crimea. The Russian armed forces airlifted him from Crimea for Russia.

The Speaker of the Ukrainian Parliament (Rada) Alexander Turchinov declared himself the interim President of Ukraine. A government under the Premiership of Arseniy Yatsenyuk (one of the leading figures in Maidan protests) took charge. We now know that the Atlantic Alliance was complicit in what happened in Maidan and afterwards.

Obama Administration's Assistant Secretary of State for European Affairs Victoria Nuland offered last-minute instructions to US Ambassador to Ukraine Geoffrey Pyatt that Arseniy Yatsenyuk should be the Ukrainian prime minister and Vitali Klitschko should not enter government as his Deputy. She also says that Vice President Joe Biden approves of the plan. A recording of the leaked conversation can be viewed here https://www.youtube.com/watch?v=WV9J6sxCs5k.[11] Appendix A offers a full transcript of the leaked conversations.

All states within the Atlantic Alliance swiftly recognised the new unconstitutional government. Following the unconstitutional power grab in Kiev, anti-Maidan protests broke out in the eastern parts of the country. Again, Western actions in Ukraine were based on the premise that Russia is too weak to offer a firm response and therefore could easily be taken advantage of. It was a miscalculation. Russia moved swiftly, secured Crimea with its already stationed 25,000 troops, and organised a referendum. Unsurprisingly the people of Crimea who are majority ethnic Russians overwhelmingly voted in favour of joining the Russian Federation. Following the

[11]Link accessed on 18 July 2020.

referendum, the government of Russia recognised that the people of Crimea exercised their right to self-determination. The Republic of Crimea was accepted as a subject of the Russian Federation.

Many dispute the legality of the referendum and view Russian actions in Crimea as annexation. Others dispute the validity of the referendum results as it was done in the absence of any international observers. Scholars also make legal arguments both in favour and against. Ukraine, Russia, the United States, and the United Kingdom are signatories to the Budapest Memorandum which was concluded during the December 1994 OSCE meeting in Budapest. The Memorandum guarantees independence and territorial integrity of Ukraine. Russian actions in Crimea are in contravention to the Memorandum. Predictably, the Russian government does not accept this argument. They argue that the Republic of Crimea exercised its right to self-determination and left Ukraine on its own volition. This was perfectly legitimate at a time when Ukrainian constitution was void due to the unconstitutional power garb following Maidan. Therefore, Russia did not violate its obligations under the Memorandum by accepting Crimea as a Russian subject.

It also remains an open question to what extent the post-Maidan Ukrainian government is an independent sovereign republic. American and by extension the Atlantic Alliance's involvement in Ukraine is extensive to the extent of choosing Prime Ministers, Prosecutor Generals, and other officials as demonstrated by the conversations of Victoria Nuland and Joe Biden. I have already discussed the conversation between Obama Administration's Assistant Secretary of State for European Affairs Victoria Nuland and US Ambassador to Ukraine Geoffrey Pyatt regarding the appointment of Arseniy Yatsenyuk as the Prime Minister of post-Maidan Ukraine. Arseniy Yatsenyuk indeed became the Prime Minister. On 23 January 2018 in a Foreign Affairs issue launch[12] event hosted by the US Council on Foreign Relations (CFR) Vice President Joe Biden admitted that in December 2015 he personally and directly intervened in Ukraine's governance by ordering the dismissal of the Ukrainian Prosecutor General[13] Viktor Shokin from office. Joe Biden insisted at the CFR event that the dismissal was necessary because Viktor Shokin was corrupt. Subsequent leaked conversation[14] between Joe Biden and Ukrainian President Petro Poroshenko revealed that investigations by the

[12]Foreign Affairs is a leading American journal on international relations and geopolitics published by the CFR. Former Vice President Joe Biden was at the CFR event to launch the January/February issue of the journal in which he penned an article (co-authored with Michael Carpenter) entitled, 'How to Stand Up to the Kremlin: Defending Democracy Against Its Enemies'. The former Vice President and his co-author Michael Carpenter was at the event discussing the said article. The full transcript of the event is available at https://www.cfr.org/event/foreign-affairs-issue-launch-former-vice-president-joe-biden. Link accessed on 18 July 2020. Also see Appendix B.

[13]The Prosecutor General in Ukraine is equivalent in stature to the US Attorney General.

[14]This conversation was leaked by Ukrainian Rada Deputy (or Member of Parliament) Andrii Derkach. The conversation took place on 3 December 2015 and was leaked to the media by Derkach on 19 May 2020. It can be viewed at https://www.youtube.com/watch?v=EbmDLhJ43cU. Link accessed on 18 July 2020. For full transcript see Appendix C.

Ukrainian government did not find any evidence of wrongdoing against Viktor Shokin. President Poroshenko fired Prosecutor General Viktor Shokin because that is what he promised to deliver to Vice President Biden.[15] The relevant transcripts and link to videos are presented in Appendices C and D respectively. The above events demonstrate that in spite of the Great Power guarantees of independence in the December 1994 Budapest Memorandum, post-Maidan Ukraine increasingly resembles a neo-colonial client state of the United States and Atlantic Alliance as opposed to an independent sovereign constitutional republic operating under the rule of law.

Regardless of the principled position one takes, the reality is that Crimea is now under Russian possession and will remain so in the foreseeable future barring a major conflict. Ukraine on its own does not have the capability to take Crimea militarily. Any such attempt would likely be a repeat of Georgia in 2008. Great power involvement in such a conflict could easily turn into a nuclear confrontation.

Events in Crimea and deep distrust in the nationalist Maidan government triggered separatist movements in the east. Initially, many in the pro-Russian regions of Odessa and Kharkov revolted. However, violent clashes erupted between anti-Maidan protesters and nationalist battalions in these regions. The violence in the Odessa Trade Union House where more than 40 anti-Maidan protesters lost their lives is a testament to the severity of this violence. The most pro-Russian regions of Lugansk and Donetsk organised themselves as armed resistance group against the Maidan government. They held referendums and unilaterally declared independence from Ukraine with the hope that they would also be absorbed into the Russian Federation. The interim President Alexander Turchinov declared war against the breakaway regions in April 2014.

Ukrainian Armed Forces and Nationalist volunteer battalion groups many of whom are openly Nazis took charge of the military campaign against the eastern regions. The interim Ukrainian government received unequivocal diplomatic, logistical, and material support from the Obama Administration and the EU. Obama Administration escalated diplomatic and economic pressure on Russia. Initially, the EU was reluctant to go along with economic sanctions but the attitude changed following the shoot down of the Malaysian Airlines MH17 flight over the conflict zone. The EU imposed harsh financial and economic sanctions on Russia. In response, Russia imposed sanctions on agricultural imports from the EU, the United States, and allied countries. I discuss this separately in the next subsection.

The Atlantic Alliance unanimously held the rebels and Russia responsible or the MH-17 tragedy even before the investigations began. Malaysia, who is now part of

[15]The real reason behind Biden ordering Poroshenko to remove Viktor Shokin could have been to shut down the corruption investigation into the Ukrainian Natural Gas Company 'Burisma Holding Limited (Cyprus)'. The company was registered in Cyprus perhaps due to its widely known status as a tax haven. Vice President Biden and Secretary of State John Kerry's family members were involved in 'Burisma Holding Limited (Cyprus)' as board members. These family members were receiving generous remunerations from the natural gas company. Viktor Shokin was leading this investigation.

the joint investigative team along with the Netherlands, Australia, Belgium, and Ukraine is reluctant to apportion blame on the rebels and Russia and questions the impartiality of the investigations.

High-intensity combat ensued in eastern Ukraine. The rebels with military assistance from the Russians arrested the advance of the Ukrainian Army and allied nationalist battalions. The Ukrainian Armed Forces suffered heavy defeat at the hands of the rebels in Ilovaisk and Amvrosiivka. Following these defeats, in September 2014 Ukraine entered into an OSCE and Russia brokered ceasefire agreement with the rebels known as the Minsk Protocol. It did not last as combat operations resumed in January 2015. The Ukrainian Army suffered a further heavy defeat in Debaltsevo. This time it entered into another Germany, France, and Russia brokered ceasefire agreement known as Minsk II.

Sporadic low-intensity fighting still continues at the frontline and the dispute remains unresolved. Minsk Protocol, Minsk II, and the associated Steinmeier Formula stipulate that Ukraine should grant special status to the breakaway regions by changing its constitution before organising elections there. Control of the Russia–Ukraine border should come next. Ukraine insists on changing the terms of the Protocol as it deems legislating on special status is not practical before taking full control of the territory.

Ukraine remains a key flashpoint in the new US–Russia confrontation. Syria is the other flashpoint. I have already discussed Syria in Chap. 10 and therefore will not do so here again.

11.3.4 Sanctions and Energy War

The initial reason for the EU and US economic sanctions on Russia was 'annexation of Crimea'. Subsequently, the stated reason shifted as more and more sanctions were imposed revealing the real reason to be geopolitical rivalry. Sanctions are used as a foreign policy tool and the full economic consequences are not very well understood. I intend to discuss the economic consequences of sanctions here following which I will discuss the Energy War between the United States and Russia.

US and EU sanctions included travel bans and individual sanctions on Russian officials who they deemed to be behind what ensued in Crimea and Ukraine. More importantly, the sanctions barred access to long-term credit for Russian banks, financial institutions, and businesses in the European and American credit markets. Europe kept the provision of Russian borrowing with a term structure of maximum 2 weeks effectively cutting them off from Euro and dollar denominated credit.

Almost simultaneously, negative dynamic took hold in the oil market. The Federal Reserve announced the possibility of a future rise in the Funds rate. This put downward pressure on oil prices. More importantly, Saudi Arabia declared war on the US shale oil industry and started producing significantly more oil to price them out of the market. This led to a collapse in oil prices from 100 US dollars a barrel in 2014 to 30 US dollars a barrel in 2015. It remains unclear whether the potential Funds rate rise and the Saudi Arabian decision to increase production were coordinated. Nevertheless, the financial sanctions and a collapse in oil price generated a perfect storm for Russia.

The macroeconomic challenges for Russia were significant. The collapse in oil price had adverse implications for the Russian federal budget. It went into deficit. Furthermore, it significantly reduced Russia's trade surplus. There was downward pressure on the rouble. The Russian Central Bank initially responded with measures to support the rouble using foreign currency reserves. This exposed Russia to speculative attacks and Russia was burning reserves at a rapid pace. The Russian Central Bank gave up supporting the rouble and allowed free float. The rouble depreciated significantly against the dollar moving from 28 roubles to 100 roubles against the dollar and finally settling around 65 roubles.

The Russian sovereign debt-to-GDP ratio was very low at the time. However, Russian corporations had external foreign currency denominated loans, which they needed to service. Therefore, there was a steady demand for dollar and euro liquidity from the sanctioned Russian large corporations. In the absence of access to such liquidity in the Western markets, these corporations had to rely on liquidity supplied by the Russian Central Bank. This meant that there were further claims on the reserves weakening the rouble even further. Russian sovereign and corporate credit ratings were downgraded increasing external borrowing costs even further.

A weak rouble increased the cost of imports triggering inflation. Russia was a net food importer at that time and therefore depreciation of the national currency triggered food price inflation. Russian Central Bank reacted swiftly by floating the currency and increasing the benchmark interest rate. The currency float and subsequent devaluation protected the Russian budget as government received more roubles per dollar earned from exports. The rate rise arrested inflation by triggering a recession. The recession was shallow and short lived. Overall Russia lost 3.5 percent of its GDP over 3 quarters. Russian economy returned to growth in 2016 and by 2017 made up for the GDP loss.

Russia imposed counter sanctions on agriculture imports from the EU and the United States. It also instituted import substitution. The strong money policy pursued by the central bank along with the import substitution measures aided structural change in Russia. A shift towards low inflation reduced uncertainty and encouraged investments. Continual improvements in the business climate as evidenced by the World Bank's Doing Business Survey also did the same. The high rates also led to financial consolidation with the central bank actively liquidating bad banks.

The counter-sanctions on EU agriculture and targeted lending led to very high output growth in the agriculture sector. Import substitution also did the same in other sectors and allowed diversification of the Russian economy. Overall, the sanctions shock failed to deliver the intended negative politico-economic chain reaction in Russia. The economic impact was limited. It did not alter Russia's foreign policy posture. It made the Russian economy less dependent on external credit. None of this was surprising given that economic restrictions hardly affects continent-sized economies endowed with all the factors of production.

Over time the sanctions war escalated as it became a containment tool as opposed to a tool for manufacturing political change. It spilled over into the energy market. With the growth of the shale oil and gas industry, the United States once again became a net exporter of petroleum. As a result, it became a direct competitor of Russia in the European energy market. The struggle this time was between Russian pipeline gas and the American liquefied natural gas (LNG).

Russia inherited a gas pipeline network from the USSR spanning Eastern Europe and Germany. This network delivered natural gas from the USSR to the socialist economies of Eastern Europe and Germany. The initial network was land based and concentrated on the territory of Ukraine. Therefore, by default following the dissolution of the USSR independent Ukraine became a major transit country for Russian pipeline gas exports to Europe. As demand for Russian gas in Europe increased, Russia added new pipelines to the network and diversified away from Ukraine as the transit route. Three notable new pipelines were the Nord Stream 1, the Turk Stream, and the Blue Stream. Nord Stream 1 is an undersea pipeline directly linking Russia and Germany via the neutral waters of the Baltic Sea. It was concluded in 2012 and is owned by the Nord Stream AG. Russian state company Gazprom is the majority shareholder. Both the Turk and Blue Stream pipelines link Russia and Turkey via the Black Sea. They were concluded in November 2018 and February 2003. Both are joint ventures involving Eni (Italy), BOTAS (Turkey), and Gazprom (Russia). Khrennikova et al. (2019) based on data from the Agency for Cooperation of Energy Regulators illustrates the pipeline network and its market penetration within the EU.

These projects envisaged creation of energy hubs in Germany and Turkey. The former is to cater for the Northern and Central European markets while the latter is to address demand in Turkey and Southern Europe. These projects faced significant opposition from the United States as it feared that growing Russian economic influence in Europe would compromise its economic, political, and security influence in the continent. Americans found allies within the EU in the form of the Baltic States, Poland, and the United Kingdom. The new pipeline infrastructure reduced the importance of pre-existing pipelines in Eastern Europe thereby jeopardising transit fees for the affected countries. Nevertheless, they were built as the economic interests of the Western European nations' trumped geopolitics.

Following the new shale technology fuelled petroleum boom in the United States in the 2010s, it once again became a net exporter. Therefore, it was directly competing with the Russian producers for market share in Europe and elsewhere. The new production method however was not cost effective. The unit cost of production is significantly higher than conventional gas. Furthermore, the unit cost of transportation is significantly higher than pipeline gas as shale gas would need to be liquefied under pressure, shipped and then reconverted before use. Liquefied natural gas imports require port infrastructure with LNG terminals which are not inexpensive and takes time to build. In contrast, pipeline gas is inexpensive and ready to use. In spite of high hopes, American LNG failed to win market share in Europe as fundamental economic forces dictated the outcome. Nevertheless, political posturing continued. In late 2019, the Americans sanctioned all the companies participating in the Nord Stream 2 project. Facing the prospect of losing access to the

American credit market, Swiss pipe laying firm 'All Seas' pulled out of the project with 90 percent of the undersea segment already completed. This did stop the project temporarily. It is unlikely to have any effect on the project long term as Gazprom owns an undersea pipe laying vessel 'Akademik Chertsky' with identical capabilities. Eventually, the project will be completed increasing Gazprom's gas delivery capacity to the European market.

11.3.5 The New Arms Race

The collapse of the ABM Treaty triggered a new arms race. Russian alarm over the placement of nuclear capable missiles in Poland and Romania meant that they were slowly upgrading their nuclear triad. New generation of submarines, bombers, and missiles were gradually introduced into the armed forces. The existing submarines, bombers, and missiles received upgrades. A wide array of both conventional and nuclear weapon systems arrived in the 2010s. A new battle tank Armata and associated frames for armoured personnel carriers were introduced in 2017. New fourth- and fifth-generation fighter aircrafts such as MiG35, SU35, and SU57 were introduced into the air force. Manufacturing of medium-sized battleships gained momentum. The Russian Navy on average received 10 new ships every year throughout the 2010s. Many of the medium-sized ships were corvettes fitted with nuclear capable short-, medium-, and long-range missiles.

In the late 2010s, Russia introduced the supersonic cruise missile Kalibr. It was successfully combat tested during the Syrian campaign. Several Russian battleships launched Kalibr missiles from the Caspian Sea to successfully hit targets in Western Syria. New air defence systems such as the S-400 and Pantsir entered service with NATO member Turkey acquiring the former. New hypersonic missiles such as the Zircon and Kinzhal were also introduced into service along with new generation of Inter-Continental Ballistic Missiles (ICBMs).

America responded to the new Russian weapon systems by reactivating its own weapons programme. In 2019, the Trump Administration walked away from the Intermediate-Range Nuclear Forces (INF) Treaty by notifying Russia and citing Russian violations with the Iskander system. Russia denied such violations. In the same year, the Administration approved a historic 700 billion US dollars Pentagon budget to support defence procurement, hypersonic missile development, nuclear triad upgrade, and space force creation. In 2020, Trump Administration also indicated that it is not in favour of renewing the Strategic Arms Reduction Treaty (START). On 23 May 2020, the Trump Administration informed Russia that it is withdrawing from the Treaty on Open Skies. The Treaty has 35 state parties and is one of the pillars of promoting international transparency on military activities, especially in the Euro-Atlantic region. It came into force in January 2002 and allows for aerial unarmed surveillance flights over territories of its participants. Russia indicated that they will stay with the Treaty in spite of American withdrawal. Nevertheless, the new arms race is now in full swing. A future Joe Biden administration is unlikely to significantly change the dynamic. Biden administration's Russia policy is laid out by Nuland (2020).

11.4 Russia–China Strategic Partnership

Under pressure from the Atlantic Alliance Russia increasingly looked eastward. Economic sanctions from the west necessitated reorientation of its economy towards the Chinese and Asian markets. Russia invested heavily in its Strategic Partnership with China.

China facing increasing pressure from America and Japan regarding its trade and security posture responded positively to the Russian overtures. China's own security challenge at the South China Sea meant that it was looking for diplomatic allies. More importantly, it anticipated risks for its resource-poor economy in the event of serious tensions along its sea-bound trade route. China imports fuel and other raw materials and exports finished goods using the South China Sea trade route.

Russia offered an alternative land-based trade route. In addition, resource endowments of the two economies matched perfectly well making them ideally suited for a symbiotic trade relationship. Russia is labour scares, skill intensive, and resource abundant while China is labour abundant, skill intensive but resource poor. The two economies have different comparative advantages. Russia specialises in high-end defence manufacturing, aircraft building, space industries, extractive industries, and agriculture while China specialises in consumer durables, heavy industries, and telecommunications. This makes them ideally suited for bilateral trade. The Russian–Chinese partnership concluded major energy infrastructure projects such as the Power of Siberia pipeline in 2019. Tanas et al. (2019) based on data from Gazprom and Xinhua News Agency illustrates this network. Trade turnover between the two countries increased steadily since 2015 reaching the record 110 billion US dollars figure in 2019.

In addition to collaboration at the international level in AIIB, BRI, BRICS, and G20, the new Sino-Russian strategic partnership established a joint investment fund, aircraft manufacturing joint venture CRAIC,[16] joint media holdings, and space cooperation. This relationship and trade turnover is likely to grow as these initiatives start delivering results.

[16]The China-Russia Commercial Aircraft International Corporation Limited (CRAIC) is a 50–50 joint venture between Commercial Aircraft Manufacturing Corporation of China (COMAC) and the Russian United Aircraft Corporation (UAC). Current project included the development of a wide body commercial aircraft.

11.5 BRICS

BRIC (acronym for Brazil, Russia, India, and China) was initiated in 2009 as a loose formation of four major emerging economies. The association's key objective at the time of inception was for its members to coordinate actions within international financial organisations such as the IMF and the World Bank. In addition, the members wanted to coordinate their actions within international forums such as the G20. One of the key unifiers for the members were their lack of representation within international financial organisations relative to their contributions. In the 2000s and the 2010s, emerging economy contributions to the IMF and the World Bank increased steadily. Yet, this was not reflected in their voting rights. The BRIC member countries wanted to speak with one voice on this issue.

As the association started gaining momentum following its first successful summit meeting in Yekaterinburg (Russia), its scope became ambitious. Spatial diversification and regional engagement became one of the key agendas of the association. In 2010, Brazil hosted the second summit meeting in Brasilia and invited South African President Jacob Zuma as the Chief Guest in line with the association's spatial diversification agenda. BRIC had representation from Latin America, Europe, South Asia, and Southeast Asia but had no representation from Africa. South Africa joined the association in 2010 as the fifth member and the association's name was changed to BRICS. South Africa participated in the 2011 summit meeting in Sanya (China) as a full member.

Following South Africa's inclusion, the association's spatial diversity objective became a reality. During the 2012 summit meeting in New Delhi (India), important joint infrastructure initiative such as the BRICS Cable was launched. BRICS Cable is a fibre optic submarine telecommunication system currently under construction. Regional outreach activities of the association received new impetus during the 2013 summit meeting in Durban (South Africa). Chairpersons of the African Union and the African Union Commission along with eight African leaders representing the eight regional economic groupings attended the summit. This trend continued during the next five summit meetings over the period 2014 to 2018. During the Fortaleza (Brazil) summit in 2014, BRICS outreach activities included leaders of the Union of South American Nations (UNASUR) and the Southern Common Market (MERCOSUR). In addition, important initiatives of the BRICS New Development Bank (with 100 billion US dollars initial capitalisation) and the BRICS Contingent Reserve Arrangement were launched. The 2015 Ufa (Russia) summit brought BRICS together with the Shanghai Cooperation Organization (SCO) and the Eurasian Economic Union (EAEU). In 2016, India contributed to the BRICS regional outreach activity by inviting leaders of seven countries involved in the Bay of Bengal Initiative, which is a South Asian economic cooperation organisation. The following year China widened the scope of the outreach strategy by introducing BRICS+, which included key economies such as Egypt, Mexico, and Thailand. South Africa formalised the BRICS+ approach the following year by inviting Argentina (Chair of the G20 and MERCOSUR member), Indonesia (influential

ASEAN member), Egypt (major Middle East and North Africa (MENA) economy), Jamaica (Chair of Caribbean Community (CARICOM)), and Turkey (Chair of Organisation of Islamic Cooperation (OIC)).

The outreach strategy of BRICS is aimed at delivering market integration in trade and finance along with security coordination. Market integration with the regional partners goes hand in hand with delivering strong returns to the shareholders from potential investments by the BRICS New Development Bank. Note that the BRICS shareholders are the constituent sovereigns who are pooling their financial resources and technical assistance capabilities in order to exploit scale economies from their investments. The Bank is mandated to support public or private sector projects in member and non-member countries through loans, guarantees, equity participation, technical assistance, and other financial instruments. Non-member countries include but are not limited to countries within BRICS+ and other regional groupings part of BRICS outreach.

The BRICS Contingency Reserve Agreement (CRA) is a competitor to the IMF. This is a common financial stability mechanism for the member countries and is independent of the IMF. China holds 21 billion US dollar drawing rights and 39.95 percent voting rights commensurate to its capital contribution. Brazil, Russia, and India each hold 18 billion US dollar drawing rights and 18.10 percent voting rights while South Africa holds 10 billion US dollar drawing rights and 5.75 percent voting rights.

What started as an informal grouping to coordinate actions within the American led Euro-Atlantic financial system, gradually evolved into an independent, ambitious, and influential organisation. Within a decade of its inception, BRICS transformed itself from a lobby group within the Euro-Atlantic structure to an independent organisation. The launch of the New Development Bank and the BRICS CRA is a clear indication that the member countries increasingly see their destiny as future great powers working outside the Euro-Atlantic system with independent institutions. In spite of their short history, the competing nature of these institutions relative to the IMF and the World Bank cannot be understated. Indeed, the current mandate of the BRICS financial institutions is to cooperate with other international organisations but nonetheless they remain independent from the Euro-Atlantic system. These initiatives are likely to gain momentum as the relative strength of the BRICS economies increase. They are also likely to compete more with the older institutions within the Euro-Atlantic system and diverge from them.

11.6 Summary

The dissolution of the USSR and the collapse of the rival socialist block did induce initial expansion of the Atlantic Alliance into the void left by the former. However, this was short lived as the pendulum started to shift again in the 2000s and the 2010s. The 2000s and the 2010s witnessed a significant strengthening of the BRICS economies thereby increasing their power and influence in international affairs.

Initially, there was little appetite for coordination. However, towards the end of 2000s and especially following the 2008 financial crisis, the emerging BRICS economies started coordinating their actions more closely.

With momentum behind their initiatives, BRICS created independent institutions. At the same time, with a much weakened and overleveraged economy Western influence in international affairs weakened. Aggressive policies towards Russia and China coupled with militarism in the Middle East eroded Western influence even further. Therefore, a transition appears to be inevitable. It is worth noting that the new institutions created by BRICS, EAEU, BRI, and the emerging security architecture led by SCO are the building blocks of an emerging international system which is likely to be multipolar. BRICS and the United States are likely to be key members of that new system. In the next chapter, I discuss how that new system will look like.

Bibliography

Ahluwalia, M. (2002). Economic reforms in India since 1991: Has gradualism worked. *The Journal of Economic Perspectives, 16*(7), 67–88.

Bajpai, N., & Sachs, J. (1999). Fiscal policy in India's economic reforms. In J. Sachs, A. Varshney, & N. Bajpai (Eds.), *India in the era of economic reforms*. New Delhi: Oxford University Press.

Banerjee, A., & Iyer, L. (2005). History, institutions, and economic performance: The legacy of colonial land tenure systems in India. *The American Economic Review, 95*, 1190–1213.

Bayly, C. (1983). *Rulers, townsmen, and bazaars: North Indian society in the age of British expansion, 1770–1870*. Cambridge: Cambridge University Press.

Bhagwati, J., & Desai, P. (1970). *Planning for industrialization: A study of India's trade and industrial policies since 1950*. Cambridge: Cambridge University Press.

Bhattacharyya, S. (2009a). Unbundled institutions, human capital, and growth. *Journal of Comparative Economics, 37*, 106–120.

Bhattacharyya, S. (2009b). Root causes of African underdevelopment. *Journal of African Economies, 18*(5), 745–780.

Broadberry, S., & Gupta, B. (2005). *The early modern great divergence: Wages, prices and economic development in Europe and Asia, 1500–1800*. Unpublished manuscript, University of Warwick.

Brzezinski, Z. (1997). *The grand chessboard: American primacy and its geostrategic imperatives*. New York: Basic Books.

Brzezinski, Z. (2004). *The choice: Global domination or global leadership*. New York: Basic Books.

De Long, B. (2003). India since independence: An analytical growth narrative. In D. Rodrik (Ed.), *In search of prosperity: Analytical narratives on economic growth*. Princeton, NJ: Princeton University Press.

European Union. (2009). *Independent international fact-finding mission on the conflict in Georgia*. Report, Volumes I–III, September. Accessed July 18, 2020, from https://web.archive.org/web/20091007030130/http://www.ceiig.ch/pdf/IIFFMCG_Volume_I.pdf

Khrennikova, D., Shiryaevskaya, A., & Krasnolutska, D. (2019). Why the Russia – Ukraine Gas Dispute Worries Europe? *Bloomberg Quick Take*, 6 December 2019. Accessed July 18, 2020, from https://www.bloomberg.com/news/articles/2019-12-06/why-the-russia-ukraine-gas-dispute-worries-europe-quicktake

Kohli, A. (1989). Politics of economic liberalization in India. *World Development, 17*(3), 305–328.

Kotwal, A., Ramaswami, B., & Wadhwa, W. (2009). *Economic liberalization and Indian economic growth: What's the evidence?* Unpublished Manuscript, February.

Krueger, A. (1974). The political economy of the rent-seeking society. *The American Economic Review, 64*(3), 291–303.

Mukherjee, R. (1939). *The economic history of India: 1600–1800*. London: Longmans, Green and Company.

Nehru, J. (1947). *The discovery of India*. London: Meridian Books.

Nuland, V. (2020). *Pinning Down Putin: How a confident America should deal with Russia*. Foreign affairs, The Council on Foreign Relations, July/August, 2020.

Odling-Smee, J. (2006). The IMF and Russia in the 1990s. *IMF Staff Papers, 53*(1), 151–194.

Raychaudhuri, T. (1983). The mid-eighteenth-century background. In D. Kumar & M. Desai (Eds.), *The Cambridge economic history of India* (Vol. II). Cambridge: Cambridge University Press.

Rodrik, D., & Subramanian, A. (2004). *From 'Hindu Growth' to productivity surge: The mystery of the Indian growth transition*. NBER working paper 10376, March.

Srinivasan, T., & Tendulkar, S. (2003). *Reintegrating India with the world economy*. Washington, DC: Institute for International Economics.

Tanas, O., Shiryaevskaya, A., & Murtaugh, D. (2019). How Russia – China gas pipeline changes energy calculus. *Bloomberg Quick Take*, 25 November 2019. Accessed July 18, 2020, from https://www.bloomberg.com/news/articles/2019-11-25/how-russia-china-gas-pipeline-changes-energy-calculus-quicktake

Williamson, J., & Zagha, R. (2002). *From slow growth to slow reform*. Washington, DC: Institute for International Economics.

Part IV
Going Forward: What to Expect?

Chapter 12
Rivalry, Expansionism, and the Future of the International System

Abstract This chapter revisits the main thesis of the book—capitalism is an expansionist system fraught with risks of violent confrontation. History should guide us to manage these conflicts effectively and draw lessons from them. Barring major armed or nuclear conflicts (flashpoints of such incidents are many), the world will perhaps converge towards multipolarity whereby the economic and political powers of the BRICS nations are likely to increase at the expense of Western Europe and the United States. This process will be accelerated by the ongoing public health crisis and the global economic crisis. The international trade and financial systems are also likely to change. Whether this transition will take place in a peaceful and orderly manner is an open question. Given the dangers of a nuclear-armed great power conflict, it is likely that a Thucydides' Trap would be avoided this time.

'The Coronavirus pandemic will forever alter the world order. The United States must protect its citizens from disease while starting the urgent work of planning for a new epoch'. Henry A. Kissinger (2020)

Chapters 10 and 11 describe the gradual geopolitical transformation since 1991. In its desire to expand rapidly first into the post-Soviet space and later elsewhere, the American led Atlantic Alliance overextended itself. Unsuccessful military campaigns in Iraq and Afghanistan coupled with economic malaise following the 2008 financial crisis significantly weakened the Atlantic Alliance. In contrast, the emerging powers within BRICS focused on rebuilding their economies and exploiting scale economies internationally without overextending themselves. As a result, we are now approaching a critical juncture where a switch in geopolitical balance of power appears inevitable. This process is further accelerated by the ongoing SARS-COV-2 or COVID-19 (commonly known as Coronavirus) pandemic and public health crisis. The sharp economic downturn because of the pandemic is likely to have a profound impact on the geopolitical balance of power. In what follows, I discuss the potential economic consequences of the pandemic. Following which I present a brief assessment of the potential effects of the pandemic on the geopolitical positions of the United States, China, Russia, India, and the EU.

S. Bhattacharyya, *A History of Global Capitalism*, Frontiers in Economic History,
https://doi.org/10.1007/978-3-030-58736-9_12

12.1 The Economic Consequences of COVID-19: An Initial Assessment

12.1.1 The Genesis and Spread of the Pandemic

The coronavirus pandemic is caused by the highly contagious virus COVID-19. The virus spreads from people to people during close contact and causes lower respiratory tract infection. High temperature, persistent cough, sneezing, and fatigue are some of the common symptoms of this disease. At a later stage among many patients, the virus triggers a severe immune response leading to weakening of the immune system. A weakened immune system also invites bacterial and fungal infections that are not treatable using common antibiotics. It causes untreatable and potentially fatal pneumonia in patients.

First human infection with the virus was identified in the city of Wuhan in China in December 2019. It is identified to be common among certain animals such as bats. However, human infections were not recorded prior to the case in Wuhan. It is believed that the virus was first transmitted to a human from animals in a Wuhan seafood market. The first human-to-human transmission was identified soon after. Due to the highly contagious nature of this virus, it spread rapidly across the city of Wuhan and then to the neighbouring Hubei province. By January 2020, the disease reached an epidemic proportion and started spreading all across China.

Following the initial outbreak in China, the disease was transmitted to other countries through air travel. By mid-January, the disease already spread to other parts of Asia and arrived at the continents of Europe and America. At the time of writing on 20 July 2020, the disease reached every continent of the world except the southernmost continent of Antarctica. Data from the John Hopkins University indicates that there are over 13 million recorded infections around the world with over 600,000 fatalities and around 7.3 million recoveries. Note that these are recorded figures and the actual infections and fatalities are likely to be much higher. Many countries including developed ones do not have a sufficient number of testing kits and therefore many infections stay unrecorded. Furthermore, some countries solely record hospital deaths making it harder to ascertain the actual number of fatalities.

The disease currently has no proven treatment. It causes breathing difficulties in patients and therefore respiratory support is essential for saving lives. If left untreated, fatality rates could be significantly higher. Due to the lack of medication or any proven treatment, it takes very long to treat patients and thereby imposing additional pressure on the public health system.

In order to minimise the rate of spread of this disease, countries around the world have largely followed the World Health Organisation (WHO) guidelines and imposed 'social distancing' regimes. 'Social distancing' implies limiting people-to-people contact by closing down places of social gathering, transport, air travel and asking citizens mainly to stay home. This strategy is commonly known as 'lock-downs'. Lockdowns have severely restricted mobility.

12.1.2 *Macroeconomic Effects of the Pandemic*

12.1.2.1 Public Health to Macro Economy: Identifying the Channels

In order to understand the short- and long-term economic effects of the pandemic and lockdowns we would need to revisit the key principles of a globalised capitalist economic system. Even though we are addressing an empirical question, the discussion below is theoretical in nature. Thus, the actual effect could very well turn out to be different. In the absence of sufficient and reliable data, this is perhaps the best analytical way forward in understanding the macroeconomic effects of the pandemic.

The globalised economic system depends on the movement of goods, services, labour, capital, and raw materials.[1] Goods and services move from the locations where they are produced to the locations where they are consumed. They could be final goods and services reaching the final consumers or they could be intermediate goods and services moving between producers. Labour moves from its place of residence to the factories or offices to work. Fixed capital (office buildings etc.) could be stationary but capital goods travel long distances between producers to facilitate production. The same applies to raw materials that typically travel around the globe to reach factories where they are transformed into final or intermediate goods.

The movement of goods, services, and factors of production takes place via the supply chain. In the process, they change hands and these transactions take place in markets. Movement requires the use of transport services. Transactions even in an age of electronic communications require significant degree of human contact. All of this is made possible in a modern globalised economy due to relatively low and continually declining transport costs. The pandemic, subsequent lockdowns, and the sharp decline in economic activity have demonstrated to what extent modern economies rely on transport and human contact in order to conclude transactions.

By disrupting transport, limiting contact, and reducing transactions the pandemic and the restrictive measures have partially frozen the lifeblood of the world economy. Given the intensity and geographical expanse of the pandemic, it can now be said that it will leave a profound impact on the world economy. The impact on individual economies would of course vary. I will discuss the individual effects in the next section. Here, I will describe the theoretical demand and supply-side effects of the pandemic.

---

[1]Labour, capital, and raw materials are otherwise known as factors of production.

12.2 Demand Response

As the disease started spreading from China to other parts of the world, the initial demand response was positive. Predictably, large sections of the population panicked on the face of uncertainty. Therefore, consumers in large numbers brought forward their purchases accumulating inventory of essential commodities anticipating a future lockdown. This positive demand shock disrupted supply chains with retailers and distributors struggling to maintain their stock on shop floors due to unusually high demand. This, however, was short lived. After four to five weeks following the panic demand started to fall. As the epidemic intensified, governments imposed lockdowns restricting movement. This undoubtedly restricted the ability of consumers to visit shops. Many switched online. However, online platform and associated delivery infrastructure were not fit for purpose to manage such high volume. It is impossible to add logistical capacity overnight. Vans need to be purchased; drivers need to be appointed etc. Therefore, the supply chain for online purchases also collapsed contributing to the general fall in demand.

The first casualty of the restrictive measures was the airline industry. With the advent of budget air travel, this industry typically operates with a fairly slim margin. National carriers may receive subsidies from the state budget but this cannot be said about a large array of private passenger carriers. In a competitive marketplace such as passenger transport, companies are under continuous pressure to issue cheaper tickets to lure passengers. With relatively high fuel, personnel, and rental costs the profit margins of most carriers are not significant. As a result, following restrictions on air travel many companies are under stress and steadily laying off workers in order to survive the shock.

The second casualty is the hospitality industry. Hotels, restaurants, cafes, bars, and clubs rely on tourists and outdoor life. Restrictions on movement and zero influx of tourists meant they had to shut down. Some of the workers received temporary government assistance. However, as the pandemic perseveres, unemployment in the hospitality industry is likely to be high. The overall negative outlook for the hospitality industry is likely to continue for a long time as government support for the industry is gradually withdrawn.

The third casualty is transport and retail. As demand shrinks and retailers shut down their stores, the demand for transport services would continue to fall. This will also contribute to job losses. This is likely to have a more severe impact in Western nations where a significant proportion of the non-graduate male workforce engage in driving for a living. Truck driving, local removal services, taxis, and couriers are common semiskilled professions in Western developed economies.

Some workers are temporarily compensated by their employers or the government due to the economic hardship imposed by the lockdown. However, as the pandemic perpetuates, many of the short-term unemployed are likely to become long-term unemployed thus significantly aggravating labour market and macroeconomic challenges.

With high unemployment, household income falls over time delivering a second round medium-term contractionary effect from the demand side. The Keynesian multiplier could potentially magnify such contractionary effect as it passes through the economy. The magnitude of the contractionary effect in a country would depend on its initial condition and parameter values. The initial conditions and parameter values vary across countries. Therefore, the contractionary effects would also vary across countries.

12.3 Financial Market Volatility in the Short Run

Predictably, the uncertainty associated with the pandemic caused turmoil in the financial markets. The equity market is spooked by the pandemic and is sceptical about the medium run revenue prospects of the listed companies. The markets suspect that transport, tourism, retail, energy, and airline sectors would encounter a prolonged drop in revenue thereby making it difficult for them to service their current credit obligations. Firms in these sectors are unlikely to churn out profits and pay dividends. Many of them might not survive the pandemic. These effects might spread to other sectors of the economy through the credit channel (derivatives) or supply chain. Therefore, the overall sentiment in the equity market remains negative with large sell-offs not seen since the Great Depression. On average equity markets around the world collapsed by approximately 30 percent during the first four months following the COVID-19 outbreak. Even though the market stabilised after the initial turmoil, the sentiment remains overwhelmingly negative. Likewise, the outlook going forward is also negative and uncertain.

The initial movement in the equity market is expectation induced. As investors sold off shares, the demand for bonds and dollar liquidity increased strengthening the dollar against all currencies. Capital inflow into the United States also increased. This is the first sign of financial panic as investors typically flee to the safe haven. Holding US dollar liquidity (cash) or buying government bonds (US Treasury bonds) are considered safe relative to holding equity. Demand for US government bonds increased sharply reducing Treasury bond yields to historic lows. Furthermore, the demand for gold (another safe haven) also increased and continues to increase progressively.

Western governments responded swiftly to the collapse in the equity markets by announcing expansionary fiscal and monetary policies. The market was not convinced by the policy response. The slide continued albeit at a slower pace and then stabilising at a low-level equilibrium. I will discuss policy response separately below.

12.4 The Oil Shock

Amid the pandemic induced equity market chaos in March 2020, the Organisation of the Petroleum Exporting Countries (OPEC) met in Vienna along with the non-OPEC petroleum producing countries led by Russia to review their existing production cut agreement which was due to expire on 31 March 2020. This agreement is commonly referred to as the OPEC+ agreement. Petroleum prices were already sliding amid the pandemic and the financial market turmoil. Saudi Arabia, the de facto leader of OPEC demanded that the non-OPEC countries agree to an additional production cut of 1.5 million barrels a day till the end of 2020. Russia responded to this proposal by suggesting that the existing market conditions are too volatile to merit a firm decision. Therefore, their position was to extend the existing arrangement for another month (till the end of April) to get a clear view of the demand trajectory. This was not acceptable for Saudi Arabia and their representatives withdrew from further negotiations. The Saudi Crown Prince announced that Saudi Arabia would increase production instead and sell its oil at a discount in the European and American markets.

Due to the Saudi posture, crude oil prices collapsed to 20 US dollars a barrel. It was the lowest crude price recorded since the 1990s. This set financial markets into a tailspin. US Crude oil benchmark the West Texas Intermediate (WTI) collapsed even lower and turned negative for a short while threatening the viability of the entire US oil industry. Moreover, the Saudi and other Gulf country overproduction triggered a supply glut not witnessed during the post-war period. The world started rapidly running out of storage space (including offshore storage space such as oil tankers) for crude. Recognising the threat to the US oil industry, which the US government considers to be a strategic asset, the US President Donald Trump lobbied hard with OPEC and non-OPEC countries to arrive at an agreement. More on this later.

12.5 Supply Response

It is expected that the demand side contraction would be coupled with negative supply-side effects. The lockdowns imposed by governments all around the world would automatically cut production. In addition, low demand going forward would force firms to cut production. There will be low demand for consumer durables given declining disposable income. Contraction in the transport sector would limit demand for cars. The supply response facing low demand in these sectors would also be contractionary. A contractionary supply response for final goods would have contractionary knock-on effects on the capital goods, intermediate goods, and raw material sectors. It is likely that the initial contractionary demand effect would be magnified manyfold through the knock-on effects on supply. This undoubtedly would cause mass unemployment and an even weaker demand creating a vicious cycle. All of these sectors, especially in the Western world (what I have referred to as the Atlantic Alliance throughout the book) have significant credit exposure. Therefore, the risk of mass defaults and a potential transnational banking crisis remains high.

It is not difficult to envisage that there would be problems in the agriculture sector and the food supply chain. Farmers in developed countries have significant credit exposure. Many small and medium-sized farmers typically rent their plot and machinery for farming. They rely on short-term credit from financial institutions to meet their rental cost. A pandemic induced credit crunch would hit them hard. It is likely that financial institutions would charge a higher risk premium on short-term loans making credit expensive and farming unprofitable. Furthermore, fruits and vegetables farms typically use seasonal migrant workers for planting and fruit picking. Widespread travel ban and lockdowns would increase their labour cost and possibly even cause labour shortages. Facing these shocks many and especially small and medium-sized farms focusing on fruits and vegetables could go out of business. This would reduce supply and would be inflationary. Some of these effects are already apparent in food-deficit countries in Europe. The full extent of the effect will be known during the final quarter of 2020 and the first two quarters of 2021.

How about the effect of the pandemic on the grain market. Let us focus on wheat and rice. Farming in large wheat producing countries such as Russia, the United States, Canada, and Australia are capital intensive and therefore their operations are likely to be relatively less affected by the pandemic. The picture in rice could be starkly different. Let us focus on India and Thailand, two large rice producing countries. Rice cultivation in India and Thailand remain labour intensive. Plots are typically small in India and there are numerous near subsistence farmers operating in this sector. Lockdown in India coincides with the crop-planting season. Paddy planting typically relies on seasonal migrant agricultural workers who travel across provinces to work on land. They are unable to travel due to the lockdown. This will adversely affect output. Large-scale default on credit by farmers might follow further exposing financial institutions with exposure to agricultural loans. Challenges for Thailand and Southeast Asia are somewhat different. The entire region is experiencing a drought. This is negatively affecting production. The pandemic will aggravate the negative effects.

Overall, it is expected that the pandemic would push grain prices in the upward direction. Low production and supply chain disruption are the likely causes. Grain importing developing countries are the most vulnerable. The poor would suffer most from food price inflation. However, given the overall magnitude of the negative shock worldwide, developed countries are also not immune to food price inflation and shortages.

A demand and supply-side contraction of this magnitude is likely to trigger banking crisis, especially in countries where the financial system is extremely overleveraged. All the Anglophone countries (Australia, Canada, Britain, and the United States) and the EU are places to watch for a potential banking crisis, which could complicate the macroeconomic challenges even further. The risk of contagion is also high given cross-border interlinkages in banking through financial derivatives.

12.6 Policy Response and Hyperinflation Risks

Appreciating the sheer magnitude of the economic challenges, governments around the world have announced numerous stimulus packages to protect the economy from the pandemic. Here I will discuss the economic merit of these measures and the underlying risks.

So far, the measures have included monetary policy and fiscal policy. The former is primarily to ensure financial and price stability while the latter is to mitigate the negative effects of the pandemic on the labour market and businesses. In all the advanced economies of the Atlantic Alliance (the United States, Britain, and the European Union), central banks have committed themselves to unlimited asset purchases. This implies that central banks would continue to purchase all the assets including equity not absorbed by the other agents indefinitely. Where would the central bank get resources to conduct such operations? All the central banks who have committed to unlimited Quantitative Easing (QE) also reduced their target interest rate to either zero or near zero. Note that QE is electronic money printing where the central bank creates electronic money for the commercial banks encouraging them to lend. The current QE is intended to provide unlimited liquidity to the interbank lending market. Furthermore, it is intended to support the central bank's asset purchase programmes. This level of market intervention and extension of central bank balance sheets is unprecedented in post-war history. The monetary policy operations can be summed up as a ginormous corporate debt monetisation programme not seen in recent economic history.

On the fiscal side, countries have announced a wide array of policies ranging from helicopter money, direct payments to the temporary unemployed to loan guarantees. The Trump Administration in the United States instituted helicopter money by offering 1000 US dollars payment to all households. They have also instituted waiver of student loans and loan guarantee for small and medium-sized businesses. Britain instituted loan guarantees for small businesses and direct time-limited payments (up to 80 percent of income) to the temporarily unemployed and the self-employed. I will not discuss the details of these policies here. Instead, I will focus on the macroeconomic consequences of these policies.

Fiscal policies instituted by the governments undoubtedly eased short-term pain in the labour market. It has also stabilised demand up to an extent in the short term. However, longer the pandemic persists and longer the lockdowns are kept in place, these measures are likely to be insufficient to support demand. Moreover, they would jeopardise fiscal sustainability of the individual governments. Some governments do have more fiscal space than others. For example, the United States government have more borrowing capacity than Britain because the dollar is the world reserve currency while the pound sterling clearly is not. Nevertheless, all the sovereigns within the Atlantic Alliance (with the exception of Germany) remain heavily indebted. Therefore, their borrowing capacity is not unlimited.

Another source of macroeconomic and financial instability is the energy market. After several weeks of turmoil following the failure of OPEC+ to reach an agreement in early March, some stability appears to have been restored. OPEC+ agreed on a new deal to gradually cut production by 9.7 million barrels starting 1 May 2020 for two months following which the cuts will decline to eight million barrels and would stay so till the end of 2020. OPEC+ expects other non-OPEC large oil exporters such as the United States, Canada, and Norway to voluntarily cut production by additional ten million barrels to stabilise price. Canada and Norway oil ministers have already confirmed that they will comply. The United States indicated that the market realities would force a drop in their production, especially in the shale patch.

As I have identified above, the source of inflation could be from the supply side and therefore traditional monetary policy through the interest rate channel may not be effective. Moreover, the monetary policy measures and especially debt monetisation could significantly magnify the risk of hyperinflation which I discuss next.

Under normal circumstances, governments finance their expenditure by collecting taxes. If the expenditure exceeds tax revenue then the government runs a budget deficit and borrows from the credit market by issuing bonds. The realities of the ongoing economic crisis and the promised fiscal response would force governments to drift beyond the usual. The scale of debt creation in already heavily indebted Atlantic Alliance economies would necessitate debt monetisation. Debt monetisation or seignorage is a practice where the central bank prints money to buy government bonds through the asset purchase programme to finance government expenditure. This happens when there are not enough buyers of government bonds.

Let me explain why the risk of a bond market collapse (i.e. a drastic decline in bond price due to lack of demand) now is real. Within the Euro-Atlantic economic space (I am also including Japan here) all sovereigns are heavily indebted. Germany has a relatively cleaner balance sheet but Germany would need to finance its own expenditure following the contractionary shock. The same applies to the corporate sector, which is also highly leveraged. Countries that have the cleanest sovereign and corporate balance sheets are Russia and China. They are geopolitical rivals of the Atlantic Alliance and therefore unlikely to buy sovereign bonds issued by the latter unless major concessions are offered. Therefore, the existing financial system would be unable to absorb such a massive excess supply of bonds. Debt monetisation would be the only viable option.

The economics of what I described above is straightforward. A country's current account is defined as net payments received from abroad due to exports or ownership of foreign assets. Therefore, it is a measure of the country's external financial balance. A current account deficit implies foreigners have more claims on the country's economy. Similarly, a current account surplus implies locals have more claims on the foreign economy. The laws of macroeconomics dictate that a country's external financial balance (or current account) should equate to its internal financial balance. Internal financial balance is the sum of government financial balance and the private sector financial balance. In other words, current account should be equal to the sum of net government saving and private sector saving.[2]

Now consider the typical Atlantic Alliance country with current account deficit, large budget deficit and sovereign debt, and large private sector deficit (a highly leveraged private sector). Any attempt to borrow further can only take place either by increasing private sector savings (i.e. selling bonds to the private sector—corporates, pension funds) or by reducing the current account deficit. A highly leveraged and exposed private sector cannot buy more bonds without triggering a sharp recession. Central bank led QE and asset purchase programmes are trying to encourage more private sector borrowing which is exactly opposite of private sector buying government bonds (i.e. saving or deleveraging). Reducing the current account deficit for countries with large trade deficits imply reducing net foreign asset positions. In other words, encouraging foreigners to buy bonds. However, as I have illustrated above all other members of the Atlantic Alliance are already saturated with debt and are trying to sell their bonds at the same time. Countries (Russia and China) with strong sovereign balance sheets are unlikely to be interested. Therefore, the risk of a bond market crisis is relatively high. The risk could be minimised through international policy coordination, but international cooperation and goodwill are in short supply in the current environment.

Failure to sell bonds implies there is only seignorage or debt monetisation left as an option to finance the deficit. Seignorage is directly increasing in money growth. However, it is also indirectly decreasing in money growth through its relationship with inflation expectations and money demand. This is demonstrated by the equation $S = \frac{\Delta M}{M} \overline{Y} L\left(\overline{r} + \frac{\Delta M}{M}\right)$ where *S*, *M*, *Y*, *r*, *L*(.) are seignorage, money supply, output, real interest rate, and money demand, respectively. A stagnant or falling output and potentially high inflation expectation working from the supply side could increase the need for debt monetisation beyond the optimal level. If tax revenue collapses then more and more seignorage would be necessary fuelling inflation expectations even further. A negative real interest rate would not be able to outweigh the money demand collapse due to persistent high inflation expectation. Open capital account and free movement of capital would complicate the challenges even further. In an open economy, $\overline{r} + \frac{\Delta M}{M} = i* - \Delta E^e_{t+1}$ where $i*$, ΔE^e_{t+1} are the world interest rate and the expected appreciation in nominal exchange rate, respectively. Seignorage and high inflation expectation would mean high money growth which could lead to rapid depreciation of the national currency triggering a currency crisis. A currency crisis would invariably trigger hyperinflation and end badly. Even though hard to imagine under normal circumstances, the risks are now real and should be given due consideration.

[2]For the more mathematically minded $(S^p_t - I_t) + S^g_t - CA_t = 0$, $CA_t = NFA_t - NFA_{t-1}$, and $CA_t = NX_t + rNFA_t$ where $S^p_t, I_t, S^g_t, CA_t, NX_t, NFA_t$ are private saving, investment, government saving, current account, net exports, and net foreign assets, respectively.

12.7 Asset Markets and the Macro Economy: Long-Run Effects

The long-term outlook for the developed country asset market is negative. The global economy has not witnessed twin contractionary demand and supply-side shocks since the Second World War. Indeed, we are in uncharted territory and predicting the future is not easy. Nevertheless, the risk of a financial crisis is real.

The pandemic is already causing mass unemployment. The labour market challenges would intensify over time. If the pandemic persists and governments have to impose lockdowns in order to contain it then the current short-term unemployed risk becoming long-term unemployed. Search costs and other labour market frictions would not make it easy for the long-term unemployed to return to the workforce. High unemployment is correlated with mortgage defaults. Households in advanced economies of the Atlantic Alliance have very high exposure to mortgage debt. It is difficult to measure the magnitude of the problem at this stage. If indeed defaults are widespread then banks and mortgage lenders would be unlikely to absorb all the losses. Some of them might fold. If the other surviving financial institutions are exposed to the bad assets through financial derivatives then the contagion would be large. We would be experiencing a serious financial crisis.

12.8 The United States, China, Russia, India, and the EU: Key Powers in a Future System?

The transition towards a multipolar international system that was already set in motion after the dissolution of the USSR will only accelerate going forward. In what follows, I analyse what effect this transition will have on each of the major powers.

12.8.1 The United States

> The surreal atmosphere of the Covid-19 pandemic calls to mind how I felt as a young man in the 84th Infantry Division during the Battle of the Bulge. Now, as in late 1944, there is a sense of inchoate danger, aimed not at any particular person, but striking randomly and with devastation. But there is an important difference between that faraway time and ours. American endurance then was fortified by an ultimate national purpose. Now, in a divided country, efficient and farsighted government is necessary to overcome obstacles unprecedented in magnitude and global scope. Henry A. Kissinger (2020)

The United States overextended itself since the conclusion of the cold war in 1991. Some of its major weaknesses going forward would be its highly leveraged economy, near unsustainable sovereign debt-to-GDP ratio, erosion of its industrial base, extremely high military spending, expensive social entitlement programmes, and overreliance on the service sector. In addition to sovereign debt, the United States has very high exposure to household and corporate debts. Its budget and trade deficits continue to grow and it relies heavily on capital inflow from abroad. In other words, it maintains a large current account deficit which is growing over time. Its net foreign asset position is negative and growing over time.

So far, this has been manageable due to the global reserve currency status of the dollar. There is significant external demand for the dollar as it is widely used in international trade-related transactions, especially in the market for raw materials (petroleum, industrial metals etc.). However, an unprecedented pandemic induced demand and supply shock is likely to put immense pressure on the dollar. The US macroeconomic balance sheet is weak thus increasing the risk of a currency crisis and hyperinflation.[3] The policy response following the pandemic and lockdown relies heavily on increasing leverage even further.[4] Furthermore, it also offers an unprecedented fiscal stimulus (2 trillion dollars) effectively doubling the US Federal budget in a month. Such policy framework assumes that the pandemic induced lockdown is not going to last beyond 8–12 weeks. Therefore, the recession that would follow a lockdown is functional and not structural. Following the relaxation of lockdown, recovery from a functional recession would be swift and thus expanding leverage is not a risky strategy.

There are two major downsides to this strategy which is worth noting here. First, the United States economy has deep structural problems. As I have discussed above, its economy is highly leveraged. Therefore, the recession following a lockdown is unlikely to be functional if the pandemic lasts for 12 weeks or more. Job lost in the service sector, an important sector for the United States economy, would be difficult to regain within a short span of time. The pandemic would unleash unpredictable political forces, which could alter the current model of globalisation. It is highly likely that the rules of engagement in international trade and finance would change. These changes may not be favourable to the reserve currency status of the dollar. A highly leveraged economy would not work in favour of the dollar.

Due to the reasons outlined above, the impending structural recession in the United States would be deep and protracted. Undoubtedly, the effect of this economic contraction would not be uniform across society. This would likely unleash bitter distributional conflicts within the American polity. The sharp division in American politics following the election of Donald J. Trump is not a favourable starting point. Failure to unite the country could make distributional conflicts sharp and debilitating. The litmus test for national unity would be period after the presidential election in November.

Nevertheless, being a continental economy America has vast reserves of resources. Therefore, in the medium to long run it is likely to recover. However, its global military footprint would decline. The economic necessities would force

[3]See the previous section for a discussion on the economics of hyperinflation.

[4]See discussion on unlimited asset purchase in the previous section.

America to retreat. Its aggressive military and foreign policy posture would wane. In spite of the weaknesses and challenges, it will remain a great power in the future.

12.8.2 China

China has vast amount of resources. It has massive financial reserves and low sovereign debt. It did increase private sector leverage following the 2008 financial crisis, but it is sustainable. China has strong macroeconomic balance sheet with large and persistent trade surplus and current account surplus. It has a large internal market of over a billion people. The economy mainly relies on manufacturing and it has a relatively low exposure to services. China definitely has policy space to grow its economy by boosting internal consumption. The OBR initiative and its close coordination with the Russian led EAEU would work in favour of the Chinese economy. These projects encompass economies with unutilised capacity. Therefore, realisation of the common infrastructure projects and market integration within the OBR-EAEU space would deliver scale economies to China sustaining its economic expansion.

Chinese foreign policy stance is less militaristic compared to the United States or the Atlantic Alliance. China's military spending is approximately 10 times less than the United States and miniscule compared to the entire Atlantic Alliance. This would work in China's favour going forward.

China is the only country so far to have successfully contained the COVID-19 epidemic. Therefore, it can start operating its economy at near capacity. It would suffer knock-on effects from the ongoing global recession but it is likely to be mild and brief. China has policy space. It will focus on domestic demand to ride the short-term negative demand induced shock. It will recover fast once the world reaches a permanent solution to the COVID-19 induced public health crisis.

Unlike the United States or Russia, China is not a continental economy. It is labour abundant but resource poor. However, it has strong neighbourhood advantages. The combined resources of a Russia–China alliance surpass any other alliance. Chinese authorities appear to be acutely aware of this fact and invest heavily in maintaining good relations with Russia. With the realisation of integration projects within OBR and EAEU, the China–Russia alliance will gain strength. Therefore, overall China is likely to have significantly more influence in international affairs barring a repeat of the Sino-Soviet split of the 1960s. Such split looks unlikely in the near future.

12.8.3 Russia

Russia enters the COVID-19-induced economic crisis with the strongest macroeconomic balance sheet of all the major economies. It has massive reserves relative to the size of its economy and extremely low sovereign debt. Its corporate external debt is also very low. Its banks are well capitalised as it underwent banking reforms following the 2015 sanctions and oil price induced negative shock. Banks have very little exposure to external debt, as they cannot borrow on the Western financial markets due to sanctions. Russia leads a large market of 170 million people within the EAEU. The economy relies on agriculture and industry including raw materials and manufacturing. It has a service sector footprint mainly in urban areas but it is not as large as other advanced Western economies. It has high per capita income measured using the purchasing power parity (PPP) exchange rate.

Being a continental economy, it has all the resources required for economic expansion. It is labour scarce but resource and skill abundant. Following the EU and American imposed sanctions regime in 2015, it has successfully pursued import substitution policy rapidly diversifying its economy. It is self-sufficient in food and the largest exporter of grains (wheat and wheat-based products) in the world. It has a highly competitive raw materials sector. It also operates R&D intensive high-tech manufacturing industries such as aviation, space, automobiles, nuclear energy, and petrochemicals. It also has a vibrant information technology (IT) industry that is growing at a rapid pace.

Russia also has strong neighbourhood advantages. It is rapidly integrating its economy with the fast-growing economies of Asia and especially China. As I have mentioned earlier, the combined resources of a Russia–China alliance surpass any other alliance. Russian authorities like the Chinese authorities also appear to be acutely aware of this fact. Multi-level integration is currently underway using the EAEU, OBR, and SCO platforms.

Being the third largest exporter of crude following the United States and Saudi Arabia, Russia has significant influence on the market for this strategic resource. It has influences on a significant number of key market participants within OPEC and beyond. Therefore, in spite of the relatively moderate size of its economy, Russia's economic influence around the world cannot be underestimated.

As the successor of a superpower such as the USSR, Russia's diplomatic influence around the globe cannot be underestimated either. Russia is a permanent member of the United Nations Security Council. It has a strong conventional military force and a very competitive military industrial complex. It is the second largest exporter of armaments only next to the United States. It has strong military defence relationships with large countries such as India, Algeria, and Egypt. Its trade relationships with these countries are growing. The Syrian and Ukrainian conflicts are a testament to the military and diplomatic powers of Russia. It has successfully lured NATO power Turkey into acquiring Russian anti-aircraft missile system such as the S-400.

Undoubtedly, Russia will suffer from the negative consequences of the pandemic. The pandemic reached Russia late and remains largely contained. The human losses so far are less significant relative to the rest of the world. It has one of the lowest fatality rates from the pandemic. Russia is self-sufficient in medicine to tackle the pandemic. It has sufficient stocks of the locally produced drug Avifavir to treat the virus. It is also the first country in the world to complete clinical testing of its coronavirus vaccine. Nevertheless, the pandemic drained Russian government resources. It caused high unemployment mainly in the urban services sector. However, the negative effects are small relative to other major economies. Given Russia's strong macroeconomic fundamentals and its proximity to the Chinese and Asian markets, the ongoing recession is unlikely to be structural. Therefore, it is likely that the Russian economy will bounce back fast.

The long-term economic outlook also appears to be positive given the scale economy opportunities that the EAEU and OBR integration projects will unleash. The Russian government is currently investing heavily into infrastructure (hospital, roads, housing). It is also digitising the economy and modernising public services at a rapid pace. These are likely to deliver significant productivity dividends in the medium to long term. Overall, it is expected that the Russian influence in international affairs would only grow.

12.8.4 India

India's macroeconomic balance sheet is stable. However, it would face major challenges in the short run. It has a relatively high stock of corporate debt. Bank balance sheets in India are not strong as most banks carry a large burden of non-performing assets (or loans). Many loans issued by the banks are unlikely to be repaid even though they remain on the bank's ledger as assets.

India also has high exposure to FDI-dependent service sector jobs. India specialises in the offshoring economy and especially the back office functions of large multinational corporations. These formal sector jobs are related to the health of the parent company. Therefore, India is particularly vulnerable to external financial market volatility. If there are losses in the value of the parent company in the global financial markets, then local job losses will follow. These losses could very well be structural if there are policy changes in the home country of the multinational corporation.

Job losses in the formal sector could have adverse knock-on effects on the large informal sector. In spite of India's recent economic success, it still remains one of the poorest in the world. In fact, World Bank estimates that the total number of absolute poor residing in India is far greater than the same in Africa. A crisis in the formal sector would present significant challenges for the Indian informal sector.

Moreover, the pace of the COVID-19 epidemic in India appears to be rapid. There are question marks concerning testing and reliability of the published data on infections and fatalities. Therefore, the actual extent of the pandemic could be even more severe. Eventually, India like all other countries will recover from this crisis even though the losses would be far greater than comparable economies. India's success would depend on reorienting its economy towards the rapidly growing Southeast Asia and the strengthening of its vast internal market. Indeed, India has strong neighbourhood advantages. It also has untapped potential, a seemingly unlimited supply of young workforce (demographic dividend), and a very large internal market. The degree of Indian engagement into the integration projects of EAEU and OBR would define India's destiny going forward.

12.8.5 The European Union

What's at stake is the survival of the European project. The risk we are facing is the death of Schengen. Emmanuel Macron, President of France, 26 March 2020, Source: Reuters

The European Union entered the pandemic-induced economic crisis ill prepared. The public health crisis rapidly escalated in Italy, Spain, France, and elsewhere. The European Union member countries have extremely weak macroeconomic balance sheet. Almost all the major EU economies have unsustainable sovereign debt. They are also locked into a common currency that makes their economy uncompetitive. The corporate balance sheets are not sustainable either. Sovereign debts in Italy, Spain, France, and Portugal are extremely high. Major European banks have very high exposure to this debt. The sovereign debt position is likely to worsen even further with the COVID-19 induced public health crisis and lockdowns. The ongoing recession is likely to be deep and protracted.

Even though the Euro is the second most used currency in the world, it does not have the same privileges as the dollar. Therefore, it is much more fragile and essentially relies on the macroeconomic balance sheet of Germany.

The public health crisis exposed weakness of the European projects as the member states had to fend for themselves. No meaningful help arrived from Brussels. It became very apparent that national governments are more effective in tackling public health challenges than supranational structures.

On economic issues, the heavily indebted nations of Greece, France, Italy, and Spain pushed for debt mutualisation. Their joint position during the recent EU Commission meeting was fiscal consolidation and the issuance of joint Eurobonds. If adopted, such proposal would imply a common tax system and more taxes in the future for the surplus countries of Germany, the Netherlands, Denmark, Austria, Finland, and Slovakia. In other words, taxpayers in the surplus countries would have to pay for the debt of the deficit countries. The joint French, Spanish, Italian, and Greek position in support of debt mutualisation was flatly rejected by the surplus countries. There is no realistic prospect of such proposal passing a German veto as this is against a ruling by the German Constitutional Court, which deems European debt mutualisation 'unconstitutional'. As an alternative, Germany proposed strengthening the European Stability Mechanism (ESM) from the current 500 billion Euro to a trillion Euro. It is questionable whether this will ward off an impending sovereign debt crisis. Even if it does, the ESM would impose more austerity on the deficit countries weakening their economies even further. It remains to be seen whether the indebted countries would accept such a debt trap.

Regardless of the outcome of current round of negotiations on the ESM, the Euro remains unsustainable. It is likely that the deficit countries would have to eventually exit the Euro. The pandemic-induced economic crisis and another round of austerity imposed by the creditors behind the new ESM would unleash unpredictable political forces that could permanently change the European political landscape. The already battered European Union may not survive such a political earthquake.

12.9 Final Word

We are standing on the threshold of a multipolar world order. This new order was long time in the making but the pace of transformation accelerated following the ongoing coronavirus pandemic. As it appears so far, the pandemic is disproportionately affecting the Western Alliance, especially the United States and the EU. However, the risk of a second wave elsewhere remains significant. It is beyond doubt that the pandemic will leave indelible impact on the international system. In the emerging multipolar world order, China, Russia, and perhaps India are likely to have leading roles. Given the resource endowments and mutual compatibility, the combined economic power of China and Russia is likely to surpass that of any other competing alliances. So far India has maintained a safe distance from any potential alliance but the post-pandemic economic realities may very well change this position. It is likely that India will increasingly align with Russia and China on economic issues and with the United States on security issues. The United States is likely to remain a significant player in a multipolar order but its overleveraged and fragile economy will force it to retreat. It is unlikely to remain a hyper power. The future of the European Union appears to be uncertain. It may or may not survive the existential challenge thrown its way by the pandemic. The pandemic has exposed inherent weaknesses of its overleveraged economy and institutions. It does not possess military power of any significance. The outcome of the existential challenge will decide whether the European Union will have a seat on the high table.

We are witnessing a critical juncture in economic history where the future is likely to be significantly different from the past. The international economic system, especially since 1991 has relied on three fundamental principles namely free movement of goods and factors of production, financial leverage, and greed. The pandemic-induced public health crisis has rudely exposed weakness of that system. The impending economic crisis would force many countries to rethink the three fundamental principles of global engagement. I suspect many would choose a system based on need, less leverage, and factor movement restrictions. This undoubtedly would shape elite feuds and imperial expansions of the future.

Bibliography

Kissinger, H. (2020). The coronavirus pandemic will forever alter the world order. *The Wall Street Journal*, 3 April, 2020.

Part V
A Survey of the Literature

Chapter 13
Long-Run Economic Development: A Survey of the Literature

Abstract This chapter presents a review of the literature on long-run economic development. It may not be exhaustive and I am sure I have missed many. Nevertheless, this should offer the reader a wide spectrum of views in this literature.

Discussing the causes of economic expansion, Samuelson (1976) writes, '*No new light has been thrown on the reason why poor countries are poor and rich countries are rich*'. A large literature followed attempting to identify the sources of economic expansion (Sachs and Warner 1997a; Easterly 2009). Easterly (2001) and Easterly and Levine (2001) offer reviews of the early literature. More recently, Bhattacharyya (2011) presents a review of the theories of long-term economic and political expansion. Here I present a summary of that review.[1]

Institutions and Economic Development:

> Little else is required to carry a state to the highest degree of opulence from the lowest barbarism, but peace, easy taxes and tolerable administration of justice; all the rest being brought about by the natural course of things—Adam Smith (cited in Jones 1981, pp. 253).

This is how Adam Smith described the role of institutions in economic expansion. Even though many scholars have referred to the role of institutions as an organising principle of society, the contemporary definition of institution is associated with North (1981, 1989, 1994). North (1994) defines institutions as humanly devised constraints that shape human interaction. The constraints are in the form of rules. They comprise of formal and informal rules and in practice depend on how they are enforced. These rules shape economic and political incentives of a society in the very long run. For example, North (1989) demonstrates that the economic and political effects of the United States Constitution and the British Common Law are divergent from the centralised enforcement mechanism of Spain. The recent empirical literature tests these predictions (Hall and Jones 1999; Acemoglu et al. 2001; Easterly and Levine 2003; Rodrik et al. 2004) including a potential relationship between political

[1]Note that large sections of Chap. 13 is a reproduction of my earlier work Bhattacharyya (2011) with permission from the publisher.

S. Bhattacharyya, *A History of Global Capitalism*, Frontiers in Economic History,
https://doi.org/10.1007/978-3-030-58736-9_13

institutions and growth (Tavarez and Wacziarg, 2001). However, there are obvious challenges concerning causality (Glaeser et al. 2004; Bhattacharyya 2009a).

North's work subsequently led to numerous contributions exploring the effects of property rights on development. For example, Knack and Keefer (1995) and Hall and Jones (1999) argue that the key to success is private property rights and contract enforcement. Therefore, Western European prosperity could be explained by adherence to the institutional principles of private property and contract enforcement. These institutions migrated with the Western Europeans to the temperate colonies of the new world. Thus, institutional quality could be measured by the distance from the equator, the fraction of the population speaking English, and the fraction of population speaking other Western European languages. The key message thereof is that a significant presence of Western Europeans in a country is indicative of better institutional quality, fair redistributive justice, and economic expansion.

In a similar vein, Acemoglu et al. (2001) discuss the role of colonisation on institutional and economic divergence.[2] In colonies with temperate climate (Australia, New Zealand, the United States, and Canada) the disease environment was similar to Western Europe. As a result, the mortality rates of the colonisers were relatively low. In contrast, the disease environments faced by the colonisers in tropical colonies were hostile with higher incidence of malaria and yellow fever. As a result, the mortality rates for the colonisers were relatively high. This influenced the settlement decisions of the colonisers. In temperate climates, the colonisers established settlement colonies with institutions of private property and enforceable contracts. In tropical climates, the colonisers established extractive colonies where expropriation of private poverty and violation of contracts became the norm. The long-run consequence of such institutional divergence was economic divergence driven by economic expansion of the imperial core and secular decline of the non-temperate colonial periphery. In a subsequent study, Acemoglu et al. (2002) argue that the settlement decision of the European settlers also depended on the rate of urbanisation prior to 1500, the start of the period of colonisation. A high density of population in the colonies ruled out the possibility of settlement for the settlers and they erected extractive institutions. In contrast, low population density in the colonies encouraged the settlers to erect settlement colonies and build institutions conducive for capitalism.

The above explanation seems plausible. However, a key conundrum is the economic and institutional divergence across the settlement colonies in North and South America. Engerman and Sokoloff (2001) argue that such divergence could be due to initial conditions such as factor endowments. They write, '. . .a hemispheric perspective across the range of European colonies in the New World indicates that although there were many influences, the factor endowment or initial conditions more generally had profound and enduring impacts on the evolution of economic institutions, on the structure of the colonial economies, and ultimately on their

[2]Historians refer to the economic divergence between the West and the East as Great Divergence (see Broadberry and Gupta 2005).

long-run paths of institutional and economic development. While all began with an abundance of land and other resources relative to labour, at least after the initial depopulation, other aspects of their factor endowments varied—contributing to extreme differences in the distributions of land holdings, wealth, and of political power'.

In support of their factor endowment thesis, Engerman and Sokoloff (2001) argue that the climatic conditions of the North were favourable to mixed farming of grains and livestock that exhibited limited scale economies. This encouraged the development of small family farms and a relatively homogeneous population in terms of the distribution of wealth and political power. The result was better institutions favouring broader access to economic opportunities, more extensive domestic markets, and better overall growth. In contrast, the South and the Caribbean were endowed with vast mining resources and climates and soil conditions conducive to commercial crops such as sugar, tobacco, and cotton. To exploit these resources that exhibited large scale economies, it was efficient for the colonizers to set up large mining firms and plantations. These operations were run with African slave labour. This led to the establishment of a society where a large section of the population remained impoverished with no political or economic rights, whereas a small section, the political and economic elite, and appropriated all the wealth. The high level of inequality in the distribution of wealth and political power created institutions that are extractive, exploitative, and extremely unjust. These institutions persisted over time causing persistent inequality and economic stagnation. The highly concentrated landholdings and extreme inequality in Mexico, Colombia, and Peru during the colonial period are supportive of their story.

As institutions and distributive justice influence economic and political expansions, the converse may also hold. For example, initial endowment of resources dictate initial income and wealth, which in turn influences initial distribution of political power. Over time, such distribution of political power is reflected in the formal political institutions. Formal political institutions dictate the rules of the game for the future thereby influencing future economic growth and distribution. Future economic growth and distribution influences the future distribution of political power and political institutions. If a country gets dislocated from its institutional equilibrium, new demands for distributive justice may emerge leading to widespread changes in institutions and political regimes.

Acemoglu et al. (2005a) formalise these ideas. They distinguish between two components of political power—*de jure* and *de facto*. They define political power originating from formal political institutions in a society as *de jure* political power. Examples of formal political institutions are Monarchy, Democracy, Autocracy, Dictatorship etc. In contrast, *de facto* political power originates from informal political institutions which could potentially challenge the formal institutions. Examples of informal political institutions are economic and social interest groups etc. Acemoglu et al. (2005a) posit that the existing formal institutions determine the distribution of *de jure* and *de facto* political power in a society. *De facto* political power at a particular point in time also depends on the distribution of resources in that period. This shapes economic and political institutions. Current economic institutions influence current economic performance and future distributional outcomes. Future distribution of resources and future political institutions in turn influence subsequent distribution of political power, economic institutions, and economic performance. The following schematic diagram summarizes the link:

$$\left\{ \begin{array}{l} PI_t \Rightarrow djPP_t \& dfPP_t \\ DR_t \Rightarrow dfPP_t \end{array} \right\} \Rightarrow \left\{ \begin{array}{l} EI_t \Rightarrow Y_t \& DR_{t+1} \\ PI_{t+1} \end{array} \right\}$$

where *PI*, *DR*, *djPP*, *dfPP*, *EI*, & *Y* are political institutions, distribution of resources, *de jure* political power, *de facto* political power, economic institutions, and economic performance, respectively.

In a subsequent paper, Acemoglu et al. (2005b) show that the origin of capitalist institutions in early modern Europe is due to Atlantic trade. In particular, Atlantic trade and colonialism strengthened the political power of the seafaring merchants in Britain and the Netherlands. Over time, the merchants became stronger than the crown and imposed constraints on the monarchs. These constraints evolved in the form of property rights and contract enforcement. In contrast, in Portugal and Spain the crown maintained absolutist control over trading activities and therefore the institutional and economic outcomes were different from Britain and the Netherlands.

Subsequent work explores extension of franchise under the Anglo-American political model. Acemoglu and Robinson (2000) argue that the extension of franchise was a consequence of working-class struggle against the bourgeois elite. In particular, the Anglo-Saxon elite offered political concessions by extending franchise being fearful of mob violence similar to revolutionary France. This led to the demise of class society. In contrast, Galor and Moav (2006) identify technological progress as the main driver of extension of franchise. With the advent of the steam engine and skill intensive technological progress, the demand for skilled labour increased manyfold which led to investments in mass education and extension of political rights.

North et al. (2009) present a framework to explain open access and restricted capitalism. It states that the restricted capitalist states protect the monopoly power and rent of the politically influential elite by restricting entry. Violence, expropriation of private property, and higher taxes are the typical instruments used by the state to restrict entry. Entry restriction yields weak institutions that limit economic expansion in the long run.

In a similar vein, Thelen (1999, 2000) discusses the role of critical junctures in history that shapes institutions and economic progress. Rodrik (2005) and Shleifer and Vishny (1998) offer strategies of institutional reforms that could promote growth.

13.1 Religion, Culture, and Economic Development

> Respect the altar of every belief. Spanish America, limited to Catholicism to the exclusion of any other religion, resembles a solitary and silent convent of nuns…To exclude different religions in South America is to exclude the English, the Germans, the Swiss, the North Americans, which is to say the very people this continent most needs. To bring them without their religion is to bring them without the agent that makes them what they are.—Juan Bautista Alberdi (cited in Landes 2000, p. 5)

Nineteenth-century Argentine political theorist Juan Bautista Alberdi described religion, culture, and other informal institutions as significant in shaping the destiny of nations. Max Weber also repeated the same argument only half a century later in his thesis *The Protestant Ethic and the Spirit of Capitalism.* Weber (1930) argues that the epoch-making Protestant Reformation changed society and sowed the seeds of modern capitalism. Protestantism's emphasis on industry, thrift, and frugality along with its moral approval of risk taking and financial self-development created a social environment conducive to investment and the accumulation of private capital. This became an inspirational force in transforming traditional societies into modern capitalist ones. Catholicism on the other hand considered trade and accumulating riches to be sinful, an attitude which was quite inimical to economic progress.

Samuelsson (1993) points out that Weber's theory hardly applies to Lutheranism, which retained the traditional attitudes of Catholicism towards trade and commerce at least at the time of its inception. However, it undoubtedly applies to Calvinism which supports trade and commerce. One of the central themes of Calvinism is predestination. According to this belief, some individuals are chosen and saved by God while others are not. This process of selection by God is predestined and unalterable. Calvin in his discourse did not mention who had been chosen. Therefore, the only practical way for the followers of Calvin to attain salvation was by performing intense worldly activities. Calvin's doctrine encourages economic activity but condemns enjoying the fruits of such activity by means of leisure. The followers of Calvin consider morality to be a virtue not because it can bring salvation but because it helps in acquiring moral credit. All these characters of Calvinism are essential preconditions for economic progress. Thus, Weber (1930) concludes that Calvinism influences economic performance. Given the provocative nature of Weber's thesis, it is not hard to understand that it fails to achieve universal acceptance. In an influential study on religion and growth, Tawney (1926) rejects Weber's view. He argues that the English economy took off in the sixteenth century when the religious influence in the society was replaced by secular attitudes. Furthermore, Weber's thesis appears to be Eurocentric and unable to explain the development trajectories in locations with faith diversity.

Weber's emphasis on hard work and thrift reappears (even though in different forms) on numerous occasions in the literature. In particular, Landes (1998, 2003), Grief (1994), Putnam (1993) Clark (2007) and Kuran (1997) returns to this theme. Landes (1998) argue that the profit motive of the entrepreneurial class coupled with invention and productivity growth is the elixir of economic progress. Therefore, societies that encourage hard work, scientific thinking, and profit making are likely to be materially successful in the long run. He uses eighteenth-century Britain as an example to illustrate the effects of Protestant work ethic and values on economic performance. Landes (1998) argues that the supportive and tolerant role played by the church created the moral preconditions for Britain's numerous scientific successes during the industrial revolution. In contrast, Landes (1998) concludes that the Catholic Church in Portugal, Italy, and Spain were unsupportive of scientific enquiry and critical thinking thus halting progress even though these societies were the first to make significant progress in cartography and ocean navigation. He cites 'Roman Inquisition' in sixteenth-century Europe as evidence of religious intolerance and orthodoxy of the Catholic Church. The intolerance of the Inquisition stalled the European renaissance, Landes (1998) concludes. In summary, Landes' main argument is that the culture of intolerance in Catholicism and Islam limits the potential of a country to grow its economy. Protestantism, on the other hand, facilitates economic growth by encouraging hard work and scientific research.

Grief (1994) argues that the same set of formal institutions could produce different outcomes if there are differences in religion and culture. Clark (2007) also emphasises the role of hard work and thrift in economic expansion which he names as 'middle class virtues'. He argues that industrial revolution took place in Britain because the middle-class virtues spread down the social scale in the sixteenth and seventeenth century. The poor experienced relatively high death rates during this time. Therefore, they did not have enough surviving children. In contrast, the infant survival rate amongst the rich was higher. As a result, many of the rich offspring were forced down the social scale in marriage carrying middle-class virtues with them. This led to a change in work ethic of the entire society and rapid economic progress. Clark's thesis is criticised by many including Allen (2008) for the lack of evidence. Allen (2008) concludes that the evidence provided by Clark appears to be unreliable. Putnam (1993) analyses the negative effects of Catholicism on economic growth. He argues that Catholicism undermines horizontal bonds and generalised trust thus increasing transaction costs. Stulz and Williamson (2001) focus on the anti-usury stance of Catholicism and argue that it harms economic expansion in the long term. Temple (1998) tests the effect of informal institutions on economic progress using cross-national data and finds social capital and trust have significant effect on growth and especially in Africa.

13.2 Geography and Economic Development

Jared Diamond in his influential book *Guns, Germs and Steel* describes how geography affects living standards and history over the very long run. He writes,

> …the striking differences between the long-term histories of peoples of the different continents have been due not to innate differences in the peoples themselves but to differences in their environments…if the populations of Aboriginal Australia and Eurasia could have been interchanged during the Late Pleistocene, the original Aboriginal Australians would now be the ones occupying most of the Americas and Australia, as well

as Eurasia, while the original Aboriginal Eurasians would be the ones now reduced to downtrodden population fragments in Australia.—Jared Diamond (1997), Guns, Germs and Steel, p. 405.

The geography view of economic development could be divided into five different categories: the climate view, the agriculture view, the market proximity view, the disease view, and the sophisticated geography view.

The climate view could be traced back to Montesquieu (1748). It posits that the population in the tropics is not industrious enough largely due to the energy-sapping heat. Natural availability of food in abundance also makes tropical people idle. This has a direct and negative effect on human productivity and hence economic growth. In a recent study, Parker (2000) supports Montesquieu's argument. According to Parker (2000), an individual's desire to maximize utility is dependent on motivation, homeostasis and neural, autonomic, and hormonal adjustments. These physiological factors are governed by the hypothalamus. The activity of the hypothalamus is heavily dependent on thermodynamics. In hot conditions, the hypothalamus secretes hormones that negatively affect motivation and enterprise; whereas in the cold climate individuals are naturally hard working. These tendencies affect the steady-state level of income in these two regions. The average steady-state income in the cold climate is naturally higher than the average steady state in the hot climate. Hence, climate explains two-thirds of the per capita income differences between the tropics and the temperate. However, Parker (2000) and Montesquieu (1748) fail to explain why tropical and subtropical geographies were relatively more prosperous in the sixteenth century prior to European contact.

The agriculture view is due to Gallup and Sachs (2000) and maintains that high relative humidity and high night-time temperature in the tropics cause high plant respiration and slows down plant growth. Such deficiency in plant growth in the tropics is also related to the lack of nutrients in tropical soil. Humid tropical soils (alfisols, oxisols, and ultisols) are typically low in nutrients and organic matters. This limits plant growth and also causes soil erosion and acidification. In addition, the lack of frost allows a greater number of pests and pathogens to survive and breed. These factors have a debilitating impact on agricultural productivity and inhibit economic progress. In addition, Diamond (1997) contributes to the agriculture view by arguing that prior to the period of European colonisation of the tropics, Europeans used technology that was well suited for the temperate climate. In the late eighteenth and early nineteenth century, when the Europeans embarked on a colonisation drive, they introduced these technologies in the colonies. They worked well in the colonies with temperate climate but failed to deliver the same crop yield in the tropical climate. This explains the low productivity of tropical agriculture and hence slow economic progress.

The market proximity view is due to Sachs and Warner (1995b, 1997b), and Gallup et al. (1998). It is widely accepted that trade and commerce generate wealth and prosperity (Smith 1776). One of the important preconditions for trade is easy access to major markets. According to the market proximity view, unfavourable geographic location characterised by no or limited access to ports or ocean navigable waterways, being landlocked, is a major impediment to trade and commerce. Access to ports or major markets for landlocked geographies often involve crossing international borders thus raising transport cost, High transport cost discourages international trade thus limiting the size of the market. Absence of international trade in these economies confines all commercial activities into small internal markets. This causes an inefficient division of labour and underdevelopment. Sachs and Warner (1997b) note that poorer countries in Africa are typically inland and landlocked thus preventing these countries from effectively participating in international trade. Sachs and Warner (1997b) estimate that transport costs for these countries are typically too high.

The disease view is due to Gallup and Sachs (2001), Bloom and Sachs (1998), and Gallup et al. (1998). According to this view, malaria has a debilitating effect on human productivity thus directly affecting economic performance. Gallup and Sachs (2001) point out that the countries with intensive malaria grow their per capita income 1.3 percentage point slower than countries without malaria and a 10 percentage point reduction in malaria could result in a 0.3 percentage point increase in annual per capita income growth. Bloom and Sachs (1998) also report that the high incidence of malaria in sub-Saharan Africa reduces the annual growth rate by 1.3 percentage point a year. In other words, eradication of malaria in 1950 would have resulted in a doubling of current per capita income. Sachs (2003a) and Carstensen and Gundlach (2006) in their empirical study report strong and negative effects of malaria on economic progress even after controlling for institutions and openness. Sachs (2005) discusses the effects of malaria on economic progress in Africa and some potential remedies. Easterly (2006) presents a counterargument suggesting that the best way to tackle malaria is by improving living standards.

There is also a large literature on diseases that examine the effect of malaria in contemporary Africa and how malaria-affected African economic history. In particular, the former deals with the economic burden of malaria in contemporary Africa, while the latter deals with the historical impact of malaria and diseases on the continent's long-run economic development. I would group the former as the 'contemporary malaria view' whereas the latter as the 'historical malaria view'.

The 'contemporary malaria view' is due to Sachs (2003b). According to this view, malaria dramatically lowers labour productivity, the return on foreign investment, and raises transaction cost of international trade limiting development. Sachs (2003b) notes that these challenges are typically apparent in sub-Saharan Africa. I have already discussed some of the studies involved in this literature above.

Sachs (2003a) in a cross-country empirical study shows that institutions do matter but not exclusively. He highlights the prevalence of malaria as another important factor that should not be underestimated. In a series of studies Bloom and Sachs (1998), Gallup et al. (1998), and Gallup and Sachs (2001) show that infectious malaria has a debilitating effect on human productivity and directly affects economic performance. Sachs et al. (2004) argue that with malaria and subsequent low productivity of labour an agricultural labour in sub-Saharan Africa cannot generate enough marketable surplus, which also limits the prospect of market development.

Markets even if it develops remain concentrated at a local level. This is indicative of a 'low level equilibrium trap' in these economies.

Acemoglu et al. (2003) take a long view on the effect of malaria. They argue that disease environment influenced the balance of power between previously isolated populations when they come into contact. The local disease environment influenced the colonisation strategy and settlement decision setting up the path for future institutional development (Acemoglu et al. 2001, 2002). Therefore, disease environment affected the level of development indirectly through institutions. Their thesis is closely related to Phillip Curtin's work on the epidemiology of the new world and Africa (Curtin 1968). In this study, Curtin shows that epidemiological factors have influenced economic decisions and development patterns of the new world (particularly tropical America) and Africa.

In a similar vein, Miller (1982) uses Portuguese traveller records, missionary and church documents to show that frequent epidemics of malaria and yellow fever caused massive depopulation in the agriculturally marginal zones of West-Central Africa. Dias (1981) documents a similar population trend in nineteenth and twentieth century Angola. Stevenson (1968) reviews the effects of epidemics on morbidity and political systems in Africa. These studies collectively find that the effects of disease, epidemics, and famines were far more powerful than the slave trade in depopulating the region. They also argue that the rapid growth in slave trade was an outcome of local epidemiology and poor agriculture rather than strong Atlantic demand. For example, Miller (1982) writes, 'The slave trade appears in some ways less a cause of depopulation than a consequence of it when viewed in terms of droughts and demographic changes in West-central Africa'. Therefore, disease environment had direct effects on the demography and economic development of the region. Inikori (1992) and Manning (1981, 1982) disagree and show that these effects were not strong enough to have a large enough impact on the African population compared to the strong Atlantic demand for slaves.

Bhattacharyya (2009b) shows that malaria explains long-run economic development in Africa. All other variables including institutions and slave trade turned out to be statistically insignificant in a regression model estimated by the study.

Finally, the sophisticated geography view is due to Jared Diamond (1997). Diamond in his book entitled 'Guns, Germs and Steel' asks the question: why did history unfold so differently on different continents? He argues that geography and biogeography moulded the contrasting fates of human lives in different continents. His thesis can be summarised as follows.

Diamond (1997) argues that geography has endowed mankind with different sources of food and livestock. The Eurasian climate, especially southwest Asia, which he calls the 'Fertile Crescent'[3], was best suited for the growth of maximum number of edible wild grains and large mammals. Early hunter-gatherers living in this region domesticated these wild grains and adopted a sedentary agriculture-based

[3]The Fertile Crescent spans a part of the modern day Israel, Palestine, and Jordan valley. For further reference, see map in Diamond (1997) p. 135.

lifestyle. They domesticated large mammals for meat, milk, and brawn, which they could use for farming. The use of large mammals in agriculture immensely improved farm productivity yielding more and more food surplus. This technology and knowledge spread all across Eurasia along the same latitude. Close contact with the large mammals also led to frequent outbreaks of epidemic diseases among the human population in this region. This helped Eurasians to develop immunity to many of these diseases over the long run. The gift of food surplus and a sedentary lifestyle allowed them to invest more time into the development of guns, steel swords, ocean-going ships etc. The societal structure became hierarchical and far more complex compared to the earlier society of the hunter-gatherers.

This, however, was not the case in other continents. In New Guinea, humans were left with very limited choices of food. No wild grains or large mammals were available for domestication. Therefore, humans in New Guinea remained hunter-gatherers. In the Americas, corn was the major domesticated crop. Other grains were not available. The continent also lacked large mammals for domestication. Llamas were the only candidate for domestication. However, they are weak and yield less meat and milk compared to cows, goats, and sheep. The indigenous American population were not familiar with horses and they lacked immunity from the fatal Eurasian infectious diseases. As a result, the Europeans faced little or no resistance from the indigenous American population in their colonial conquest. The Aztecs, the Incas, and the Mayas were fighting an unequal battle with the Europeans powered with guns, steel swords, horses, and germs. More than two-thirds of the population were wiped out by smallpox epidemic following the initial European contact. Riding on the power of guns, germs, and steel the Europeans colonized most of the known world getting access to a large pool of resources, which helped them to develop an advanced industrialised society. The Americas, Australia, and New Zealand gained from European technology and migration. The rest of the world remained largely impoverished. The technology and living standards gap widened over time.

13.3 Trade Openness and Economic Development

Adam Smith's pioneering thesis on trade openness and economic development is widely known. Emphasizing the role of trade and division of labour in his pioneering thesis the Wealth of Nations, Smith writes,

> The greatest improvement in the productive power of labour, and the greater part of the skill, dexterity, and judgement with which it is any where directed, or applied, seem to have been the effects of the division of labour. . .This division of labour, from which so many advantages are derived, is not originally the effect of any human wisdom, which foresees and intends that general opulence to which it gives occasion. It is the necessary, though very slow and gradual, consequence of a certain propensity in human nature which has in view no such extensive utility; the propensity to truck, barter, and exchange one thing for another—Adam Smith [1776 (1960)], Wealth of Nations, Chaps. 1 and 2, pp. 7 and 17.

Smith's main thesis runs as follows. Openness to trade increases the size of the market thereby triggering scale economy and division of labour. Division of labour improves productivity and triggers economic growth delivering sustained improvement in living standards.[4]

The neoclassical theory, however, holds a somewhat different view. It posits that reduction in trade barriers unleash factor movement within the economy in line with its comparative advantage. Labour and capital move towards their highest valued use improving overall productivity and the welfare of the economy. Growth takes place in the economy due to transitional dynamics. In other words, growth takes place only during the movement of the economy between steady states. Once the economy arrives at a new steady with new levels of capital and output per worker, growth stops.

Technology transfer through trade also induces economic growth. I would call this the technology transfer view. In a closed economy neoclassical growth model, given technology at a particular point in time a country accumulating more physical and human capital grows faster than a country accumulating less of the same but all of them converge to the same long-run steady-state equilibrium rate of growth (Solow 1956; Swan 1956; Mankiw et al. 1992). In such a model, income per capita grows in the long run only when there is exogenous technological progress. However, we hardly observe convergence of income. What we actually notice is that the rich countries grow faster than the poor countries and the gap between the rich and the poor widens over time.[5] Coe and Helpman (1995) argue that this gap is due to variable rate of technological progress. They report that technology catch up or Research and Development (R&D) spillover bridges this gap. Dowrick and Rogers (2002) report that the gap is due to variable rates of capital accumulation as well as technological progress. Howitt (2000) presents a theoretical model showing that due to technology transfer, R&D performing countries converge to parallel growth paths whereas others stagnate. Several other studies including Coe and Helpman (1995) identify trade openness as a main medium of technology transfer. In other words, these studies argue that technology is typically embodied and therefore cross border transfer of goods and services induce knowledge transfer. Therefore, participation in international trade is growth promoting as it triggers knowledge transfer and economic growth in the long run.

Other influential studies in the openness and growth literature are Sachs and Warner (1995a) and Frankel and Romer (1999).

Sachs and Warner (1995a) use the growth accounting approach to show that trade openness is a key determinant of growth. They calculate trade openness using information on average tariff levels, non-tariff barriers, black market premium,

---

[4]Yang and Borland (1991) uses a growth model to formalise Adam Smith's notion of division of labour.

[5]This is disputed by many if we consider the last 50 years. World income distribution has increased over the last 50 years especially with the impressive growth performances of India and China over the last two to three decades. But the diverging trend certainly holds over a longer period.

state monopoly on major exports etc. Their results indicate that on average 'open' economies grow 2–3 percentage points faster than 'closed' economies.[6] Their study is not free from criticism. Rodrik and Rodriguez (2000) show that the Sachs and Warner measure of openness suffers from over-reliance on the black market premium and state monopoly on major export criterion. Other notable studies of trade liberalisation and growth are Shepherd and Alburo (1991), Wacziarg (2001), and Warner (2003).

Frankel and Romer (1999), on the other hand resort to level accounting using instrumental variable regressions to conclude that trade openness is a key factor influencing economic development. They construct an instrument by separating out the influences of income, population size, and land area, which they call the constructed openness. This variable arguably yields accurate estimate of the relationship between openness and per capita income. They report a strong positive effect of openness on income per capita.

Even though there has been wide agreement on the empirical association between trade openness and economic growth, recently these results have come under scrutiny from a series of studies. These studies argue that trade openness loses importance once institutional quality is introduced as a control variable in a regression model. Rodrik et al. (2004) reach a similar conclusion which I have discussed before. One possible explanation is openness facilitating institutional development. Therefore, a regression model with openness and institutions as controls may not picking up any individual effect of openness on income. The effect of openness could be working via institution. Wei (2000) supports this thesis and suggests that more open economies face greater losses from corruption than less open economies. The loss from corruption is potentially much higher in case of foreign transactions. Therefore, open economies have a greater incentive to strengthen institutions.

Another explanation is from Dollar and Kraay (2003). They argue that cross-country regressions of log-level per capita GDP on instruments of institutions and openness do not reflect the relative importance of these variables in the long run. The high correlation between institutions and openness does not allow regression models to estimate the actual relationship accurately. In contrast, regression of changes in decadal growth rates on instrumented changes in trade and changes in institutional quality show a significant effect of trade openness on growth. They note that trade openness and institutions are important for economic growth in the very long run, but trade has a relatively larger role over institutions in the short run. They do not control for geography, religion, and culture. Furthermore, their study explains changes in growth rates rather than growth itself. Changes in growth rate is a measure of growth acceleration. Growth accelerations are hard to observe in the long run (Jones 1995). This also brings about the question whether the growth spurt

[6]Wacziarg and Welch (2003) improve the Sachs and Warner (1995a) measure and extend it to the 1990s. Their measure, however, is not free from the basic criticisms of Rodrik and Rodriguez (2000). Bhattacharyya (2012) examine the effect of trade openness on institutions.

resulting from the changes in institutions and openness is a mere impulse that tapers off in the long run or something that is sustainable.

In a recent study, Chang (2008) argues that overtly strong commitment to free trade is not good for growth. As an alternative strategy, he promotes 'heterodox capitalism' which includes a combination of protectionism, government promotion of favoured industries, strong state-owned enterprise, and heavy regulation of foreign direct investments. Chang's key evidence in support of this argument is as follows. He shows that the developing countries have grown at a rate two times faster during the 'heterodox' era of 1960s and 1970s than the 'free trade' era of 1980 onwards. Chang notes that the average growth rate for the developing countries during the 1960s and 1970s, is 3 percent. In contrast, the average growth rate during the period 1980 to 2002 for the same country group is 1.7 percent. Easterly (2009), however, finds several inconsistencies in the figures reported by Chang. For example, the result alters if the 1980 turning point is shifted to 1983 or 1982. He also shows that the average growth rate for the developing countries for the period 1983 to 2008 is 2.7 percent. It is, in fact, higher than the same for the period 1960 to 1982 (2.6 percent). Therefore, Chang's argument heavily relies on picking 1980 as the turning point. Easterly (2009) also shows that picking 1980 as the turning point in itself is misleading as trade liberalisation was first pushed by the IMF and the World Bank in the aftermath of the Third World debt crisis in 1982.

On balance, the view put forward by this literature is that there are gains from trade. Trade undoubtedly is a driver of economic expansion. However, the outcome could be divergent across and within societies. If the rules and institutions governing the distribution of gains from trade are skewed in favour of one group then trade may not deliver uniform expansion of living standards. It can also shift political alignments within societies (Rogowski 1989).

13.4 Knowledge, Human Capital, and Economic Development

Technology and knowledge is a key driver of economic expansion. Technology shapes the best use of scarce resources in producing goods and services for mass consumption. Joel Mokyr (1990) in his book The Lever of Riches writes,

> Technological progress predated capitalism and credit by many centuries, and may well outlive capitalism by at least as long.—Joel Mokyr (1990), The Lever of Riches, p. 6.

Joseph A. Schumpeter also demonstrates the role of technology in economic expansion in his book *The Theory of Economic Development*. Schumpeter (1934) introduces the notion of 'creative destruction' as the fundamental driver of economic progress. He describes firms in a market economy with monopolistically competitive markets are constantly seeking to distinguish their products from their rivals either by improving quality or creating new products. The aim of such product differentiation is to reduce the market share of their rivals. Success in creating new ideas and new products could mean monopoly power for that firm within that product space. Schumpeter describes this competitive process of continuous innovation as creative destruction.

Joel Mokyr (1990) in his book supports the Schumpeterian idea of creative destruction. He catalogues inventions going back in time that has played a major role in fostering innovation and economic expansion. The book emphasizes the complementarity between invention and innovation. Mokyr writes invention in itself may not be a meaningful concept, but without it, it is impossible to develop applications for immediate commercial usage. At the other extreme, without innovation, an inventor will have little economic incentive to pursue new ideas.

In Part III of Mokyr's book, he goes on to argue that the complementarity between invention and innovation explains why many societies failed to be technologically creative. Invention requires individual brilliance and an inventor expects social recognition as a reward for the work. Therefore, a society more receptive to new ideas and willing to reward human inquiry is more likely to produce more scientists and researchers. Innovation, on the other hand, requires interaction with other individuals and an in-depth knowledge of the market. Hence, it is more social and economic in nature. Therefore, a society that encourages business enterprise is more inclined towards producing innovations that are more successful. However, invention and innovations cannot take place independently of each other in the long run. A society has to fulfil multiple conditions to generate both invention and innovation. Mokyr provides support for his argument using evidence from the Chinese and the European history of technology.

Even though China entered the early modern era as a technology leader, soon after it lost its advantage to Europe. China suffered technology stagnation over the next three centuries. In contrast, Europe acquired most of the early technologies from China and the east through direct and indirect means and went on to develop them further which led to the industrial revolution. Mokyr enquires why such technology divergence took place. His explanations are as follows. First, social groups trying to sabotage and block new technology were far less potent in Europe than in China. Second, a market for technology developed fairly rapidly in early modern Europe, which created an economic as well as socially rewarding environment for the scientists and innovators. This encouraged private initiatives in the development of new technology. Therefore, the change in the character of the state did not affect investments in technology by much. Even if it did, it led to a decline of that state in the European economic hierarchy. For example, Spain and Portugal were early movers but lost the initiative to the Netherlands and Britain. This made every state or monarch in early modern Europe conscious of the costs of conformism. In contrast, Chinese scientific activities and technology development were largely state sponsored. This prevented the development of private initiatives and hence a technology market. A change in the character of the state often led to hostile behaviour towards innovation and nonconformism. The abrupt ending of the famous Zheng He voyages in 1433 is a classic illustration. A change in the ruler and internal power structure in the Ming Dynasty in 1433 led to the closure of shipyards and production of ocean-going vessels. The continuous threat to potential innovators from rival factions had perhaps forced them to shy away from novel scientific ideas.

In a recent paper, Glaeser et al. (2004) explore the relative importance of human capital and institutions in economic expansion across a sample of former colonies. They argue that human capital is embodied and therefore cannot be dissociated from a settler. Hence, it follows that the settlers who arrived to the new world from Western Europe undoubtedly brought their skills with them. The same cannot be inferred about institutions as these are abstract social constructs.

Allen (2009) also supports the knowledge and human capital theory of economic expansion. Allen's scholarly work investigates how the Industrial Revolution in eighteenth-century Britain led to economic expansion unprecedented in human history. He identifies high wages, relatively low cost of capital, and cheap energy due to the abundance of coal as the main factor behind the Industrial Revolution in Britain. The favourable factor endowment and initial conditions underpinned capital and energy-intensive technological progress. As a result, the unit cost of steam power was far less relative to livestock or labour. New technology increased profitability of production manyfold. Relatively high wages in pre-industrial Britain also made schooling and apprenticeship affordable securing the supply of skilled labour. What ensued was a cumulative skill and energy intensive but labour-saving technological progress.

Galor and Moav (2006) reinforce the above argument. Investigating the demise of the class society in industrial Britain they argue that the increased demand for skilled labour with cumulative skill-biased technological progress compelled capitalists to invest in schools. The capitalists realised that without a steady supply of skilled labour their profit margins would be compromised. Therefore, they actively supported education and apprenticeship that in turn dismantled the class society. They provide empirical evidence to support the hypothesis. They explore the voting patterns of the legislators on England's education reform bill, the Balfour Act of 1902. This bill was meant to create a publicly supported secondary school system. They show that legislators' support for this bill is positively correlated with the industrial skill-intensity level of the counties. Legislators representing counties with high industrial skill-intensity levels overwhelmingly supported this bill whereas the others did not. By assuming that the legislators received financial backing from the industrialists of their respective counties, they argue that this result reflects the eagerness of the capitalists owning skill-intensive industries to invest in human capital.

A large literature also associate health with human capital. Reduced morbidity affects growth by increasing labour productivity. Schultz (2002) and Weil (2005) offer good examples of studies of this nature.

13.5 State Formation, War, and Economic Development

Another body of work investigates the role of state capacity in economic expansion. Notable among them is North et al. (2009). They write in their book entitled *Violence and Social Orders*,

> All societies must deal with the possibility of violence, and they do so in different ways. . .Most societies, which we call natural states, limit violence by political manipulation of the economy to create privileged interests. These privileges limit the use of violence by powerful individuals, but doing so hinders both economic and political development. In contrast, modern societies create open access to economic and political organisations, fostering political and economic competition.—Douglass C. North, John Joseph Wallis, and Barry R. Weingast (2009), Violence and Social Orders, p. 1.

Max Weber was perhaps the first to highlight the connection between violence, state capacity, and institutions. He argued that high density of population and scarcity of land in early modern Europe led to intense territorial competition among the monarchs and feudal lords. Therefore, warfares for the control of scarce resources and land were extremely common and frequent. Taxation was the main instrument used by small and medium-sized states to mobilise and finance their war expenditure. In other words, the symbiotic financial relationship between the ruler and his or her subjects became ever more powerful during this time. Weber posits that this relationship is fundamental to the formation of statehood and perhaps is at the heart of the construct of a modern state.

Recent research by economists and political scientists suggest that state formation and state capacity plays a major role in economic development. Herbst (2000) following Weber's thesis also argues that state weakness explains the lack of development in Africa. As I have discussed earlier, Herbst's work predominantly focuses on the question why African states are weak and ineffective in curbing lawlessness and establish order. He comes up with the following answer. He argues that Africa was land abundant and labour scarce. This is reflected by the low population density figures across the continent. Therefore, the pre-colonial states in the continent did not fight over land but they fought over people. This explains why property rights over people were so well defined in the form of slavery whereas property rights over land were not so well defined. Lands in pre-colonial Africa were held communally. This implies that it was not necessary for the pre-colonial states to defend a well-defined territory as there was no fierce competition over land. In other words, there was less need to invest in defence and maintain bureaucracies. Therefore, tax collections in pre-colonial African states were poor and often non-existent. This allowed African states to survive without having to engage in institution building (tax collection, invest in defence, maintain bureaucracies, and provide rule of law) which made them very fragile. The trend of almost no external threat coupled with low population density persisted during the colonial period. Therefore, the colonisers had little incentive to develop institutions either. After independence, the situation did not change. The United Nations decision to enforce the colonial boundaries as national boundaries and the Cold War politics reinforced this trend.

Hence, what we observe in contemporary Africa is a legacy of weak state institutions.

Besley and Persson (2008, 2009) also present theory and evidence on why the lack of state capacity may lead to poor development outcomes. They argue that state's institutional capacity to levy taxes and support markets is typically constrained by her history of investments in legal and fiscal capacity. States with weak legal systems and imperfect taxation institutions are unlikely to be capable enough to adequately levy taxes and support markets. In other words, state capacity would be fairly limited. This would lead to poor development outcomes. They also show that investments in common interest public goods, such as fighting external wars, political stability, inclusive political institutions are all conducive to building state capacity. In contrast, civil war, internal conflict, and restrictive political institutions are all damaging to state capacity.

In a similar vein, North et al. (2006, 2009) argue that the nature of the social order characterised by the nature of the existing state can explain the process of modern social development. Their framework suggests that in a natural state the actors use political power within the existing political system to limit entry and protect rent. These rents are then used to stabilise the political system and limit violence. However, restrictive economic entry and restrictive political institutions are not conducive to long-run economic growth as it suffocates enterprise, free market, and innovation. They argue that this is the natural way most human societies are organised and hence the name natural state. In contrast, a handful of developed countries have developed open access social order where open access to economic and political organisations facilitates competition and supports market. In other words, social order in these states are sustained by competition and not rent creation.

The obvious question, however, is how the transition from 'natural state' to 'open access state' takes place. According to North et al. (2006), war and the threat of violence plays a crucial role. In the event of an external war, the incumbent state requires more tax revenue and general support from its subjects. In order to increase revenue, the state typically increases taxation of citizens. In return, the state offers widespread political rights. O'Brien (2001, 2005) show that in early modern Britain the state borrowed heavily from the bourgeoisie to finance continental wars. In return, the state extended political rights to the merchants. This led to the development of an efficient financial and revenue management system conducive for economic development.

In summary, one could argue that the development of the state has played a crucial role in prosperity. The factors that influenced state development are taxation, legal institutions, external conflict, and internal conflict. Evidence suggests that external conflict boosts state capacity whereas the reverse is observed if the conflict is internal in nature.

Bibliography

Acemoglu, D., Johnson, S., & Robinson, J. (2001). The colonial origins of comparative development: An empirical investigation. *The American Economic Review, 91*(5), 1369–1401.

Acemoglu, D., Johnson, S., & Robinson, J. (2002). Reversal of fortune: Geography and institutions in the making of the modern world income distribution. *Quarterly Journal of Economics, 117*, 1231–1294.

Acemoglu, D., Johnson, S., & Robinson, J. (2005a). Institutions as the fundamental cause of long-run growth. *Handbook Economic Growth, 1*, 385–472.

Acemoglu, D., Johnson, S., & Robinson, J. (2005b). The rise of Europe: Atlantic trade, institutional change and economic growth. *The American Economic Review, 95*, 546–579.

Acemoglu, D., Johnson, S., Robinson, J., & Thaicharoen, Y. (2003). Institutional causes, macroeconomic symptoms: Volatility, crises and growth. *Journal of Monetary Economics, 50*, 49–123.

Acemoglu, D., & Robinson, J. (2000). Why did the west extend the Franchise? Democracy, inequality and growth in historical perspective. *Quarterly Journal of Economics, 115*, 1167–1199.

Allen, R. (2008). A review of Gregory Clark's a farewell to alms: A brief economic history of the world. *Journal of Economic Literature, 46*(4), 946–973.

Allen, R. (2009). The British industrial revolution in global perspective. Cambridge University Press, Cambridge

Besley, T., & Persson, T. (2008). War and state capacity. *Journal of the European Economic Association, 6*(2–3), 522–530.

Besley, T., & Persson, T. (2009). The origins of state capacity: Property rights, taxation, and politics. *The American Economic Review, 99*(4), 1218–1244.

Bhattacharyya, S. (2009a). Unbundled institutions, human capital, and growth. *Journal of Comparative Economics, 37*, 106–120.

Bhattacharyya, S. (2009b). Root causes of African underdevelopment. *Journal of African Economies, 18*(5), 745–780.

Bhattacharyya, S. (2011). *Growth miracles and growth debacles: Exploring root causes*. Cheltenham: Edward Elgar.

Bhattacharyya, S. (2012). Trade liberalization and institutional development. *Journal of Policy Modeling, 34*, 253–269.

Bloom, D., & Sachs, J. (1998). Geography, demography, and economic growth in Africa. *Brookings Papers on Economic Activity, 2*, 207–295.

Broadberry, S., & Gupta, B. (2005). *The early modern great divergence: Wages, prices and economic development in Europe and Asia, 1500–1800*. Unpublished manuscript, University of Warwick.

Carstensen, K., & Gundlach, E. (2006). The primacy of institutions reconsidered: Direct income effects of malaria prevalence. *World Bank Economic Review, 20*, 309–339.

Chang, H.-J. (2008). *Bad Samaritans: The myth of free trade and the secret history of capitalism*. New York: Bloomsbury Press.

Clark, G. (2007). *A farewell to alms: A brief economic history of the world*. Princeton: Princeton University Press.

Coe, D., & Helpman, E. (1995). International R&D spillovers. *European Economic Review, 39*(5), 859–887.

Curtin, P. (1968). Epidemiology and the slave trade. *Political Science Quarterly, 83*(2), 181–216.

Diamond, J. (1997). *Guns, germs and steel: The fate of human societies*. New York: W.W. Norton.

Dias, J. (1981). Famine and disease in the history of Angola, 1830–1930. *The Journal of African History, 21*, 349–378.

Dollar, D., & Kraay, A. (2003). Institutions, trade, and growth. *Journal of Monetary Economics, 50*, 133–162.

Dowrick, S., & Rogers, M. (2002). Classical and technological convergence: Beyond the Solow-Swan growth model. *Oxford Economic Papers, 54*, 369–385.

Easterly, W. (2001). *The elusive quest for growth: Economists' adventures and misadventures in the tropics*. Cambridge, MA: The MIT Press.

Easterly, W. (2006). The Big Push Déjà Vu: A review of Jeffrey Sachs's the end of poverty: Economic possibilities for our time. *Journal of Economic Literature, XLIV*, 96–105.

Easterly, W. (2009). The anarchy of success. *New York Review of Books, LVI*(15), 28–30.

Easterly, W., & Levine, R. (2001). It's not factor accumulation: Stylized facts and growth models. *World Bank Economic Review, 15*(2), 177–219.

Easterly, W., & Levine, R. (2003). Tropics, germs, and crops: How endowments influence economic development. *Journal of Monetary Economics, 50*(1), 3–39.

Engerman, S., & Sokoloff, K. (2001). *Inequality, institutions, and differential paths of growth among new world economies*. Working paper. University of California, Los Angeles.

Frankel, J., & Romer, D. (1999). Does trade cause growth? *The American Economic Review, 89*(3), 379–399.

Gallup, J., & Sachs, J. (2000). Agriculture, climate, and technology: Why are the tropics falling behind? *American Journal of Agricultural Economics, 82*, 731–737.

Gallup, J., & Sachs, J. (2001). The economic Burden of Malaria. *The American Journal of Tropical Medicine and Hygiene, 64*(1–2), 85–96.

Gallup, J., Sachs, J., & Mellinger, A. (1998). *Geography and economic development*. NBER working paper no. w6849, December.

Galor, O., & Moav, O. (2006). Das Human-Kapital: A theory of the demise of the class structure. *The Review of Economic Studies, 73*, 85–117.

Glaeser, E., LaPorta, R., Lopez-de-Silanes, F., & Shleifer, A. (2004). Do institutions cause growth? *Journal of Economic Growth, 9*, 271–303.

Grief, A. (1994). Cultural beliefs and the organization of society: A historical and theoretical reflection on collectivist and individualist societies. *Journal of Political Economy, 102*(5), 912–950.

Hall, R., & Jones, C. (1999). Why do some countries produce so much more output per worker than others? *Quarterly Journal of Economics, 114*(1), 83–116.

Herbst, J. (2000). *States and power in Africa: Comparative lessons in authority and control*. Princeton: Princeton University Press.

Howitt, P. (2000). Endogenous growth and cross-country income differences. *The American Economic Review, 90*(4), 829–846.

Inikori, J. (1992). *The chaining of a continent: Export demand for captives and the history of Africa South of the Sahara, 1450–1870*. Institute of social and economic research, University of the West Indies, Mona, Jamaica

Jones, E. (1981). *The European miracle: Environments, economies and geopolitics in the history of Europe and Asia*. Cambridge: Cambridge University Press.

Jones, C. (1995). Time series tests of endogenous growth models. *Quarterly Journal of Economics, 110*(2), 495–525.

Knack, S., & Keefer, P. (1995). Institutions and economic performance: Cross-country tests using alternative institutional measures. *Economics and Politics, 7*(3), 207–227.

Kuran, T. (1997). *Private truths, public lies: The social consequences of preference falsification*. Cambridge, MA: Harvard University Press.

Landes, D. (1998). *The wealth and poverty of nations: Why some are so rich and some so poor*. London: Abacus.

Landes, D. (2000). Culture makes almost all the difference. In L. Harrison & S. Huntington (Eds.), *Culture matters: How values shape human progress*. New York: Basic Books.

Landes, D. (2003). *The unbound prometheus: Technological change and industrial development in Western Europe from 1750 to the present*. Cambridge: Cambridge University Press.

Mankiw, G., Romer, D., & Weil, D. (1992). A contribution to the empirics of economic growth. *Quarterly Journal of Economics, 107*(2), 407–437.

Manning, P. (1981). The enslavement of Africans: A demographic model. *Canadian Journal of African Studies, 15*(3), 499–526.
Manning, P. (1982). *Slavery, colonialism and economic growth in Dahomey, 1640–1960*. Cambridge: Cambridge University Press.
Miller, J. (1982). The significance of drought, disease and famine in the agriculturally marginal zones of West Central Africa. *The Journal of African History, 23*, 17–61.
Mokyr, J. (1990). *The lever of riches: Technological creativity and economic change*. New York: Oxford University Press.
Montesquieu, C. (1748 [1989]). *The spirit of laws*. New York: Cambridge University Press.
North, D. (1981). *Structure and change in economic history*. New York: Norton.
North, D. (1989). Institutions and economic growth: An historical introduction. *World Development, 17*(9), 1319–1332.
North, D. (1994). Economic performance through time. *The American Economic Review, 84*(3), 359–368.
North, D., Wallis, J., & Weingast, B. (2006). *A conceptual framework for interpreting recorded human history*. NBER working paper no. 12795, December.
North, D., Wallis, J., & Weingast, B. (2009). *Violence and social order*. New York: Cambridge University Press.
O'Brien, P. (2001). *Fiscal exceptionalism: Great Britain and its European rivals*. Department of economic history working paper no. 65/01, London School of Economics, October.
O'Brien, P. (2005). *Fiscal and financial preconditions for the rise of British naval hegemony 1485–1815*. Department of economic history working paper no. 91/05. London School of Economics, November.
Parker, P. (2000). *Physioeconomics: The basis for long-run economic growth*. Cambridge, MA: The MIT Press.
Putnam, R. (1993). *Making democracy work: Civic traditions in modern Italy*. Princeton University Press: Princeton.
Rodrik, D. (2005). Growth strategies. *Handbook Economic Growth, 1*(1), 967–1014.
Rodrik, D., & Rodriguez, F. (2000). Trade policy and economic growth: A skeptics guide to cross-national evidence. In B. Bernanke & K. Rogoff (Eds.), *NBER macroeconomics annual 2000*. Cambridge, MA: MIT Press.
Rodrik, D., Subramanian, A., & Trebbi, F. (2004). Institutions rule: The primacy of institutions over geography and integration in economic development. *Journal of Economic Growth, 9*, 131–165.
Rogowski, R. (1989). *Commerce and coalitions: How trade affects domestic political alignments*. Princeton: Princeton University Press.
Sachs, J. (2003a). *Institutions don't rule: Direct effects of geography on per capita income*. NBER working paper no. w9490, February.
Sachs, J. (2003b). Institutions matter, but not for everything. *Finance and Development, 40*(2), 38–41.
Sachs, J. (2005). *The end of poverty: How we can make it happen in our lifetime*. London: Penguin Books.
Sachs, J., McArthur, J., Schmidt-Traub, G., Kruk, M., Bahadur, C., Faye, M., & McCord, G. (2004). Ending Africa's poverty trap. *Brookings Papers on Economic Activity, 1*, 117–240.
Sachs, J., & Warner, A. (1995a). Economic reform and the process of global integration. *Brookings Papers on Economic Activity, 1*, 1–118.
Sachs, J., & Warner, A. (1995b). *Natural resource abundance and economic growth*. NBER working paper no. w5398, December.
Sachs, J., & Warner, A. (1997a). Fundamental sources of long-run growth. *The American Economic Review, 87*(2), 184–188.
Sachs, J., & Warner, A. (1997b). Sources of slow growth in African economies. *Journal of African Economies, 6*(3), 335–376.

Samuelson, P. (1976). Illogic of Neo-Marxian doctrine of unequal exchange. In D. A. Belsley et al. (Eds.), *Inflation, trade and taxes: Essays in honor of Alice Bourneuf* (pp. 96–107). Columbus: Ohio State University Press.

Samuelsson, K. (1993). *Religion and economic action: The protestant ethic, the rise of capitalism, and the abuses of scholarship*. Toronto: University of Toronto Press.

Schultz, P. (2002). Wage gains associated with height as a form of health human capital. *The American Economic Review, 92*(2), 349–353.

Schumpeter, J. (1934). *The theory of economic development*. Cambridge, MA: Harvard University Press.

Shepherd, G., & Alburo, F. (1991). The Philippines. In D. Papageorgiou, M. Michaely, & A. Choksi (Eds.), *Liberalizing foreign trade*. Cambridge, MA: Basil Blackwell.

Shleifer, A., & Vishny, R. (1998). *The grabbing hand: Government pathologies and their cures*. Cambridge, MA: Harvard University Press.

Smith, A. (1776 [1976]). *The wealth of nations* (Cannan ed.). Chicago: University of Chicago Press

Solow, R. (1956). A contribution to the theory of economic growth. *Quarterly Journal of Economics, 70*(1), 65–94.

Stevenson, R. (1968). *Population and political systems in tropical Africa*. New York: Columbia University Press.

Stulz, R., & Williamson, R. (2001). *Culture, openness and finance*. NBER working paper no. w8222, April.

Swan, T. (1956). Economic growth and capital accumulation. *The Economic Record, 32*, 334–361.

Tawney, R. (1926). *Religion and the rise of capitalism*. London: John Murray.

Temple, J. (1998). Initial conditions, social capital and growth in Africa. *Journal of African Economies, 7*(3), 309–347.

Thelen, K. (1999). Historical institutionalism in comparative politics. *Annual Review of Political Science, 2*, 369–404.

Thelen, K. (2000). Timing and temporality in the analysis of institutional evolution and change. *Studies in American Political Development, 14*, 101–108.

Wacziarg, R. (2001). Measuring the dynamic gains from trade. *World Bank Economic Review, 15* (3), 393–429.

Wacziarg, R., & Welch, K. (2003). *Trade liberalization and growth: New evidence*. NBER working paper no. 10152, December.

Warner, A. (2003). *Once more into the breach: Economic growth and integration*. Center for global development working paper no. 34, December.

Weber, M. (1930). *The protestant ethic and the spirit of capitalism*. London: Allen and Unwin.

Wei, S.-J. (2000). *Natural openness and good government*. NBER working paper no. w7765, June.

Weil, D. (2005). *Accounting for the effects of health on growth*. NBER working paper 11455, July.

Yang, X., & Borland, J. (1991). A microeconomic mechanism for economic growth. *Journal of Political Economy, 99*, 460–482.

Appendix

(A) Transcript of the Leaked Conversation between Obama Administration's Assistant Secretary of State for European Affairs Victoria Nuland and US Ambassador to Ukraine Geoffrey Pyatt.

The conversation was leaked to the media on 4 February 2014. Conversation can be viewed at https://www.youtube.com/watch?v=WV9J6sxCs5k. Link accessed on 18 July 2020.

Victoria Nuland: What do you think?

Geoffrey Pyatt: I think we're in play. The [Vitaly] Klitschko piece is obviously the complicated electron here. Especially the announcement of him as deputy prime minister and you've seen some of my notes on the troubles in the marriage right now. So we're trying to get a read really fast on where he is on this stuff. But I think your argument to him, which you'll need to make. I think that's the next phone call you want to set up is exactly the one you made to Yats [Arseniy Yatsenyuk] and I'm glad you sort of put him on the spot on where he fits in this scenario. And I'm very glad that he said what he said in response.

Victoria Nuland: Good. So I don't think Klitsch [Vitaly Klitschko] should go into the government. I don't think it's necessary. I don't think it's a good idea.

Geoffrey Pyatt: Yeah. I mean, I guess. . .you think. . .what? In terms of him not going into the government. . .just let him stay out and do his political homework and stuff. I'm just thinking, in terms of, sort of the process moving ahead. We want to keep the moderate democrats together. The problem is going to be [Oleh] Tyahnybok and his guys, and you know I'm sure that's part of what [President Viktor] Yanukovych is calculating on all of this. Ah, I kind of . . .

Victoria Nuland: I think Yats [Arseniy Yatsenyuk] is the guy who's got the economic experience, the governing experience. He's the guy, you know. What he needs is Klitsch [Vitaly Klitschko] and [Oleh] Tyahnybok on the outside. He needs to be talking to them four times a week, you know. I just think Klitsch

S. Bhattacharyya, *A History of Global Capitalism*, Frontiers in Economic History, https://doi.org/10.1007/978-3-030-58736-9

[Vitaly Klitschko] going in, he's going to be at that level working for [Arseniy] Yatsenyuk—it's just not going to work.

Geoffrey Pyatt: Yeah, no, I think that's right. Okay, good. Do you want us to set up a call with him as the next step?

Victoria Nuland: My understanding from that call, that you tell me was that the big three were going into their own meeting, and that Yats [Arseniy Yatsenyuk] was going to offer in that context a three-way, you know, a three-plus-one conversation or three-plus-two with you. Is that not how you understood it?

Geoffrey Pyatt: No. I think ... I mean that's what he proposed ... but I think, just knowing the dynamic that's been with them where [Vitaly] Klitschko's been the top dog. He's going to take a while to show up for whatever meeting they've got. He's probably talking to his guys at this point. So I think you reaching out directly to him helps with the personality management among the three and it gives you also a chance to move fast on all this stuff and put us behind it—behind it before they all sit down, and he ... ah, he explains why he doesn't like it.

Victoria Nuland: Okay, good. I'm happy. Why don't you reach out to him and see if he wants to talk before or after?

Geoffrey Pyatt: Okay, will do. Thanks.

Victoria Nuland: Okay, I've now written—oh, one more wrinkle for you Geoff [Geoffrey Pyatt].

Geoffrey Pyatt: Yeah.

Victoria Nuland: Ah, [I] can't remember if I told you this or if I only told Washington this, but when I talked to Jeff Feltman [Jeffrey David Feltman, United Nations Under-Secretary-General for Political Affairs and former American diplomat] this morning, he had a new name for the UN guy—Robert Serry [a Dutch and UN Diplomat who was sent to Crimea by the UN in March 2014 as a mediator]. Did I write you that this morning?

Geoffrey Pyatt: Yeah, I saw that.

Victoria Nuland: He's now gotten both [Robert] Serry and [UN Secretary General] Ban Ki-moon to agree that [Robert] Serry could come in Monday or Tuesday.

Geoffrey Pyatt: Okay.

Victoria Nuland: So that would be great I think to help glue this thing and to have the UN help glue it and, you know ... [profanity] the EU.

Geoffrey Pyatt: No, exactly. And I think we've got to do something to make it stick together because you can be pretty sure that if it does, if it does, start to gain altitude the Russians will be working behind the scenes to try to torpedo it. And again the fact that this is out there right now. I'm still trying to figure out in my mind why [President Viktor] Yanukovych [did] that? In the meantime there's a Party of Regions faction meeting going on right now and I'm sure there is a lively argument going on in that group at this point. But anyway we could, we could land jelly side up on this one if we move fast. So let me work on, let me work on [Vitaly] Klitschko. And if you can just keep... I think, we want to try to get somebody with an international personality to come out here and help to midwife this thing. Then the other issue is some kind of outreach to [President Viktor]

Yanukovych but we probably regroup on that tomorrow as we see how things start to fall into place.

Victoria Nuland: So on that piece, Geoff [Geoffrey Pyatt], when I wrote the note, [US National Security Advisor Jake] Sullivan's some back to me VFR saying you need [Vice President Joe] Biden, and I said probably tomorrow for an 'atta-boy' and get the 'deets' [details] to stick. So [Vice President Joe] Biden's willing.

Geoffrey Pyatt: Okay. Great. Thanks.

(B) Transcript of Vice President Joe Biden Admitting his Direct Role in the Dismissal of the Ukrainian Prosecutor General Viktor Shokin:

The full transcript of the Council on Foreign Relations 23 January 2018 event can be viewed at https://www.cfr.org/event/foreign-affairs-issue-launch-former-vice-president-joe-biden. Link accessed on 18 July 2020.

The full video of the event can be viewed at https://www.youtube.com/watch?v=Q0_AqpdwqK4&feature=emb_title. Link accessed on 18 July 2020.

Following is the transcript of the relevant segment of Vice President Biden's presentation. Biden here is referring to the 1 billion dollars loan guarantee to the Ukraine that the Obama Administration threatened to withhold if the Prosecutor General Viktor Shokin is not removed from office.

Joe Biden: 'Do I think they're—I think the Donbas has potential to be able to be solved, but it takes two things. One of those things is missing now. And that is I'm desperately concerned about the backsliding on the part of Kiev in terms of corruption. They made—I mean, I'll give you one concrete example. I was—not I, but it just happened to be that was the assignment I got. I got all the good ones. And so I got Ukraine. And I remember going over, convincing our team, our leaders to—convincing that we should be providing for loan guarantees. And I went over, I guess, the 12th, 13th time to Kiev. And I was supposed to announce that there was another billion-dollar loan guarantee. And I had gotten a commitment from Poroshenko and from Yatsenyuk that they would take action against the state prosecutor. And they didn't'.

'So they said they had—they were walking out to a press conference. I said, nah, I'm not going to—or, we're not going to give you the billion dollars. They said, you have no authority. You're not the president. The president said—I said, call him'. (Laughter.)

'I said, I'm telling you, you're not getting the billion dollars. I said, you're not getting the billion. I'm going to be leaving here in, I think it was about six hours. I looked at them and said: I'm leaving in six hours. If the prosecutor is not fired, you're not getting the money. Well, [profanity]. (Laughter.) He got fired. And they put in place someone who was solid at the time'.

'Well, there's still—so they made some genuine substantial changes institutionally and with people. But one of the three institutions, there's now some backsliding'.

(C) Transcript of Leaked Conversation between Secretary of State John Kerry, Vice President Joe Biden and Ukrainian President Petro Poroshenko on the Dismissal of the Ukrainian Prosecutor General Viktor Shokin:

The conversation between John Kerry and Petro Poroshenko took place on 3 December 2015. The conversation between Joe Biden and Petro Poroshenko took place on 18 February 2016. The tapes were leaked to the media by Ukrainian Rada Deputy (Member of Parliament) Andrii Derkach on 19 May 2020. A recording of the tape can be viewed at https://www.youtube.com/watch?v=EbmDLhJ43cU. Link accessed on 18 July 2020.

3 December 2015 Conversation between John Kerry and Petro Poroshenko where John Kerry asks for Viktor Shokin's removal:

John Kerry: But before Vice President [Joe] Biden comes in, I just wanted to try to urge you to see if there is a way to get by this problem of replacing the Prosecutor General, you know, [Viktor] Shokin. Because, to my perception he's blocked the clean-up of the Prosecutor Generals' Office and I know the Vice President [Joe Biden] is very concerned about it. And I think it would be good to try to have some resolution of that before the Vice President comes, if it's possible. And have real clarity as to the steps that we are going to take forward. I think his visit and his speech to the Rada [Ukrainian Parliament] are a good opportunity to showcase your successes as we continue forward, but...

Petro Poroshenko: And I think, I doubt that any other General Prosecutor can do that, but we provide absolutely transparent procedure for the selection commission. And their procedure was widely accepted both inside the country, including my opponents, all the NGO, all the parliamentary forces. They widely accepted as an absolutely transparent and effective situation. And as I promised the very next day before the first of December, exactly as I promised to Vice President Biden, this person who was selected by the selection commission has appointed. Now, all of us should understand that the Prosecutor General Office has no any opportunity under the law to make any cases against corruption because it's immediately goes already from the first of December, the day before yesterday, to the new Anti-Corruption Bureau and the new Anti-Corruption Prosecutor's Office. And I was very proud that Jean-Claude Junker, Angela Merkel, Francois Hollande and everybody welcome it as a very strong position of Anti-Corruption Prosecutor and General Prosecutor's Office. For the Prosecutor position and for Inspector General, I am also proud that exactly as we agreed with the your Ministry of Justice guys and your embassy, the Office of Inspector General is already established. It is coordinated not by General Prosecutor but the Deputy of General Prosecutor Mr. Sakvarelidze, exactly as we agree with the Vice President and with the Ambassador. For the other continuation with the Prosecutor General [Viktor] Shokin and other things, I think I will speak with Vice President [Joe] Biden. And I doubt that it would be theoretically even possible to make any decision without any arguments before.

John Kerry: Vice President [Joe Biden] is going to take up with you and will have a more detailed discussion about it.

Petro Poroshenko: Thank you. Thank you, John [Kerry].

18 February 2016 Conversation between Joe Biden and Petro Poroshenko where Petro Poroshenko delivers the news that he forced Viktor Shokin to resign:

Joe Biden: Petro [Poroshenko], can you hear me?

Petro Poroshenko: Yes, now is better.

Joe Biden: I can hear you better too. I'm sorry, I'm sorry. You were saying. I didn't understand, I missed what you were saying.

Petro Poroshenko: Yes. So, first of all, I'm very happy to hear you. Second, this is very valuable for me, that you find time for me even in Minnesota. And I'm dreaming some days we will be together in Minnesota.

Joe Biden: Man, I tell you what, I'd like to be with you instead of Minnesota right now. But go ahead.

Petro Poroshenko: The third, I have some positive and negative news. I will start with positive news.

Joe Biden: Good.

Petro Poroshenko: Joe [Biden], I have a second positive news for you. Yesterday, I met with the General Prosecutor [Viktor] Shokin.

Joe Biden: Yes.

Petro Poroshenko: And despite of the fact that we didn't have any corruption charges, we don't have any information about him doing something wrong, I specially asked him—no, it was day before yesterday—I specially asked him to resign. In, uh, as his, uh, position as a state person. And despite of the fact that he has a support in the power. And as a finish of my meeting with him, he promised me to give me the statement on resignation. And one hour ago he bring me the written statement of his resignation.

Joe Biden: Great.

Petro Poroshenko: And this is my second step for keeping my promises.

Joe Biden: I agree.

22 March 2016 Conversation between Joe Biden and Petro Poroshenko where Joe Biden reveals his preparedness to hold a public signing of the 1 billion dollars loan guarantee following the removal of Viktor Shokin.

Joe Biden: Hey, Mr. President [Petro Poroshenko]. Joe Biden. How are you?

Petro Poroshenko: Very well, indeed. All the time when I hear your voice, it's a great pleasure for me.

Joe Biden: Well, I'm on Air Force Two and think we are going to stay connected. We just took off and I'm hoping this connection will stay open. Tell me that there is a new government and a new Prosecutor General. **I am prepared to do a public signing of the commitment for the billion dollars. Again, I'm not suggesting that that's what you want or don't want.** I'm just suggesting that that's what we're prepared to do. And again, it wouldn't be finalised until, you know, the IMF pieces are written.

Petro Poroshenko: Extremely strong motivation. One of the possible candidates was leader of my fraction [meaning faction]—[Yuri] Lutsenko who is the public figure. If you think that the political motivated figure would be not very good from your point of view, I recall this proposal. I do not propose, because nobody knows that I want to propose [Yuri] Lutsenko [as the new Prosecutor General]. In this situation I take all the political motivated figures out from this process.

Joe Biden: All right, well, look, let me, let me, when you and I finish speaking, let me huddle with my team, talk over what you and I just talked about. I agree with you, there is a sense of urgency here.

13 May 2016 Conversation between Joe Biden and Petro Poroshenko where Joe Biden congratulates Petro Poroshenko on the appointment of Yuri Lutsenko as the new Prosecutor General replacing Viktor Shokin:

Joe Biden: Hey, Mr. President [Petro Poroshenko]. Joe Biden. How are you?

Petro Poroshenko: Very well, indeed. As usual, when I hear your voice. Thank you very much.

Joe Biden: Well you are doing very well, congratulations on getting the new Prosecutor General. I know there is a lot more that has to be done, but I really, I really think that's, I think that's good. And I understand you're working with the Rada [Ukrainian Parliament] in the coming days on a number of additional laws to secure the IMF. But congratulations on installing the new Prosecutor General, it's going to be critical for him to work quickly to repair the damage [Viktor] Shokin did. And I'm a man of my word. And now that the new Prosecutor General [Yuri Lutsenko] is in place, we're ready to move forward to signing that one billion dollar loan guarantee. And I don't know how you want to go about that. I'm not going to be able to get to Kiev anytime soon, I mean, next month or so. And, and I don't know whether you could either sign it with our Ambassador or if you came here, we could sign or if you want, we're inviting [Prime Minister Vladimir] Groysman here later. I'm going to be talking to him later this morning. Not for that purpose. We're inviting him to Washington. And so I'll leave it up to you as to how you want that done and when you want it done.

Petro Poroshenko: First of all, thank you very much indeed for these words of support. Believe me, that it was a very tough challenge and a very difficult job. And Mrs. [Yulia] Tymoshenko and Mr. [Oleh] Lyashko fraction [meaning faction] tried to break this. Because we not only voted for the new Prosecutor General, which we do in a very short period of time, within one day we changed the law. By the way, in this law we are presenting the set, the new structure of the General Prosecutor's [meaning Prosecutor General's] Office, including the General Inspection [meaning Inspector General] as we agreed with you.

Joe Biden: Yeah, that's brilliant.

Petro Poroshenko: And the second thing I immediately invited [Yuri] Lutsenko and said that he should contact your embassy and I would be very pleased if you will have a certain person, who can come either from Washington or whatever. We have here—I don't remember his name—the Ukrainian origin American prosecutor. He is a little bit old. I sent to the Geoffrey [Pyatt] his name, and he was ready to come and to be assistant and adviser. He has very good experience in the American system and he can be the person of trust within new prosecution system. I think this is exactly the right time to do that. And if he's still ready to come and to cooperate from the very first step, from the very first minute of the new Prosecutor [Yuri Lutsenko], that is exactly what I'm looking for.

Joe Biden: Well, let me, let me get in contact with the [US] Justice Department and pursue that. I'll get his name. And let me find out where that is, because it is in our interest, obviously, to provide professional assistance as quick as we can. So this gets up and started it in the right direction. So I will move on as soon as hang up. I'll put that in train and I'll get back to you as to what we are, what I am able to do.

Petro Poroshenko: Absolutely. Second... Thank you very much indeed, that is exactly what I'm looking for. The second thing is that I want to thank you that you give me your word that immediately when we change the legislation and I appoint the new Prosecutor General, and it would be Yuri Lutsenko as we agreed on our previous meeting in Washington and when it happen, we can have this loan guarantee and thank you very much....

Bibliography

Acemoglu, D., Johnson, S., & Robinson, J. (2001). The colonial origins of comparative development: An empirical investigation. *The American Economic Review, 91*(5), 1369–1401.

Acemoglu, D., Johnson, S., & Robinson, J. (2002). Reversal of fortune: Geography and institutions in the making of the modern world income distribution. *Quarterly Journal of Economics, 117*, 1231–1294.

Acemoglu, D., Johnson, S., & Robinson, J. (2003). Disease and development in historical perspective. *Journal of the European Economic Association, 1*, 397–405.

Acemoglu, D., Johnson, S., & Robinson, J. (2005a). Institutions as the fundamental cause of long-run growth. *Handbook Economic Growth, 1*, 385–472.

Acemoglu, D., Johnson, S., & Robinson, J. (2005b). The rise of Europe: Atlantic trade, institutional change and economic growth. *The American Economic Review, 95*, 546–579.

Acemoglu, D., Johnson, S., Robinson, J., & Thaicharoen, Y. (2003). Institutional causes, macroeconomic symptoms: Volatility, crises and growth. *Journal of Monetary Economics, 50*, 49–123.

Acemoglu, D., & Robinson, J. (2000). Why did the west extend the Franchise? Democracy, inequality and growth in historical perspective. *Quarterly Journal of Economics, 115*, 1167–1199.

Ahluwalia, M. (2002). Economic reforms in India since 1991: Has gradualism worked. *The Journal of Economic Perspectives, 16*(7), 67–88.

Aldcroft, D. (1977). *From Versailles to Wall Street 1919–1929*. London: Allen Lane.

Alesina, A., & Drazen, A. (1991). Why are stabilizations delayed? *The American Economic Review, LXXXI*, 1170–1188.

Alesina, A., & Tabellini, G. (1989). External debt, capital flight and political risk. *Journal of International Economics, 27*, 199–220.

Allen, R. (2003). *Farm to factory. A reinterpretation of the Soviet industrial revolution*. Princeton: Princeton University Press.

Allen, R. (2008). A review of Gregory Clark's a farewell to alms: A brief economic history of the world. *Journal of Economic Literature, 46*(4), 946–973.

Allen, R. (2009). The British industrial revolution in global perspective. Cambridge University Press, Cambridge

Allison, G. (2017). *Destined for war: Can America and China escape Thucydides's Trap*. Boston: Houghton Mifflin Harcourt.

Atkinson, A., & Leigh, A. (2007). The distribution of top incomes in Australia. *The Economic Record, 83*(262), 247–261.

S. Bhattacharyya, *A History of Global Capitalism*, Frontiers in Economic History,
https://doi.org/10.1007/978-3-030-58736-9

Bagchi, A. (1976a). Deindustrialisation in India in the nineteenth century: Some theoretical implications. *Journal of Development Studies, 12*, 135–164.

Bagchi, A. (1976b). Deindustrialisation in Gangetic Bihar 1809–1901. In B. De et al. (Eds.), *Essays in Honour of Prof. S.C. Sarkar*. New Delhi: People's Publishing House.

Bairoch, P. (1982). International industrialization levels from 1750 to 1980. *Journal of European Economic History, 11*, 269–333.

Bajpai, N., & Sachs, J. (1999). Fiscal policy in India's economic reforms. In J. Sachs, A. Varshney, & N. Bajpai (Eds.), *India in the era of economic reforms*. New Delhi: Oxford University Press.

Banerjee, A., & Iyer, L. (2005). History, institutions, and economic performance: The legacy of colonial land tenure systems in India. *The American Economic Review, 95*, 1190–1213.

Bayly, C. (1983). *Rulers, townsmen, and bazaars: North Indian society in the age of British expansion, 1770–1870*. Cambridge: Cambridge University Press.

Beard, M. (2015). *SPQR: A history of ancient Rome*. London: W.W. Norton.

Beaud, M. (2000). *A history of capitalism: 1500–2000*. New York: Monthly Review Press.

Besley, T., & Persson, T. (2008). War and state capacity. *Journal of the European Economic Association, 6*(2–3), 522–530.

Besley, T., & Persson, T. (2009). The origins of state capacity: Property rights, taxation, and politics. *The American Economic Review, 99*(4), 1218–1244.

Bhagwati, J., & Desai, P. (1970). *Planning for industrialization: A study of India's trade and industrial policies since 1950*. Cambridge: Cambridge University Press.

Bhattacharyya, S. (2009a). Unbundled institutions, human capital, and growth. *Journal of Comparative Economics, 37*, 106–120.

Bhattacharyya, S. (2009b). Root causes of African underdevelopment. *Journal of African Economies, 18*(5), 745–780.

Bhattacharyya, S. (2011a). *Growth miracles and growth debacles: Exploring root causes*. Cheltenham: Edward Elgar.

Bhattacharyya, S. (2011b). Five centuries of economic growth in India: The institutions perspective. In R. Jha (Ed.), *Handbook of South Asian Economics* (pp. 32–43). London: Routledge.

Bhattacharyya, S. (2012). Trade liberalization and institutional development. *Journal of Policy Modeling, 34*, 253–269.

Bhattacharyya, S. (2016). The historical origins of poverty in developing countries. In D. Brady & L. Burton (Eds.), *Oxford handbook of the social science of poverty, Chapter 12* (pp. 270–292). New York: Oxford University Press.

Bhattacharyya, S., & Williamson, J. (2011). Commodity price shocks and the Australian economy since federation. *Australian Economic History Review, 51*(2), 150–177.

Bhattacharyya, S., & Williamson, J. (2016). Distributional consequences of commodity price shocks: Australia over a century. *Review of Income and Wealth, 62*(2), 223–244.

Blattman, C., Hwang, J., & Williamson, J. (2007, January). The impact of the terms of trade on economic development in the Periphery, 1870–1939: Volatility and secular change. *Journal of Development Economics, 82*, 156–179.

Bleaney, M., & Greenway, D. (2001). The impact of terms of trade and real exchange rate volatility on investment and growth in sub-Saharan Africa. *Journal of Development Economics, 65*, 491–500.

Bloom, D., & Sachs, J. (1998). Geography, demography, and economic growth in Africa. *Brookings Papers on Economic Activity, 2*, 207–295.

Brewer, A. (1991). *Marxist theories of imperialism: A critical survey*. London: Routledge.

Broadberry, S., & Gupta, B. (2005). *The early modern great divergence: Wages, prices and economic development in Europe and Asia, 1500–1800*. Unpublished manuscript, University of Warwick.

Broadberry, S., & Howlett, P. (2005). The United Kingdom during world war I: Business and usual? In S. Broadberry & M. Harrison (Eds.), *The economics of world war I*. Cambridge: Cambridge University Press.

Brzezinski, Z. (1997). *The grand chessboard: American primacy and its geostrategic imperatives*. New York: Basic Books.
Brzezinski, Z. (2004). *The choice: Global domination or global leadership*. New York: Basic Books.
Carr, E. H. (1937). *International relations since the peace treaties*. London: Macmillan.
Carstensen, K., & Gundlach, E. (2006). The primacy of institutions reconsidered: Direct income effects of malaria prevalence. *World Bank Economic Review, 20*, 309–339.
Chang, H.-J. (2008). *Bad Samaritans: The myth of free trade and the secret history of capitalism*. New York: Bloomsbury Press.
Chisholm, H. (ed.) (1911). Nestor (author). *Encyclopaedia Britannica* (vol. 19, 11th ed., p. 406, 407). Cambridge: Cambridge University Press.
Clark, C. (1950). *Conditions of economic progress*. London: Macmillan.
Clark, G. (2007). *A farewell to alms: A brief economic history of the world*. Princeton: Princeton University Press.
Clarke, S. (2007). *The development of capitalism in Russia*. London: Routledge.
Clingingsmith, D., & Williamson, J. (2008). Deindustrialization in 18th and 19th century India: Mughal decline, climate shocks and British industrial ascent. *Explorations in Economic History, 45*, 209–234.
Coe, D., & Helpman, E. (1995). International R&D spillovers. *European Economic Review, 39*(5), 859–887.
Cohen, S. (2011). *Soviet fates and lost alternatives: From Stalinism to the New Cold War*. New York: Columbia University Press.
Curtin, P. (1968). Epidemiology and the slave trade. *Political Science Quarterly, 83*(2), 181–216.
Curtin, P. (1975). *Economic change in precolonial Africa: Senegambia in the era of the slave trade*. Madison: University of Wisconsin Press.
De Long, B. (2003). India since independence: An analytical growth narrative. In D. Rodrik (Ed.), *In search of prosperity: Analytical narratives on economic growth*. Princeton, NJ: Princeton University Press.
Dercon, S. (2004). *Insurance against poverty*. Oxford: Oxford University Press.
Diamond, J. (1997). *Guns, germs and steel: The fate of human societies*. New York: W.W. Norton.
Dias, J. (1981). Famine and disease in the history of Angola, 1830–1930. *The Journal of African History, 21*, 349–378.
Dollar, D., & Kraay, A. (2003). Institutions, trade, and growth. *Journal of Monetary Economics, 50*, 133–162.
Dorrell, N. (2009). *The dawn of the tsarist empire: Poltava & the Russian campaigns of 1708–1709* (pp. 52–62). Nottingham: Partizan Press.
Dowrick, S., & Rogers, M. (2002). Classical and technological convergence: Beyond the Solow-Swan growth model. *Oxford Economic Papers, 54*, 369–385.
Doyle, W. (1990). *The Oxford history of the French revolution* (2nd ed.). Oxford: Oxford University Press.
Dutt, R. (1906). *The economic history of India*, vol. I, Under Early British Rule, 1757–1837. London.
Dutt, A. (1992). The origins of uneven development: The Indian subcontinent. *The American Economic Review, 82*, 146–150.
Easterly, W. (2001). *The elusive quest for growth: Economists' adventures and misadventures in the tropics*. Cambridge, MA: The MIT Press.
Easterly, W. (2006). The Big Push Déjà Vu: A review of Jeffrey Sachs's the end of poverty: Economic possibilities for our time. *Journal of Economic Literature, XLIV*, 96–105.
Easterly, W. (2009). The anarchy of success. *New York Review of Books, LVI*(15), 28–30.
Easterly, W., & Levine, R. (1997). Africa's growth tragedy: Policies and ethnic divisions. *Quarterly Journal of Economics, 112*(4), 1203–1250.
Easterly, W., & Levine, R. (2001). It's not factor accumulation: Stylized facts and growth models. *World Bank Economic Review, 15*(2), 177–219.

Easterly, W., & Levine, R. (2003). Tropics, germs, and crops: How endowments influence economic development. *Journal of Monetary Economics, 50*(1), 3–39.

Ebrey, P. (1999). *The Cambridge illustrated history of China*. Cambridge: Cambridge University Press.

Ebrey, P., Walthall, A., & Palais, J. (2006). *East Asia: A cultural, social, and political history*. Boston: Houghton Mifflin.

Eichengreen, B. (1992). *Golden fetters: The gold standard and the great depression 1919–1939*. Oxford: Oxford University Press.

Engerman, S., & Sokoloff, K. (1994). *Factor endowments: Institutions, and differential paths of growth among new world economies: A view from economic historians of the United States*. NBER working paper no. w066.

Engerman, S., & Sokoloff, K. (2001). *Inequality, institutions, and differential paths of growth among new world economies*. Working paper. University of California, Los Angeles.

European Union. (2009). *Independent international fact-finding mission on the conflict in Georgia*. Report, Volumes I–III, September. Accessed July 18, 2020, from https://web.archive.org/web/20091007030130/http://www.ceiig.ch/pdf/IIFFMCG_Volume_I.pdf

Fafchamps, M. (2004). *Rural poverty, risk and development*. Cheltenham: Edward Elgar.

Fage, J. (1978). *A history of Africa*. London: Hutchinson.

Fatás, A., & Mivhov, I. (2006). *Policy volatility, institutions and economic growth*. INSEAD, Singapore and Fontainebleau, France, unpublished.

Figes, O. (2010). *Crimea: The last crusade*. London: Allen Lane.

Findlay, R. (1990). *The triangular trade and the Atlantic economy of the eighteenth century: A simple general-equilibrium model* (Essays in International Finance, No. 177, Princeton: Department of Economics, Princeton University)

Findlay, R., & O'Rourke, K. (2007). *Power and plenty: Trade, war, and the world economy in the second millennium*. Princeton, NJ: Princeton University Press.

Finlay, R. (2008). The Voyages of Zheng He: Ideology, state power, and maritime trade in Ming China. *The Journal of the Historical Society, 8*(3), 327–347.

Ford, M. (2015). *The rise of the Robots: Technology and the threat of a jobless future*. New York: Basic Books.

Frankel, J., & Romer, D. (1999). Does trade cause growth? *The American Economic Review, 89*(3), 379–399.

Gaidar, Y. (2007). *Collapse of an Empire. Lessons for modern Russia*. Washington, DC: Brookings Institution Press.

Galbraith, J. (1955). *The great crash 1929*. London: Allen Lane.

Gallup, J., & Sachs, J. (2000). Agriculture, climate, and technology: Why are the tropics falling behind? *American Journal of Agricultural Economics, 82*, 731–737.

Gallup, J., & Sachs, J. (2001). The economic Burden of Malaria. *The American Journal of Tropical Medicine and Hygiene, 64*(1–2), 85–96.

Gallup, J., Sachs, J., & Mellinger, A. (1998). *Geography and economic development*. NBER working paper no. w6849, December.

Galor, O., & Moav, O. (2006). Das Human-Kapital: A theory of the demise of the class structure. *The Review of Economic Studies, 73*, 85–117.

Gemery, H., & Hogendorn, J. (1979). The economic costs of West African participation in the Atlantic Slave trade: A preliminary sampling for the eighteenth century. In H. Gemery & J. Hogendorn (Eds.), *The uncommon market: Essays in the economic history of the Atlantic Slave trade*. New York: Academic Press.

Gerschenkron, A. (1962). *Economic backwardness in historical perspective, a book of essays*. Cambridge, MA: Harvard University Press.

Glaeser, E., LaPorta, R., Lopez-de-Silanes, F., & Shleifer, A. (2004). Do institutions cause growth? *Journal of Economic Growth, 9*, 271–303.

Grief, A. (1994). Cultural beliefs and the organization of society: A historical and theoretical reflection on collectivist and individualist societies. *Journal of Political Economy, 102*(5), 912–950.

Grossman, G. (1987). Command economy. In J. Eatwell, M. Milgate, & P. Newman (Eds.), *The New Palgrave dictionary of economics* (Vol. I, pp. 494–495). London: Macmillan.

Hadass, Y., & Williamson, J. (2003, April). Terms-of-trade shocks and economic performance, 1870–1940: Prebisch and Singer Revisited. *Economic Development and Cultural Change, 51*, 629–656.

Hall, R., & Jones, C. (1999). Why do some countries produce so much more output per worker than others? *Quarterly Journal of Economics, 114*(1), 83–116.

Hardt, M., & Negri, A. (2000). *Empire*. Cambridge, MA: Harvard University Press.

Harley, C. K. (2013). *Slavery, the British Atlantic economy and the industrial revolution*. Discussion papers in economics and social history number 113, University of Oxford.

Herbst, J. (2000). *States and power in Africa: Comparative lessons in authority and control*. Princeton: Princeton University Press.

Howitt, P. (2000). Endogenous growth and cross-country income differences. *The American Economic Review, 90*(4), 829–846.

Inikori, J. (1977). The import of firearms into West Africa, 1750–1807: A quantitative analysis. *The Journal of African History, 18*, 339–368.

Inikori, J. (1992). *The chaining of a continent: Export demand for captives and the history of Africa South of the Sahara, 1450–1870*. Institute of social and economic research, University of the West Indies, Mona, Jamaica

Inikori, J. (2000). Africa and the trans-Atlantic Slave trade. In T. Falola (Ed.), *Africa Vol 1: African history before 1885* (pp. 389–412). Durham, NC: Carolina Academic Press.

Inikori, J. (2002). *Africans and the industrial revolution in England: A study in international trade and economic development*. Cambridge: Cambridge University Press.

Jacoby, H. G., & Skoufias, E. (1997, July). Risk, financial markets, and human capital in a developing country. *The Review of Economic Studies, 64*, 311–335.

Jensen, R. (2000, May). Agricultural volatility and investments in children. *The American Economic Review, 90*, 399–404.

Jones, E. (1981). *The European miracle: Environments, economies and geopolitics in the history of Europe and Asia*. Cambridge: Cambridge University Press.

Jones, C. (1995). Time series tests of endogenous growth models. *Quarterly Journal of Economics, 110*(2), 495–525.

Kalecki, M. (1990). Political aspects of full employment. In M. Kalecki (Ed.), *Collected works of Michael Kalecki* (Vol. I). Oxford: Clarendon Press.

Kalecki, M. (1992). Central price determination. In M. Kalecki (Ed.), *Collected works of Michael Kalecki* (Vol. III). Oxford: Clarendon Press.

Kalecki, M. (1993). Introduction to the theory of growth in a socialist economy. In M. Kalecki (Ed.), *Collected works of Michael Kalecki* (Vol. III). Oxford: Clarendon Press.

Khrennikova, D., Shiryaevskaya, A., & Krasnolutska, D. (2019). Why the Russia – Ukraine Gas Dispute Worries Europe? *Bloomberg Quick Take*, 6 December 2019. Accessed July 18, 2020, from https://www.bloomberg.com/news/articles/2019-12-06/why-the-russia-ukraine-gas-dispute-worries-europe-quicktake

Kissinger, H. (2020). The coronavirus pandemic will forever alter the world order. *The Wall Street Journal*, 3 April, 2020.

Klein, M. (2001). The slave trade and decentralized societies. *The Journal of African History, 42*, 49–65.

Klein, N. (2007). *The shock doctrine: The rise of disaster capitalism*. Toronto: Knopf.

Knack, S., & Keefer, P. (1995). Institutions and economic performance: Cross-country tests using alternative institutional measures. *Economics and Politics, 7*(3), 207–227.

Kohli, A. (1989). Politics of economic liberalization in India. *World Development, 17*(3), 305–328.

Koren, M., & Tenreyro, S. (2007). Volatility and development. *Quarterly Journal of Economics, 122*(1), 243–287.

Kotwal, A., Ramaswami, B., & Wadhwa, W. (2009). *Economic liberalization and Indian economic growth: What's the evidence?* Unpublished Manuscript, February.

Krueger, A. (1974). The political economy of the rent-seeking society. *The American Economic Review, 64*(3), 291–303.

Kuran, T. (1997). *Private truths, public lies: The social consequences of preference falsification.* Cambridge, MA: Harvard University Press.

Landes, D. (1998). *The wealth and poverty of nations: Why some are so rich and some so poor.* London: Abacus.

Landes, D. (2000). Culture makes almost all the difference. In L. Harrison & S. Huntington (Eds.), *Culture matters: How values shape human progress.* New York: Basic Books.

Landes, D. (2003). *The unbound prometheus: Technological change and industrial development in Western Europe from 1750 to the present.* Cambridge: Cambridge University Press.

Lindert, P., & Williamson, J. (2003). Does globalisation make the world more unequal? In M. Bordo, A. Taylor, & J. Williamson (Eds.), *Globalisation in historical perspective.* Chicago: University of Chicago Press.

Loayza, N. V., Rancière, R., Servén, L., & Ventura, J. (2007). Macroeconomic volatility and welfare in developing countries: An introduction. *World Bank Economic Review, 21*(3), 343–357.

Lovejoy, P. (1982). The volume of the Atlantic Slave trade: A synthesis. *The Journal of African History, 23*, 473–501.

Lovejoy, P. (1994). Background to Rebellion: The Origins of Muslim Slaves in Bahia. *Slavery Abolition, 15*(2), 151–180.

Maddison, A. (2004). *The world economy: Historical statistics.* Paris: OECD.

Malenbaum, W. (1953). *The world wheat economy 1885–1953.* Cambridge, MA: Harvard University Press.

Mankiw, G., Romer, D., & Weil, D. (1992). A contribution to the empirics of economic growth. *Quarterly Journal of Economics, 107*(2), 407–437.

Manning, P. (1981). The enslavement of Africans: A demographic model. *Canadian Journal of African Studies, 15*(3), 499–526.

Manning, P. (1982). *Slavery, colonialism and economic growth in Dahomey, 1640–1960.* Cambridge: Cambridge University Press.

Marx, K. (1852/2012). *The eighteenth Brumaire of Louis Bonaparte.* New York: Digiread Books.

Meiksins Wood, E. (2003). *Empire of capital.* London: Verso Books.

Meillassoux, C. (1976). The role of slavery in the economic and social history of Sahelo-Sudanic Africa. In J. Inikori (Ed.), *Forced migration: The impact of the export slave trade on African societies* (pp. 74–99). Hutchinson: London.

Miller, J. (1982). The significance of drought, disease and famine in the agriculturally marginal zones of West Central Africa. *The Journal of African History, 23*, 17–61.

Miller, J. (1988). *Way of death: Merchant capitalism and the Angolan Slave trade, 1730–1830.* Madison: University of Wisconsin Press.

Mokyr, J. (1990). *The lever of riches: Technological creativity and economic change.* New York: Oxford University Press.

Montesquieu, C. (1748 [1989]). *The spirit of laws.* New York: Cambridge University Press.

Moore, B. (1966). *Injustice: The social bases of obedience and revolt.* New York: White Plains.

Morgenthau, H. (1948). *Politics among nations: The struggle for power and peace.* New York: Alfred A. Knopf.

Mukherjee, R. (1939). *The economic history of India: 1600–1800.* London: Longmans, Green and Company.

Nehru, J. (1947). *The discovery of India.* London: Meridian Books.

North, D. (1981). *Structure and change in economic history.* New York: Norton.

North, D. (1989). Institutions and economic growth: An historical introduction. *World Development, 17*(9), 1319–1332.
North, D. (1994). Economic performance through time. *The American Economic Review, 84*(3), 359–368.
North, D., Wallis, J., & Weingast, B. (2006). *A conceptual framework for interpreting recorded human history*. NBER working paper no. 12795, December.
North, D., Wallis, J., & Weingast, B. (2009). *Violence and social order*. New York: Cambridge University Press.
Nuland, V. (2020). *Pinning Down Putin: How a confident America should deal with Russia*. Foreign affairs, The Council on Foreign Relations, July/August, 2020.
Nunn, N. (2008). The long-term effects of Africa's Slave trades. *Quarterly Journal of Economics, 123*(1), 139–176.
O'Brien, P. (2001). *Fiscal exceptionalism: Great Britain and its European rivals*. Department of economic history working paper no. 65/01, London School of Economics, October.
O'Brien, P. (2005). *Fiscal and financial preconditions for the rise of British naval hegemony 1485–1815*. Department of economic history working paper no. 91/05. London School of Economics, November.
Odling-Smee, J. (2006). The IMF and Russia in the 1990s. *IMF Staff Papers, 53*(1), 151–194.
Parker, P. (2000). *Physioeconomics: The basis for long-run economic growth*. Cambridge, MA: The MIT Press.
Poelhekke, S., & van der Ploeg, F. (2007). *Volatility, financial development and the natural resource curse*. CEPR discussion paper 6513, October.
Popov, V. (2010). *Life cycle of the centrally planned economy: Why Soviet growth rates peaked in the 1950's*. CEFIR/NES working paper series. Working paper no 152.
Prakash, O. (2004). *Bullion for goods: European and Indian merchants in the Indian Ocean trade, 1500–1800*. New Delhi: Manohar.
Prakash, O. (2005). *The Great divergence: Evidence from eighteenth century India*. Paper presented at the GEHN Conference on Imperialism, Istanbul, September 11–12.
Putnam, R. (1993). *Making democracy work: Civic traditions in modern Italy*. Princeton University Press: Princeton.
Ramey, G., & Ramey, V. (1995). Cross-country evidence on the link between volatility and growth. *The American Economic Review, 85*(5), 1138–1151.
Raychaudhuri, T. (1983). The mid-eighteenth-century background. In D. Kumar & M. Desai (Eds.), *The Cambridge economic history of India* (Vol. II). Cambridge: Cambridge University Press.
Robbins, H. (1928). A comparison of the effects of the black death on the economic organization of France and England. *Journal of Political Economy, 36*(4), 447–479.
Robinson, J. (2002). States and power in Africa by Jeffrey I. Herbst: A review essay. *Journal of Economic Literature, 60*, 510–519.
Rodney, W. (1966). African Slavery and other forms of social oppression on the Upper Guinea Coast in the context of the Atlantic Slave trade. *The Journal of African History, 7*, 431–443.
Rodrik, D. (2005). Growth strategies. *Handbook Economic Growth, 1*(1), 967–1014.
Rodrik, D., & Rodriguez, F. (2000). Trade policy and economic growth: A skeptics guide to cross-national evidence. In B. Bernanke & K. Rogoff (Eds.), *NBER macroeconomics annual 2000*. Cambridge, MA: MIT Press.
Rodrik, D., & Subramanian, A. (2004). *From 'Hindu Growth' to productivity surge: The mystery of the Indian growth transition*. NBER working paper 10376, March.
Rodrik, D., Subramanian, A., & Trebbi, F. (2004). Institutions rule: The primacy of institutions over geography and integration in economic development. *Journal of Economic Growth, 9*, 131–165.
Rogowski, R. (1989). *Commerce and coalitions: How trade affects domestic political alignments*. Princeton: Princeton University Press.
Rosefielde, S. (2001). Premature deaths: Russia's radical economic transition in Soviet perspective. *Europe-Asia Studies, 53*(8), 1159–1176.

Roy, T. (2002). Economic history of Modern India: Redefining the link. *The Journal of Economic Perspectives, 16*, 109–130.

Sachs, J. (2003a). *Institutions don't rule: Direct effects of geography on per capita income*. NBER working paper no. w9490, February.

Sachs, J. (2003b). Institutions matter, but not for everything. *Finance and Development, 40*(2), 38–41.

Sachs, J. (2005). *The end of poverty: How we can make it happen in our lifetime*. London: Penguin Books.

Sachs, J., McArthur, J., Schmidt-Traub, G., Kruk, M., Bahadur, C., Faye, M., & McCord, G. (2004). Ending Africa's poverty trap. *Brookings Papers on Economic Activity, 1*, 117–240.

Sachs, J., & Warner, A. (1995a). Economic reform and the process of global integration. *Brookings Papers on Economic Activity, 1*, 1–118.

Sachs, J., & Warner, A. (1995b). *Natural resource abundance and economic growth*. NBER working paper no. w5398, December.

Sachs, J., & Warner, A. (1997a). Fundamental sources of long-run growth. *The American Economic Review, 87*(2), 184–188.

Sachs, J., & Warner, A. (1997b). Sources of slow growth in African economies. *Journal of African Economies, 6*(3), 335–376.

Saez, E., & Zucman, G. (2019). *The Triumph of injustice: How the rich dodge taxes and how to make them pay*. New York: W.W. Norton.

Samuelson, P. (1976). Illogic of Neo-Marxian doctrine of unequal exchange. In D. A. Belsley et al. (Eds.), *Inflation, trade and taxes: Essays in honor of Alice Bourneuf* (pp. 96–107). Columbus: Ohio State University Press.

Samuelsson, K. (1993). *Religion and economic action: The protestant ethic, the rise of capitalism, and the abuses of scholarship*. Toronto: University of Toronto Press.

Savranskaya, S., & Blanton, T. (2017). *NATO expansion: What Gorbachev heard*. Briefing Book Number 613, National Security Archive, George Washington University, 12 December 2017. Accessed July 18, 2020, from https://nsarchive.gwu.edu/briefing-book/russia-programs/2017-12-12/nato-expansion-what-gorbachev-heard-western-leaders-early

Schultz, P. (2002). Wage gains associated with height as a form of health human capital. *The American Economic Review, 92*(2), 349–353.

Schumpeter, J. (1934). *The theory of economic development*. Cambridge, MA: Harvard University Press.

Shepherd, G., & Alburo, F. (1991). The Philippines. In D. Papageorgiou, M. Michaely, & A. Choksi (Eds.), *Liberalizing foreign trade*. Cambridge, MA: Basil Blackwell.

Shleifer, A., & Vishny, R. (1998). *The grabbing hand: Government pathologies and their cures*. Cambridge, MA: Harvard University Press.

Smith, A. (1776 [1976]). *The wealth of nations* (Cannan ed.). Chicago: University of Chicago Press

Solow, R. (1956). A contribution to the theory of economic growth. *Quarterly Journal of Economics, 70*(1), 65–94.

Srinivasan, T., & Tendulkar, S. (2003). *Reintegrating India with the world economy*. Washington, DC: Institute for International Economics.

Stannard, D. (1993). *American Holocaust: The conquest of the new world*. Oxford: Oxford University Press.

Stevenson, R. (1968). *Population and political systems in tropical Africa*. New York: Columbia University Press.

Stuckler, D., King, L., & McKee, M. (2009). Mass privatisation and the post-communist mortality crisis: A cross-national analysis. *Lancet, 373*, 399–407.

Stulz, R., & Williamson, R. (2001). *Culture, openness and finance*. NBER working paper no. w8222, April.

Swan, T. (1956). Economic growth and capital accumulation. *The Economic Record, 32*, 334–361.

Tanas, O., Shiryaevskaya, A., & Murtaugh, D. (2019). How Russia – China gas pipeline changes energy calculus. *Bloomberg Quick Take*, 25 November 2019. Accessed July 18, 2020, from

https://www.bloomberg.com/news/articles/2019-11-25/how-russia-china-gas-pipeline-changes-energy-calculus-quicktake
Tavares, J., & Wacziarg, R. (2001). How democracy affects growth. *European Economic Review, 45*(8), 1341–1379.
Tawney, R. (1926). *Religion and the rise of capitalism.* London: John Murray.
Temin, P. (1971). The beginning of the depression in Germany. *The Economic History Review, 24*, 240–248.
Temple, J. (1998). Initial conditions, social capital and growth in Africa. *Journal of African Economies, 7*(3), 309–347.
Thelen, K. (1999). Historical institutionalism in comparative politics. *Annual Review of Political Science, 2*, 369–404.
Thelen, K. (2000). Timing and temporality in the analysis of institutional evolution and change. *Studies in American Political Development, 14*, 101–108.
Thorner, D. (1962). Deindustrialisation in India 1881–1931. In D. Thorner & A. Thorner (Eds.), *Land and labour in India.* Bombay: Asia Publishing House.
Thornton, J. (1980). The Slave Trade in the eighteenth-century Angola: Effects on demographic structures. *Canadian Journal of African Studies, 14*(3), 417–427.
Tomlinson, B. (1993). *The economy of Modern India 1860–1970.* Cambridge: Cambridge University Press.
Voigtlander, N., & Voth, H.-J. (2008). *The three Horsemen of growth: Plague, war and urbanization in early Modern Europe.* Department of Economics, Universitat Pompeu Fabra.
Wacziarg, R. (2001). Measuring the dynamic gains from trade. *World Bank Economic Review, 15* (3), 393–429.
Wacziarg, R., & Welch, K. (2003). *Trade liberalization and growth: New evidence.* NBER working paper no. 10152, December.
Wallerstein, I. (1983). *Historical capitalism with capitalist civilization.* London: Verso.
Warner, A. (2003). *Once more into the breach: Economic growth and integration.* Center for global development working paper no. 34, December.
Weber, M. (1930). *The protestant ethic and the spirit of capitalism.* London: Allen and Unwin.
Wei, S.-J. (2000). *Natural openness and good government.* NBER working paper no. w7765, June.
Weil, D. (2005). *Accounting for the effects of health on growth.* NBER working paper 11455, July.
Williams, E. (1944). *Capitalism and Slavery.* Chapel Hill: University of North Carolina Press.
Williamson, J. G. (2011). *Trade and poverty: When the third world fell behind.* Cambridge, MA: MIT Press.
Williamson, J., & Zagha, R. (2002). *From slow growth to slow reform.* Washington, DC: Institute for International Economics.
World Bank. (2002). *Transition the first ten years: Analysis and lessons for Eastern Europe and the Former Soviet Union.* Washington, DC: The World Bank.
Yang, X., & Borland, J. (1991). A microeconomic mechanism for economic growth. *Journal of Political Economy, 99*, 460–482.

MIX
Papier aus verantwortungsvollen Quellen
Paper from responsible sources
FSC® C105338
FSC
www.fsc.org

If you have any concerns about our products,
you can contact us on
ProductSafety@springernature.com

In case Publisher is established outside the EU,
the EU authorized representative is:
Springer Nature Customer Service Center GmbH
Europaplatz 3, 69115 Heidelberg, Germany

Printed by Libri Plureos GmbH
in Hamburg, Germany